The Gospel and Israel

The Gospel and Israel

The Edersheim Lectures

Edited by
PAUL MORRIS

WIPF & STOCK · Eugene, Oregon

THE GOSPEL AND ISRAEL
The Edersheim Lectures

Copyright © 2014 Wipf and Stock Publishers. All rights reserved. Except for brief quotations in critical publications or reviews, no part of this book may be reproduced in any manner without prior written permission from the publisher. Write: Permissions, Wipf and Stock Publishers, 199 W. 8th Ave., Suite 3, Eugene, OR 97401.

Scripture quotations are taken from the following translations:

Revised Standard Version of the Bible, copyright © 1952 by the Division of Christian Education of the National Council of the Churches of Christ in the United States of America. Used by permission. All rights reserved.

The Holy Bible, New International Version®, NIV® Copyright © 1973, 1978, 1984, 2011 by Biblica, Inc.™ Used by permission. All rights reserved worldwide.

New King James Version®. Copyright © 1982 by Thomas Nelson, Inc. Used by permission. All rights reserved.

New Revised Standard Version Bible, copyright © 1989, Division of Christian Education of the National Council of the Churches of Christ in the United States of America. Used by permission. All rights reserved.

The Holy Bible, English Standard Version® (ESV®) Copyright © 2001 by Crossway, a publishing ministry of Good News Publishers. All rights reserved.

Wipf & Stock
An imprint of Wipf and Stock Publishers
199 W. 8th Ave., Suite 3
Eugene, OR 97401

www.wipfandstock.com

ISBN 13: 978-1-62564-154-0

Manufactured in the U.S.A.

Contents

Preface | vii
Acknowledgments | ix
Contributors and Editor | xi

1. Jews and Gentiles and the Gospel of Christ
   Dr. Paul Barnett | 1

2. The Place of Israel in Systematic Theology
   Dr. Ian Pennicook | 14

3. How Jewish Is Israel in the New Testament?
   Dr. Stephen Voorwinde | 28

4. Luther and the Jews
   Dr. Mark D. Thompson | 57

5. Calvin and the Jews
   Dr. Peter Barnes | 82

6. Christian Mission to the Jews: 1550–1850
   Dr. Rowland S. Ward | 102

7. The Israel/Palestine Conflict
   Martin Pakula | 126

8. The Yes to All God's Promises: Jesus, Israel and the Promises of God in Paul's Letters
   Dr. David Starling | 147

9. Pentecost and the Plan of God
   Mike Moore | 166

Preface

THE MISSION OF THE church to the Jews is a unique one. Only of them is it written, "Salvation is of the Jews," so that we can say that every salvation blessing the world has received has come through them. Returning those blessings to them is a gospel ministry unlike any other. The biblical, theological, and practical issues are unique. The Annual Edersheim Lecture was established to explore those issues.

When Christians read the Old Testament they tend to expect great things for the gospel among the Jews. The fulfilment of the prophecies in Jesus seems so obvious to them that they assume they are equally obvious to Jewish people, "the people of the Book." However, experience teaches otherwise. The apostle Paul tells us that, because the Jewish people are a covenant people—the people of God's promises—there will always be a believing remnant among them; but, by the same token, their unbelief has led to a unique hardening to the truth of the Messiah, such that the unbelieving majority see their very identity as bound up with rejection of Jesus.

Added to that there is anti-Semitism, which is rightly called "the Longest Hatred." The fact that much of its expression over the past two thousand years has been in the name of Jesus means that the Jewish people see the Christian faith as an enemy and the principal cause of all its ills. It is a lamentable distinction, and one that has become difficult to shed.

These factors add up to make mission to the Jews uniquely difficult, requiring considerable sensitivity—and yet also full of hope, for there is promise of both a remnant and a fullness.

These lectures aim to explore the biblical, theological, and historical issues, and to relate them to Jewish mission today. Christian Witness to Israel (Australia) has organised them because of our conviction that a consideration of such issues is crucial to an intelligent, heartfelt, and persevering interest in mission to the Jewish people.

Preface

Why "Edersheim"? Alfred Edersheim is the name of the well-known nineteenth-century Jewish Christian scholar from Vienna who ministered in Romania as a missionary and in the UK as a pastor. He authored *The Life and Times of Jesus the Messiah* and other classics. Following in his footsteps, it is our desire to engage in an in-depth examination of themes relating to the Jewish people and the Christian faith.

Paul Morris
Christian Witness to Israel

Acknowledgments

THE COUNCIL OF CHRISTIAN Witness to Israel (Australia) wishes to express its gratitude to Robert J. Landberg, MDiv (ACT), MA, BA (UQ), for his work of editing and preparing for publication the first six lectures of this publication along with their corresponding author information. He was well equipped for this task having won the Reuters Prize as a university journalism student. He previously worked for CWI (Australia), producing many of their printed publications. Prior to this he also worked as a linguistics researcher, copywriter, website developer, and TESOL curriculum designer.

Contributors and Editor

Paul Barnett, PhD (Lond), ThD (ACT), is the former Anglican Bishop of North Sydney. He lectures in ancient history and New Testament at Moore College, Macquarie University, and the Presbyterian Theological Centre in Sydney. Doctor Barnett has previously lectured at Regent College, Vancouver, Canada, and is the founder of the School of Christian Studies at Robert Menzies College, Macquarie University, Sydney. He has authored *Messiah: Jesus—The Evidence of History* (Nottingham, England: InterVarsity, 2009), *The Second Epistle to the Corinthians* (NICNT; Grand Rapids: Eerdmans, 1997), and *The Birth of Christianity: The First Twenty Years* (Grand Rapids: Eerdmans, 2005), among many other works.

The chapter by Dr. Barnett is an adaptation of an oral lecture that was originally made using outline points only. This will help explain the lack of extensive footnoting and the slightly less formal style of communication.

Ian Pennicook, DMin, MA, is an ordained Anglican minister, and since joining New Creation Teaching Ministry has lectured in a number of Bible colleges in Australia and overseas, and was principal of one college for some time. Doctor Pennicook has written numerous theological books and articles, some of which deal specifically with Israel and the church, including *The Story of the Acts of God* (Blackwood, S. Aust.: New Creation, 1994, 2005), *The Church of the Living God* (Blackwood, S. Aust.: New Creation, 2001), and *Jews, Gentiles and the People of God* (Blackwood, S. Aust.: New Creation, 2007), among many other works.

Stephen Voorwinde, ThD (ACT), MTh (WTS), previously served as a pastor in the Reformed Churches of Australia for ten years. Since 1985, he has lectured in New Testament at the Reformed Theological College, Geelong, Australia. Doctor Voorwinde's doctoral dissertation was published as *Jesus' Emotions in the Fourth Gospel: Human or Divine?* (London: T. & T. Clark,

Contributors and Editor

2005), and he has had published numerous other works in established journals.

The contribution by Dr. Voorwinde to the Annual Edersheim Lecture series, titled "How Jewish Is Israel in the New Testament?," previously appeared in the *Reformed Theological Review* (67/2 [2008] 61–90), and is used here with some minor modifications and by the kind permission of the author and publisher.

Mark D. Thompson, DPhil (Oxon), MTh (ACT), previously served as an Anglican minister in a number of churches in New South Wales. He is now the Principal of Moore College, Sydney, and has been teaching since 1991, including at Oak Hill College, London. Doctor Thompson is the author of *A Sure Ground on Which to Stand: The Relation of Authority and Interpretive Method in Luther's Approach to Scripture* (Carlisle: Paternoster, 2004), and is co-editor and contributor with P. G. Bolt in *The Gospel to the Nations: Perspectives on Paul's Mission: Essays in Honour of Peter Thomas O'Brien on His Sixty-Fifth Birthday* (Leicester, Eng.: InterVarsity, 2000), among many other works.

The contribution by Dr. Thompson to the Annual Edersheim Lecture series, titled "Luther and the Jews," previously appeared in the *Reformed Theological Review* (67/3 [2008] 121–45), and is used here with some minor modifications and by the kind permission of the author and publisher.

Peter Barnes, ThD (ACT), currently serves as the minister of Revesby Presbyterian Church, Sydney. He also previously served for twenty years in pastoral ministry in Vanuatu and in Nambucca River, New South Wales. Since 1985 he has also lectured in church history at the Presbyterian Theological Centre, Sydney. Doctor Barnes has written a commentary on Galatians, *A Study Commentary on Galatians* (Darlington, Eng.; Webster, NY: Evangelical Press, 2006), *Theological Controversies in the Presbyterian Church of New South Wales, 1865–1915: The Rise of Liberal Evangelicalism* (Lewiston, NY: E. Mellen, 2008), and *John Calvin—Man of God's Word Written and Preached* (Edinburgh: Banner of Truth, 2011).

The contribution by Dr. Barnes to the Annual Edersheim Lecture series, titled "Calvin and the Jews," previously appeared in the *Reformed Theological Review* (68/3 [2009] 175–93), and is used here with some minor modifications and by the kind permission of the author and publisher.

Contributors and Editor

Rowland S. Ward, ThD (ACT), trained for the ministry at the Free Church of Scotland College in Edinburgh and has served in his hometown of Melbourne with the Presbyterian Church of Eastern Australia since 1981. Doctor Ward has written extensively on church history, historical, and theological subjects, including *God & Adam: Reformed Theology and the Creation Covenant* (Wantirna, Victoria: New Melbourne, 2003), *The Westminster Confession of Faith: A Study Guide* (Wantirna, Victoria: New Melbourne, 2004), and a commentary on Genesis 1–11, among many other works.

The contribution by Dr. Ward to the Annual Edersheim Lecture series, titled "A Passion for God and a Passion for Jews: The Basis and Practice of Jewish Mission 1550–1850," previously appeared in the *Reformed Theological Review* (70/1 [2011] 1–25), and is used here with some minor modifications and by the kind permission of the author and publisher.

Martin Pakula, MTh (ACT), is an ordained Anglican minister, who has worked in Jewish outreach, parish ministry, student ministry, and lectured in Old Testament at the Bible College of Victoria. He has written commentaries on Numbers (*Homeward Bound: Reading Numbers Today* [Sydney South: Aquila, 2006]), Nahum, Habakkuk, and Zephaniah (same series, forthcoming), and *First for the Jew—The Urgency of Jewish Mission Today* (Melbourne: Bible College of Victoria, 2007).

David Starling, BA, DipEd, MA, BTh, BMin, PhD, served as the pastor of Petersham Baptist Church, Sydney, from 2000 to 2006. David joined the faculty of Morling College, Sydney, in 2005 as a part-time lecturer in New Testament, and in 2007 became a full-time member of faculty, teaching New Testament and theology. Doctor Starling's PhD studies were at the University of Sydney and his thesis, on Paul's use of exile imagery, was published as *Not My People: Gentiles as Exiles in Pauline Hermeneutics* (BZNW 184; New York: De Gruyter, 2011).

The contribution by Dr. Starling to the Annual Edersheim Lecture series, titled "The Yes to All God's Promises," previously appeared in the *Reformed Theological Review* (71/1 [April 2012] 185–204), and is used here with some minor modifications and by the kind permission of the author and publisher.

Contributors and Editor

Mike Moore is the general secretary of Christian Witness to Israel. He was converted in his home city of Hull at an Elim Pentecostal Church and served as a minister in two of the denomination's churches before founding Weymouth Independent Reformed Church in 1980. In 1984 he joined CWI and served for nineteen years as the Society's communications officer before being appointed general secretary in 2002. Mike has contributed to a number of Christian magazines and journals as well as the *CWI Herald* and writes a regular column for *The British Church Newspaper*. He is the author of *The Importance of Being Ernest: A Jewish Life Spent in Christian Mission* (Sevenoaks, Eng.: CWI, 2003), the story of veteran Hebrew Christian missionary Ernest Lloyd.

Editor

Paul Morris completed the theological training course of the Evangelical Movement of Wales, was ordained in a member church of the Fellowship of Independent Evangelical Churches in the UK, and began to serve as an evangelist to the Jews with CWI in 1979. In the UK he ministered in Brighton and London and in the 1990s travelled into countries of Eastern Europe and Russia to establish new CWI ministry. He led CWI's work in Australia from 2001 to 2011, where he established the Annual Edersheim Lecture. Paul is the author of *Telling Jews about Jesus* (London: Grace, 1994) and *Jewish Themes in the New Testament* (Milton Keynes: Paternoster, 2013).

1

Jews and Gentiles and the Gospel of Christ

—Dr. Paul Barnett

I. HISTORICAL REFLECTION

Jewish people are rightly sensitive to their relationship with Christians over two thousand years, having suffered at times greatly at the hands of Christians. But it is worth remembering that Jews faced enormously difficulties from the Greek and Roman world beforehand. Anti-Semitism didn't begin with Christianity.

In New Testament times the population of the Roman Empire is estimated at fifty-five to sixty million people. As many as 15 percent of that number were Jewish people, though only a minority of them were living within the historical land of Israel. The great majority were living in the Diaspora, six or seven million of them. The family of Saul of Tarsus comes to mind as an example of a Jewish family in the Diaspora.

These Diaspora non-Palestine Jews were for the most part Greek speaking. They met in synagogues and heard the Old Testament read in the Greek Septuagint or some other Greek-language Bible. Many of them made pilgrimages to Jerusalem. In the early 1900s, archaeologists discovered an inscription dedicated to a man called Theodotus whose synagogue and guesthouse was devoted to the accommodation of visiting Jewish people from outside Palestine. We can imagine that such facilities were numerous—a synagogue with a guesthouse attached.

The Gospel and Israel

In addition to this very large number of Jewish people in the Greek and Roman world there were also a considerable number of Gentiles who had become disaffected with the polytheism and temple-based paganism of the day, with its lax morality, its numerous gods (who had no morality at all). They were attracted to the monotheism of Israel, to the ethics expressed in the Ten Commandments, to the high standard of family life, and to the stability of family life that Jewish people upheld. Jewish people refused altogether to have anything to do with the termination of the unborn, which of course was prevalent in the Roman world; divorce similarly. And so there was something about the stability and order of family life among the Jewish people that attracted vast number of God-fearers, sometimes called Jewish sympathisers. Hear the words of Josephus:

> The masses have long since shown a keen desire to adopt our religious observances, and there is not one city, Greek or Barbarian, nor single nation, to which our custom of abstaining from work on the seventh day has not spread, and where the fasts and the lighting of lamps and many of our prohibitions in the matter of food are not observed.[1]

There are passages that indicate that Gentile people in large numbers would gather Sabbath by Sabbath, sit in the synagogue, and listen to the Law of the Prophets read and the prayers offered. That is on one side.

On the other side, however, there was hostility toward Jewish people in the Greek and Roman world. It is true that the early Julio-Claudian Caesars (Augustus and Tiberius) protected the Jews. Not that they were particularly drawn to the Jews, but they recognised that there were so many of them in the empire, and they were such a tight community with such an incredible network, that they were a group of people you would not want to alienate because they could do you damage.

So the earlier Julio-Claudian emperors gave Jews a right of assembly in synagogues; they were permitted to meet in ways that other groups were not. They were not required to engage in military service, and there were quite a number of other items that were matters of concession for Jewish people.

Then, on the other hand, we only have to turn to classical authors like Tacitus to see the mockery and scorn with which many intellectuals regarded the Jews. They attacked them for their refusal to eat with other people, to fraternise around the meal table. They mocked them for worshipping

---

1. Josephus, *Against Apion* 2.282.

the sky; they worshipped no depiction of a god, but nothing at all—just the open sky! "Atheists," they called them, as they would soon also call the Christians. They mocked Jews for venerating pigs of all things (for not eating pork), and they regarded them as lazy (because they would not work on the seventh day), and so on.

So we find a writer like Josephus engaged in writing apologetics for his fellow Jews. In the period after the New Testament, Christian writers engaged in apologetics to explain misunderstandings about the Christian faith. So too did Philo and Josephus, for Judaism.

Something of a sea change occurred in the Julio-Claudian period under Tiberius Caesar, who retired as a semi-recluse to the island of Capri and handed over the reign of government to the sinister Praetorian prefect Sejanus, who, it would appear, was strongly anti-Semitic. Evidence points to the fact that his appointee, one Pontius Pilate, was actually dispatched to Judea with the brief to subvert the Jewish people. Pontius Pilate was a minor player in the fairly unimportant province of Judea, and yet there is quite a lot written about him in ways that are quite unexpected given his relative unimportance. It appears that Pilate came to Judea to stir up the Jewish people. He had his military troops march into Jerusalem with a depiction of the gods of Rome on the military standards, something previous governors had been careful not to do. Pilate deliberately did this. He introduced coinage into Judea that portrayed the emperor of the day as a god or demigod. Whereas other Roman governors has been careful not to upset the Jewish people, it appears that Pontius Pilate took every opportunity to upset them.

Caligula's tenure was for a mercifully short period: AD 37–41. He had delusions of grandeur, and not only of grandeur, but also of being a god. So it comes as no surprise that he came into headlong conflict with Jewish people. During his watch, near civil war broke in Alexandria between the very large Jewish community there and the remainder of the Graeco-Egyptian population. Similarly, something approaching civil war occurred also in Antioch in Syria. We know that the same Caesar gave orders that the statue of himself be erected in the temple in Jerusalem, creating a crisis of the magnitude as under Antiochus IV that provoked the rise of the Maccabees in 175 BC. Caligula's crisis is possibly hinted at in 2 Thessalonians 2:4, which speaks about the man of sin taking his place in the temple. Caligula was succeeded by Claudius, who was friendly to the Herod family but not particularly friendly to the Jews as a people. Whereas Jews hoped for a higher status of citizenship around the empire on an equal footing, one to

The Gospel and Israel

one, Claudius would do no more than grant them a kind of corporate recognition, but refused entirely to grant them individual citizenship rights.

Nero, who succeeded Claudius, was more interested in acting, singing, and town planning than governing. During his reigning years (AD 54–68), there was a succession of incompetent and corrupt governors appointed to the province of Judea.

And so Judea slid towards the war that broke out in AD 66 with the destruction of much of the city in Jerusalem and the temple itself in AD 70. That occurred under the new Flavian dynasty, whose Caesars were particularly harsh towards the Jewish people. Vespasian decreed that the temple in Jerusalem was to be rebuilt for the Roman god Jupiter.

There were further wars between the Jews and the Romans: in AD 112 and 132–135 (the Bar Kokhba revolt). Jewish people were then expelled from their homeland in 135.

In the period that follows, we now see the development of Mishnaic and Talmudic Judaism—what we would call Rabbinic Judaism. Judaism today is a development out of the Judaism that followed the 132–135 period.

It is within this set of documents we find a few references to Jesus. These are, without exception, negative; they account for his virgin birth in term of an illicit liaison between a Roman soldier named Pandera and a Jewish girl, Miriam (Mary).

Well, so much for this brief sketch.

During this period we see that the Christians were very much identified as within Judaism in the beginning, and only later did they emerge in their own right. In Acts 18, in the incident involving the governor Gallio—dated about AD 51–52—the believers are still part and parcel of Judaism. And the accusation against them, said Gallio, must be sorted out by them, "in house," not by the civic authorities. Yet just a dozen years later in the year 64 we have the great fire of Rome. Christians (not the rabbinic Jewish community) are scapegoated by Nero as the cause of the fire and persecuted accordingly. By that time, just a dozen years after Gallio's verdict, in the eyes of the Romans Christians are a group distinct from the Jewish community.

The Gospel of Matthew, written in the 70s, makes references to *"their* synagogues," which certainly implies a distinction from Christian "synagogues," or churches. The Book of Revelation refers several times to the synagogue of Satan, also implying separation of church from synagogue. The Jerusalem church—Christians in Jerusalem—escaped from the war zone to the city of Pella, one of the cities in Decapolis, on the eastern side of the Jordan River, for the duration of the war, 66–70. But they came back to Jerusalem after the war in AD 70, and the Christian historian Eusebius gives us a list of bishops of that Jewish Christian church, many of whom were relatives of Jesus.

But Jewish Christianity after a period degenerates into a heresy called Ebionism—a set of beliefs where Jesus is the Messiah, but his deity is questioned. He was not born of a virgin; he is not regarded as God; there is still an emphasis on legalism, circumcision, Sabbath keeping; and the apostle Paul is not spoken well of. So Ebionism, which is referred to by the early Christian writers Irenaeus, Tertullian, and Hippolytus, survives for a while, but inevitably disappears since it is neither Judaism nor Christianity.

In the 90s, there is evidence from the Book of Revelation that Jews were a source of persecution against Christians. So, in the 70s the Jews lose their temple, but they still have to pay the temple tax each year for the upkeep of the temple, which, to rub salt into the wound, is now the pagan temple to the god Jupiter. Nonetheless, the payment of the *Fiscus Judaicus*, the temple tax, did purchase a kind immunity for the Jewish people, and it did purchase their ongoing special status in the Roman world. It gave them protection that the Christian believers didn't have. Colin Hemer in his important book on Revelation argues that quite a lot of the persecution that came the way of the Christians in the 90s and over into the next century was actually initiated from the Jewish quarter. This certainly was the case with the martyrdom of Polycarp, bishop of Smyrna, in the middle of the next century.

What lies in the background of a sad story of Christian anti-Semitism, which is indeed a tragic story and begins after the Constantinian settlement in early 300s, is that the persecuted church becomes the church triumphant, and is itself now a persecutor. Constantine saw a sign in the sky in the Battle of Milvian Bridge in 312 with the words "by this conquer," which was something like a crucifix or cruciform symbol. So we see the beginnings now of the coming together of Christianity *and* the Graeco-Roman Empire under Constantine. So we find a Roman Empire that is a *Christian* empire which becomes resentful of Jews and Judaism.

We move from antiquity into late antiquity and then into the early Middle Ages and then into what we might call Catholic Europe. The great symbol of Catholicism and the Orthodox Church is a cross with the crucified Christ. Where Protestants use a cross, historically it has been an empty cross. But the crucified Christ is always on the Roman Catholic and Orthodox cross.

If you travel in Europe you will see crucifixes everywhere, with letters INRI, an abbreviation of the Latin for "Jesus of Nazareth, King of the Jews."

Jewish people were continually reminded of the crucified Jesus as they were also in the Passion plays that told Christians that Jews were responsible for the crucifixion of the Son of God. Jewish people claim that whenever the Passion plays were held, as they were every few year right through Europe, those were times when synagogues were burned down and Jews persecuted. I understand the apprehension that many Jewish people had at the prospect of Mel Gibson's film being released. It came across to me (I haven't seen the movie yet) as being a kind of cinematic Passion play that might be very moving for Gentile Christians. When I put myself in a Jewish person's shoes, I can well see how it might be viewed rather differently.

Anti-Semitism is a tragic blight on the history of Europe—a tragic blight not least in Germany. While a great admirer and deeply thankful for Martin Luther, aspects of his writings are anti-Semitic.

Historically speaking, therefore, Jewish people have tended to find safe havens in Britain, and by the late 1800s we have a Jewish man as British prime minister. Jews have found safe haven in the United States. It is in the Protestant countries where Jewish people have been secure and have prospered. It is interesting to reflect on whether the relative safety for Jews in Protestant countries has been due to Protestant evangelicalism, to the long history of the British Christians' concern for the evangelisation of the Jews.

II. JESUS, PAUL, AND ISRAEL

In moving from history to some Bible teaching, it is worth considering the use of the word "first" in the New Testament.

We are reminded of Acts 3:26, where Peter says to the people in Jerusalem, "God, having raised up his servant, sent him to you *first*, to bless you in turning everyone of you from your wickedness."[2] Please note that word "first." It does turn up in great and significant texts. We must not miss the point that Peter has been sent *first* to his own people the Jews. There is a response from Israel that Peter is looking for in those words.

Paul in Acts 13:46 declares, "And Paul and Barnabas spoke out boldly, saying, ' It was necessary that the word of God should be spoken first to

---

2. Unless otherwise indicated, all Scripture quotations in this essay are from the RSV.

you. Since you thrust it from you, and judge yourselves unworthy of eternal life, behold, we turn to the Gentiles.'" Although the Jews have a first call on the gospel, says Paul, their salvation is not automatic, for they must turn to the Lord and must not thrust the word of the Lord away. Think particularly of Romans 1:16-17: "For I am not ashamed of the gospel," says Paul, "it is the power of God for salvation to every one who has faith, to the Jew *first* and also to the Greek." Once again, there is nothing automatic about the salvation of Israel, though they have "first claim," as it were, on Paul's ministry. This is not, as is sometimes suggested, just as matter of strategy, or just a matter of missionary convenience, but really it is a matter of deep-seated theology. They must be given the gospel *first*, but they too must response in faith to the gospel.

These uses of the word "first," which is so easy to miss—from Peter in Acts 3:26, from Paul in Acts 13:46, and from Paul in Romans 1:16—flow out of a word of the Lord Jesus. This word he spoke in Mark 7, in that interchange with the woman in Phoenicia whose daughter needed ministry from Jesus. He said, "Let the children *first* be fed, for it is not right to take the children's bread and throw it to the dogs." There is no doubt that "dogs" is a reference to the Gentiles and the "children" a reference to Israel. He is saying, let the children *first* be fed with the good news of the kingdom, that is, the people of Israel. It's not right to take the children's bread and throw it to dogs. She is a pretty smart lady with a quick word back at him. But Jesus' word "first" indicates the divine priority for the nation Israel, a word that seems to be so carefully picked up by both Peter and Paul in their mission preaching.

The "firstness" of Israel comes out as well as in other texts from Matthew's Gospel. For example, in the mission of the Twelve, Jesus says in Matthew 10:5-6, "Go nowhere among the Gentiles "—*nowhere among the Gentiles!*—"and enter no town of the Samaritans, but go *rather* to the lost sheep of the house of Israel." So far as we can see, apart from some exceptions—the Samaritan woman, for example—Jesus' ministry was confined to Israel.

In Matthew 15:24 Jesus says, "I was sent *only* to the lost sheep of the house of Israel." Paul (more or less) confirms those words in Romans 15:8 when he says, "For I tell you that Christ became a servant to the circumcised"—to Israel—"to show God's truthfulness, in order to confirm the promises given to the patriarchs" (see Gen 12:1-3). Paul is saying that Christ primarily came as a servant to the circumcised, to Israel. However,

The Gospel and Israel

we know that as Jesus' ministry in Israel grew to its end, he pushed it to further horizons—to the nations, the Gentiles. Matthew 24:14 says the gospel of the kingdom of God will be preached throughout the whole world, as a testimony all nations; and the end will then come. The climax is in Matthew 28:19, where he commands, " Go therefore and make disciples of all nations, baptizing them in the name of the Father and of the Son and of the Holy Spirit." But *first* it was to Israel. And that "firstness" is taken up repeatedly by both Peter and Paul.

Now, let us reflect on Paul, the Pharisee and persecutor, who was converted on Damascus road in the year AD 34. Interestingly Paul spends the next fourteen to fifteen years in relatively obscurity—in Damascus, Arabia, Damascus, Judea, Tarsus, and Antioch. Then in the year 47 it all changed dramatically. After meeting with the "pillar" apostles in Jerusalem (Gal 2:7–9), Paul and Barnabas set out on a series of westward, Rome-ward missions that will occupy Paul for the next ten years—endlessly travelling by land and sea, through steep mountains and arid countryside, facing dangers from raging rivers and bandits, flogged, thrashed and stoned—we know the story.

In the annals of human history, Paul's missionary work AD 47 must rank as one of the most remarkable. This was a burst of energy, empowered by the Spirit and motivated by Christ's love for him, that changed the course of history. After 57, Paul spent most of his remaining years in jail. He was released only briefly during last seven years of his life, between 57 and 64/65. It is true that he does write a number of letters, but they are the shorter, and perhaps the less influential letters compared with letters to the Corinthians, the Galatians, and the Romans written in that amazing decade, 47–57. Paul brought the gospel of Christ out of the Levant, out of the Jewish world, into Europe, and into the world as we know it. Had Paul not began what he did in year 47, I suspect he would have remained a footnote in history.

But why did he do it? What made him change? I suspect that in the earlier decade and a half Paul understood the Damascus commission to preach to the Gentiles in terms of a mission that was based in the synagogue to God-fearers—to Gentiles who are more or less in the orbit of the synagogue (which possibly explains all those floggings he received in the synagogues which probably come from that early period). So why did he start moving westward to preach direct to idolaters, to those outside the synagogue, who went to the pagan temples?

We can only speculate, but my speculation is that around the period 45–46, when Paul saw what was happening in Antioch, it raised his horizons to see the possibility for the ingathering of the Gentiles in numbers. At the same time, I believe Paul came to the conclusion that something was happening within Israel in fulfilment of Old Testament prophecy—that a hardening, prophesied in Isaiah 6, was now happening. We can question whether this was because Paul and others had preached the gospels to Jews in Palestine and in the Diaspora and found very little response from them. So my guess is that Paul had come to believe that this was now the time for the Gentiles, because a hardening had overtaken Israel.

I don't think Paul regarded that as a permanent hardening, and he might have been surprised that the hardening has lasted as long as it has, to this day. So, two reasons for Paul to take his new tack were, first, his conviction that Gentiles were responsive in the gospel, and, second, that the Jews had been hardened. That I think is how we might understand these well-known words in Romans, which are usually taught and preached as a challenge toward missionary service. But when you read the passages in Romans 10 carefully, they are rather sad references to Israel's rejection of the gospel.

> But how are men to call upon him in whom they have not believed? And how are they to believe in him of whom they have never heard? And how are they to hear without a preacher? And how can men preach unless they are sent? As it is written, "How beautiful are the feet of those who preach good news!" But they have not all obeyed the gospel; for Isaiah says, "Lord, who has believed what he has heard from us?" So faith comes from what is heard, and what is heard comes by the preaching of Christ. But I ask, have they not heard? Indeed they have; for
>
> "Their voice has gone out to all the earth, and their words to the ends of the world."
>
> Again I ask, did Israel not understand? First Moses says,
>
> "I will make you jealous of those who are not a nation; with a foolish nation I will make you angry."
>
> Then Isaiah is so bold as to say,
>
> "I have been found by those who did not seek me; I have shown myself to those who did not ask for me."

The Gospel and Israel

> But of Israel he says, "All day long I have held out my hand to a disobedient and contrary people." (Rom 10:14–21)

When we move into chapter 11 it is more the same. In verses 7 and 8 Israel failed to obtain what it sought and so were hardened. "'God gave them a spirit of stupor, eyes that should not see and ears that should not hear, down to this very day'" (11:8). And a bit later in verse 25, lest the brethren be wise in their own conceit, Paul says that he wants them to understand that a hardening has come upon part of Israel "until the full number of the Gentiles come in." And that picks up from Isaiah 6:

> And I heard the voice of the Lord saying, "Whom shall I send, and who will go for us?" Then I said, "Here am I! Send me." And he said, "Go, and say to this people:
>
> 'Hear and hear, but do not understand;
> see and see, but do not perceive.'
> Make the heart of this people fat,
> and their ears heavy,
> and shut their eyes;
> lest they see with their eyes . . .'"

I think that is what Paul understood as now happening within history. So again from Romans 11:1, "I ask, then, has God rejected his people?" Hardened them, yes, but rejected them, no. "By no means! I myself am an Israelite, a descendant of Abraham, a member of the tribe of Benjamin. God has not rejected his people . . ." So he asks, "have they stumbled so as to fall? By no means! But through their trespass salvation has come to the Gentiles, so as to make Israel jealous. Now if their trespass means riches for the world, and if their failure means riches for the Gentiles, how much more will their [i.e., Israel's] full inclusion mean!" (11:11–12). That is what Paul is looking to down the track—Israel's full inclusion. So he says to the Gentiles:

> Now I am speaking to you Gentiles. Inasmuch then as I am an apostle to the Gentiles, I magnify my ministry in order to make my fellow Jews jealous, and thus save some of them. For if their rejection means the reconciliation of the world, what will their acceptance mean but life from the dead? (11:13–15)

This is surely nothing less than the general resurrection at the terminus of history?

Again, in Romans 11:24, he says to the Gentiles that they have been cut out from what is by nature a wild olive tree and grafted, contrary to nature, into a cultivated olive tree. How much more (notice this question!) will their *natural* branches be grafted back into their own olive tree? So Romans 11 is full of hope, isn't it? Paul wants them to understand this mystery: a hardening has come upon part of Israel until the full number of the Gentiles comes in. With regard to election, Israel is beloved of God for the sake of the forefathers. God will honour his promises to the patriarchs.

III. CONCLUSION: HOW WILL ISRAEL BE SAVED?

Scholars are not in agreement here. Calvin and many others understood "all Israel being saved" to mean the elect, of Israel *and* the nations—the elect church. Moo, in his important commentary on Romans, understands "Israel" here to be the ethnic nation Israel at the end times. Others have said it would be the elect of Israel throughout history in a kind of retroactive sense.

A lot has been made of the text in Romans 11:26:

> So all Israel will be saved, as it is written: "The deliverer will come from Zion [viz. the second coming], he will banish ungodliness from Jacob; and this is my covenant with them when I take away their sins."

This text is made a lot of by those who are looking for some kind of—shall we say—the automatic salvation of Israel. Those who hold varieties of this view look to the Apostle Paul as a kind of special example. Paul wasn't evangelised, they say. Paul didn't repent ahead of time; God just saved him. What happened to Paul on the Damascus road is sometimes taken as a kind of paradigm of the way that God will just save the nation Israel at the end of history.

Now with great respect to those who take that view, my understanding of the New Testament is that the members of Israel will be saved the same way as everybody else is saved, that is, as a result of ministry, by evangelism. That certainly is the burden of Peter's words in Acts 3:26, and Paul's in Acts 13:46 and Romans 1:16–17.

According to Galatians 2:7–9 there were two missions: a mission to Israel led by Cephas (=Peter), and a mission led by Paul, which was to both Jews and Gentiles.

The Gospel and Israel

Today, when we think of missionary work, we basically don't think that there is a special place of mission for Jews. Yet, theologically, I believe there ought to be. The church's missionary outreach is greatly deficient if it does not specifically include missionary work among Jews. This is because I am convinced that that is the way the apostles thought. I believe that if the Apostle Paul were standing here today, he would be surprised that there is no distinct, separate, and definite mission to his people. I believe he would be really surprised. But no less surprised would be Jesus himself, who said, "Let the children *first* be fed . . ." (Mark 7:27).

We encourage people to go to Africa, Asia, Europe, and South America. But as for a discrete mission to Israel that is a mission to Jewish people, we honour those who are engaged in it, although it comes across as irregular and ad hoc.

Of course, today Jewish people object to being evangelised. They connect evangelism with persecution, and with coercive conversion. They also fear that the evangelisation of Israel would mean her extinction. But true evangelism does not demand abandonment of Israel's ethnicity or culture, including religious culture (male circumcision, dietary practices, religious calendar, etc.), just so long as these are expressions of culture and not mandatory for salvation.

To my knowledge, Protestants have generally not been coercive in evangelism of Jews. The tragedy of the Holocaust provoked appropriate sympathy for the Jewish people. The achievements of the state of Israel making the desert bloom has won appropriate worldwide admiration. Former Australian prime minister Bob Hawke was greatly taken by, and admiring of, the amazing achievements of the state of Israel since 1948.

One has only to visit the Yad Vashem museum, the Holocaust museum in Jerusalem, to be reminded of the horrific wickedness perpetrated upon continental Jews. Many Europeans feel deep guilt and shame that so many people "looked the other way" during the 1930s and 1940s, including the leaders of the Roman Catholic Church. Many Protestant Christians within the liberal tradition also feel huge shame about the Holocaust, which I believe helps explain the emergence in the last thirty years of a theological point of view called the "new perspective" on Judaism and Paul. Broadly speaking this new perspective asserts that Jews do not need to be saved because God's covenant with Israel still stands. "Justification by faith" is said by new perspective teaching to have been a Pauline construct to provide for the attachment of Gentiles to an already saved Israel. To generalise, Martin

Jews and Gentiles and the Gospel of Christ

Luther's anti-Semitic writings have led to a reaction against his teachings on "justification by faith" and the rise of the new perspective on Judaism and on Paul.[3]

So we have some strange bedfellows today: on the one hand we have "fundamentalist" Christians with dispensational theology who think that God will save Israel without evangelism, yet at the other extremity are those (generally more liberal) in the new perspective camp who also say there must be no evangelisation of Israel, for Jews do not need evangelising because, as they perceive it, the covenant still stands.

In retrospect, the sad history of Christians and Jews has been a barrier to missionary work. Yad Vashem and other memorials rightly keep the Holocaust memory alive but continue to be an issue for Jew-Christian relationship. We must remember that the Germany that perpetrated these horrors was historically a Christian country, the home also of the Protestant Reformation.

So, mission work amongst Jewish people needs to be done with sensitivity. When the Mel Gibson movie *The Passion* was showing some years back, I was invited to speak at a meeting at Shalom College in Sydney, where I gave an exposition of John's Gospel. I accompanied my words with an expression of deep regret for the past. I basically presented the Christian gospel and was given a good hearing. But I felt that expressing my regrets paved the way for a sympathetic hearing.

I think we need to gently remind the Jewish community that our Lord and his apostles and early church leaders (possibly excepting Luke) were Jews. In presenting Christ, we are not calling upon Jewish people to become Gentiles, to give up Jewish heritage, culture, and practice.

We want to say that the Jewish Scriptures—the Old Testament (or Tanakh)—is filfiled, and made sense of, by Messiah Jesus. And we want to say that the basic bottom-line needs of Jewish people are the same as the bottom-line needs of all people, namely salvation from sin and death. Sin and death are the marks of all people. But Christ crucified deals with our sin, and Christ resurrected deals with the last enemy, death. Forgiveness of sin and hope beyond the grave remain the basic needs for Jewish people, as they are for all people. So missionary work among Jewish people needs to be done with great sensitivity and patience; but it does need to be done.

---

3. In passing, let me say that while I abhor any form of anti-Semitism I strongly agree with Luther on grace as a basis for the salvation in Christ, by faith in him, for both Jews and Gentiles.

2

The Place of Israel in Systematic Theology

—Dr. Ian Pennicook

Let us begin with an assumption: that Israel ought to be a topic within systematic theology. Once that has been said, of course, we are set on a collision course with just about everybody, for the moment we ask what is meant by "Israel" and even by "systematic theology" we are, probably, going to encounter, initially at least, almost no common ground. For instance, by "Israel" do we mean ancient Israel, the descendants of Abraham through Jacob, or do we mean "the Israel of God" spoken of by Paul in Galatians 6:16 (assuming they are not one and the same), or perhaps the Israel of the twenty-first century, understood by some to be the key to eschatology? As for systematic theology, also known as dogmatics, "for every dogmatician there is a different definition."[1]

Within systematic theology, which, for the sake of simplicity, we might define as "systematic and thorough reflection on the content of the relationship which God has established with us in Christ,"[2] or as Karl Barth defines it, "the scientific self examination of the Christian Church with respect to the content of its distinctive talk about God,"[3] there are, indeed, some authors who include "Israel" as a topic for discussion. Calvin wrote:

---

1. Hendrikus Berkhof, *Introduction to the Study of Dogmatics*, trans. John Vriend (Grand Rapids: Eerdmans, 1985), 8.

2. Berkhof, *Introduction*, 9.

3. Karl Barth, *Church Dogmatics*, I/1 (Edinburgh: T. & T. Clark, 1975), 3.

The Place of Israel in Systematic Theology

... until the advent of Christ, the Lord set apart one nation within which to confine the covenant of his grace. "When the Most High gave to the nations their inheritance, when he separated the sons of Adam," says Moses, "his people became his possession; Jacob was the cord of his inheritance." [Deut. 32:8–9 p.] Elsewhere he addresses the people as follows: "Behold, to the Lord your God belong heaven and ... earth with all that is in it. Yet he cleaved only to your fathers, loved them so that he chose their descendants after them, namely you out of all peoples" [Deut.10:14, 15 p., cf. Vg.]. He, therefore, bestowed the knowledge of his name solely upon that people as if they alone of all men belonged to him. He lodged his covenant, so to speak, in their bosom; he manifested the presence of his majesty to them; he showered every privilege upon them. But—to pass over the remaining blessings—let us consider the one in question. In communicating his Word to them, he joined them to himself, that he might be called and esteemed their God. In the meantime, "he allowed all other nations to walk in vanity [Acts 14:16], as if they had nothing whatsoever to do with him. Nor did he give them the sole remedy for their deadly disease—the preaching of his Word. Israel was then the Lord's darling son; the others were strangers. Israel was recognized and received into confidence and safekeeping; the others were left to their own darkness. Israel was hallowed by God; the others were profaned. Israel was honored with God's presence; the others were excluded from all approach to him. "But when the fullness of time came" [Gal. 4:41 which was appointed for the restoration of all things, he was revealed as the reconciler of God and men; "the wall" that for so long had confined God's mercy within the boundaries of Israel "was broken down" [Eph. 2:14]. "Peace was announced to those who were far off, and to those who were near" [Eph. 2:17] that together they might be reconciled to God and welded into one people [Eph. 2:16]. Therefore there is now no difference between Jew and Greek [Gal. 3:28], between circumcision and uncircumcision [Gal. 6:15], but "Christ is all in all" [Col. 3:11, cf. Vg.]. "The nations have been made his inheritance, and the ends of the earth his property" [Ps. 2:8 p.], that "he may have unbroken dominion from sea to sea, and from the rivers even to the ends of the earth" [Ps. 72:8 p.; cf. Zech. 9:10].[4]

Calvin's point was that Israel as a nation is to be seen as having its identity within the wider purposes of God. The many blessings given to

---

4. John Calvin, *Calvin: Institutes of the Christian Religion*, ed. John T. McNeill, Ttransl. by Ford L. Battles (Library of Christian Classics 20; London: SCM, 1960), 460ff.

The Gospel and Israel

Israel served a particular goal, namely to bring about the revelation that God is the reconciler of all the nations. Theologically, Israel's place is within salvation history and not, therefore, as a topic on its own, but as part of the process by which God has brought salvation in Christ to the world.

Returning to Barth's definition above, we can see that he contends that systematic theology is the task of the Christian church in order to make certain that what is proclaimed is in conformity with the revelation of God in Christ. Referring to church history, which, from Calvin's position, would include the prior work of God through Israel, Barth has this to say:

> What is called Church history does not correspond to any independently raised question concerning Christian talk about God, and it cannot therefore be regarded as an independent theological discipline. It is an auxiliary science indispensable to exegetical, dogmatic and practical theology.[5]

This does not imply a lack of interest in Israel by Barth, as Hendrikus Berkhof demonstrates:

> Very original and still insufficiently studied is the three fold manner in which Barth deals with the way of Israel in his [*Church Dogmatics*]. First in I, 2, par.14, 2: "The Time of Expectation" (p. 71: "Revelation in the Old Testament is really the expectation of revelation or the expected revelation"); next in II, 2, par.34: "The Election of the Christian Community" ("Israel is the negative side of the Christian community, mirror of judgment, a form that passes away"); finally in IV, 3, par. 69, 2: "The Light of Life," pp. 53–72 (p. 65: "In and with the prophecy of the history of Israel there takes place in all its historical autonomy and singularity the prophecy of Jesus Christ Himself in the form of an exact prefiguration It is a true type and adequate pattern." These three approaches appear contradictory, yet are not. They are all based on the same chronological approach to the OT. Broadly speaking they can be distinguished as: the OT as preparation, as antithesis, and as identity. These three lines are found everywhere in the NT and in the history of the church. It is regrettable that Barth has not more closely related them to each other.[6]

---

5. Barth, *Church Dogmatics* I/1, 5.

6. Hendrikus Berkhof, *Christian Faith: An Introduction to the Study of the Faith* (Grand Rapids: Eerdmans, 1979), 224. In *Church Dogmatics* IV/4, §74.1, Barth says, "In the New Testament witness this covenant history as the national history of Israel is replaced (or followed and completed) by covenant history as the history of Jesus Christ and in it the history of the race intended already in that national history" (Karl Barth, *The*

The Place of Israel in Systematic Theology

In all of the material dealing with Israel—and Berkhof surveys a number of other writers, from Irenaeus in the second century to the Reformation period and then to Weber, Brunner, and Barth in the twentieth century, as well as a number of Roman catholic scholars[7]—the equation can almost always be drawn between Israel and the Old Testament.[8] The place of Israel as a nation after New Testament times is more properly the domain of historians, and then, mostly, Jewish historians. As far as I can tell, the conspicuous exception would be the Roman Catholic writer Hans Küng.[9] I am not competent to make any further observations about the post–New Testament times, except to observe that what I mean by "Israel" is not found in its successor, namely Rabbinic Judaism. So if the theologians write of Israel and in doing so limit themselves to the Old Testament and to its climax in the New Testament, I believe that they will have done their duty.

ISRAEL IN THE NEW TESTAMENT

When we go to the Scriptures to determine what is genuine, we are faced with the living world of faith that understands the things given to us; there is no abstract, speculative theology there. For instance, the Paul who wrote "And so all Israel will be saved" is the same Paul who also wrote, "Five times I have received from the Jews the forty lashes minus one." If that makes us ask about a possible distinction between "Israel" and "the Jews," then we have to ask further about the mind of the early church when faced with persecution. Acts 4 records the prohibition placed on the preaching in the name of Jesus and the reaction by the church:

> After they were released, they went to their friends and reported what the chief priests and the elders had said to them. When they heard it, they raised their voices together to God and said, "Sovereign Lord, who made the heaven and the earth, the sea, and

---

Christian Life, trans. G. W. Bromiley [Grand Rapids: Eerdmans], 10). Consistently, Barth sees Israel as part of Christology.

7. Berkhof, *Christian Faith*, 222–25.

8. See also Gordon J. Spykman, *Reformational Theology: A New Paradigm for Doing Dogmatics* (Grand Rapids: Eerdmans, 1992), 249–375. Spykman is perhaps clearest among the modern writers I have found in seeing a current relevance to "our Jewish neighbors" (370–75).

9. Hans Küng, *Judaism: Between Yesterday and Tomorrow*, trans. John Bowden (London: SCM, 1992).

everything in them, it is you who said by the Holy Spirit through our ancestor David, your servant: 'Why did the Gentiles rage, and the peoples imagine vain things? The kings of the earth took their stand, and the rulers have gathered together against the Lord and against his Messiah.' For in this city, in fact, both Herod and Pontius Pilate, with the Gentiles and the peoples of Israel, gathered together against your holy servant Jesus, whom you anointed, to do whatever your hand and your plan had predestined to take place.'" (4:23–28)[10]

Knowing that the psalm that identified the Anointed One as God's Son/King who would receive the nations as his inheritance also recognised that those nations were steadfastly contemptuous of the Lord, the believers then saw that "the peoples of Israel" stood with the Gentiles in that rebellion. Whether the phrase "peoples of Israel" simply draws on the plural of Psalm 2 (Acts 4:25) is problematical.[11] Luke insisted that the psalm has the authority of the Holy Spirit,[12] and his companion, Paul, also knew the significance of the singular/plural distinction (see Gal 3:16), but a precise meaning for the plural is hard to discern. Whatever the range of possibilities, "Israel" is, at that point in the story at least, understood in opposition to God and to the church purchased by the blood of his Son.

At this point we must observe that, as a category for theological research, Israel has hardly missed out. Just given the vast amount of work over the last thirty years, in areas with titles such as "the Third Quest for the Historical Jesus" or "the New Perspective on Paul," all of which have involved detailed and stimulating research into Second Temple Judaism, we may well find ourselves overwhelmed by the theological study of Israel. But, of course, the question of what is meant by "a Jew" or by "Israel" remains. While I have reservations about some of his methods, James D. G. Dunn has addressed the question in *The Partings of the Ways*,[13] and concludes

---

10. Unless otherwise indicated, all Scripture quotations in this essay are from the NRSV, or are the author's own translations or paraphrases.

11. See C. K. Barrett, *Acts 1–14* (ICC; Edinburgh: T. & T.Clark, 2004), 247.

12. We should note that the authority of the Scriptures is not dependent on our views of "inspiration," etc.

13. James D. G. Dunn, *The Partings of the Ways* (London: SCM, 1991), 143ff. For instance—and Dunn is not alone in doing this—he posits a supposed historical background for various New Testament documents and then proceeds to reach concrete conclusions on the basis of the suppositions. See 158ff. where the Fourth Gospel is analysed against the background of its presumed authorship in the time of the complex processes of Jewish reconstruction at the time of the council of "Yavneh."

The Place of Israel in Systematic Theology

that, for Paul, "the Jews" may be best understood as the way of defining that body of people understood in their distinction from others, ethnically and/or religiously, while "Israel" "was much more an intra muros, intra-Jewish designation ... denoting a self-understanding in terms of election and covenant promise."[14]

Dunn addresses the question of alleged anti-Jewishness within the New Testament, and in doing so says the following:

> It is important not to fall into the mistake of thinking that [Romans] chapters 9–11 are about "the church and Israel," as though already in Paul's mind these were distinct entities. Not at all! The discussion of those chapters is exclusively about Israel (9.6). Israel is the factor of continuity; the chief question is whether God's purpose has been sustained and will be fulfilled in Israel (11.26). Gentiles are only heirs of the promise and covenant as having been grafted into the olive tree of Israel—not into a different tree, but into the same tree (11.17–24). The Israel of God's purpose consists of Jew first, but also Gentile (9.24 and 10. 12—the only two references to "Jew" in chs 9–11; and note the climax to the whole argument in 15.7–12). The point of 9.6 is not to disown Israel, but to point out that Israel is defined and determined by promise and election, not by physical descent, and not by works of the law (9.7–1 1). Those who are Israelites, but who fail to recognize the covenant character of their status as Israelites, have to that extent sold their own birthright for a bowl of bread and pottage (Gen. 25.29–34). Whereas those who recognize the totally gracious character of God's call and respond in faith are Israel, whether descended from Jacob or not.[15]

While I am able to agree in general with this paragraph, there is an assumption within it with which I have problems. It is: "Gentiles are only heirs of the promise and covenant as having been grafted into the olive tree of Israel—not into a different tree, but into the same tree (11.17–24)." I want to ask whether it is indeed true that the tree is simply "Israel." A similar problem exists in my mind with the approach taken by many to Galatians 6:16, "As for those who will follow this rule—peace be upon them, and mercy, and upon the Israel of God." Let me deal with the Galatians verse first.

---

14. Dunn, *Partings*, 145.
15. Dunn, *Partings*, 148, emphasis original.

The Gospel and Israel

There are two ways in which this is translated: "and upon the Israel of God" (NRSV, ASV, KJV, NASB, RV, ESV) and "even upon the Israel of God" (NIV, cf. JB). The RSV fudges and does not translate the Greek *kai* ("and" or "even"). The former seems to assume some distinction between all who follow the rule of the new creation, being all that matters, and the Israel of God, while the latter sees that those who follow that rule actually constitute the Israel of God. A correct solution to the problem will not come from Greek grammar but from exegesis and, frankly, it is hard to see how ordinary first-century believers who received this letter from Paul would have survived the commentators!

Galatians shows us that the matters of circumcision (in particular 2:3–5) and Jewish dietary laws (2:12–13) could cause deep and tragic division in the Christian community. Paul's strong language really must not be minimised: "I wish those who unsettle you would castrate themselves!" (5:12). Circumcision was now nothing, even if it once was something. But to some, the Jewish (ethnic/religious) distinctives of circumcision, dietary laws, and Sabbath observance (Col 2:8–17) were regarded as also essential to those who were not ethnically Jewish but who had come to faith in Israel's Messiah. While Paul was a Jew and so kept Jewish observances (Acts 21:17–26), and while Peter and the others also attended the temple services (Acts 3:1, etc.), there are a couple of defining moments in Acts which show that these Jewish distinctives had had their day. Those were Acts 10 and Peter's vision of the command to eat animals that were unclean according to the Torah, and Acts 15, where circumcision was ruled out as an essential for Gentile believers. Galatians is a tract that declares that Jewishness is part of the old creation but that it is no longer a defining feature of the Christian community:

> Therefore the law was our disciplinarian until Christ came, so that we might be justified by faith. But now that faith has come, we are no longer subject to a disciplinarian, for in Christ Jesus you are all sons of God through faith. As many of you as were baptized into Christ have clothed yourselves with Christ. There is no longer Jew or Greek, there is no longer slave or free, there is no longer male and female; for all of you are one in Christ Jesus. And if you belong to Christ, then you are Abraham's offspring, heirs according to the promise. (Gal 3:24–29)

Being in Christ by faith is what matters, for only by that are we Abraham's offspring. That alone is how the new creation is known. Those who follow that rule, rather than some other outmoded one, are those upon whom Paul pronounces his blessing. And that also applies to the Israel of God, the covenant people through whom the blessing of Abraham (Gal 3:14) has come to the whole world. Israel had a significant role in the history of salvation, but that role is both complete and, by many within Israel, rejected. As Bill Dumbrell put it, "National Israel by its crucifixion of Jesus had forfeited its place in the divine purposes,"[16] whereas those who are in Christ are sons of God.

"Sons of God" (Gal 3:26), if compared with the genealogy of Jesus in Luke 3:38, would imply that the heart of the new creation is the restoration of all that was forfeited in Adam. Hence, the blessing of Abraham relates directly to the promise of the Spirit through faith (Gal 3:14).

Dunn's treatment of Romans 11:17–24 (above), arguing that the tree into which Gentiles are grafted is Israel, seems to me, therefore, to miss the point. The tree, as evidenced in Romans 4:1ff., is not Israel at all: it is Abraham, to whom the promise of global restoration was given and who stands as the classic man of faith.

ISRAEL IN THE OLD TESTAMENT

What then is the place of Israel? Although the unavoidable polemics of the New Testament make the argument seem so negative towards Israel, I do not believe that that is so at all. There is a place for Israel, and that place is in the church of God,[17] and that place is a place of honour. But it is not the defining place; that is reserved for the Last Adam, the Second Man.[18]

---

16. William J. Dumbrell, *Galatians: A New Covenant Commentary* (Blackwood, S. Aust.: New Creation Pub., 2006), 95.

17. We might ask if the use of *ekklē[<macron]sia* in Acts 7:38 is in any way intended to imply some continuity between the Christian *ekklē[<macron]sia*, previously only mentioned in Acts at 5:11, or if it is simply a general use (see NRSV's "congregation"), reflected in the more political use of Acts 19:32, 39, 41. The LXX regularly uses *ekklē[<macron]sia* to translate the Hebrew *qahal* and *sunagō[<macron]gē[<macron]* to translate *edah*. The distinctions between the terms are worth pursuing; see, e.g., L. Coenen, "Church," in *The New International Dictionary of New Testament Theology*, ed. Colin Brown (Exeter: Paternoster, 1975), 1:291–96.

18. I think it is important that we do not throw out the theological baby with the cultural bathwater here. The use of "Man" (*anthrō[<macron]pos, adam*) is not intended to convey masculine dominance or whatever. If masculinity over against femininity was the issue, then there were other perfectly clear words (*anē[<macron]r, ish*) that could be used for that purpose.

The Gospel and Israel

Paul's description of Jesus as the Last Adam and the Second Man is simple. All that Adam was created to be and to know was forfeited in the fall and is fully restored in Christ (Col 2:9–10). But what is sometimes not well stated is that Christ, the man, the Jewish Messiah, did not come out of nowhere. Thus, Romans 9:4–5:

> They are Israelites, and to them belong the adoption, the glory, the covenants, the giving of the law, the worship, and the promises; to them belong the patriarchs, and from them, according to the flesh, comes the Messiah, who is over all, God blessed forever. Amen.

The Messiah comes from the matrix of Israel, the covenant people, and we should also recall that the covenant people come from the promise made to Abraham. While this may seem axiomatic, there are also elements that need to be stressed. Israel, while seeing itself as the offspring of Abraham, must also see itself as concerned with the purpose of God through Abraham, and that, it seems to me, is one of the critical elements so often overlooked. N. T. Wright has observed:

> As later tradition puts it, Abraham will be God's means of undoing the sin of Adam. This broad theme is given significant detail by a set of recurring motifs, in which the commands given to Adam in Genesis 1.28 reappear in new guise:[LIST by verses]
>
> 1.28: And God blessed them, and God said to them "Be fruitful and multiply, and fill the earth and subdue it; and have dominion over the fish of the sea and over the birds of the air and over every living thing that moves upon the earth."
>
> 12.2f.: I will make of you a great nation, and I will bless you, and make your name great, so that you will be a blessing. I will bless those who bless you . . .
>
> 17.2, 6, 8: I will make my covenant between me and you, and will multiply you exceedingly . . . I will make you exceedingly fruitful . . . and I will give you, and to your seed after you, all the land of Canaan . . .
>
> 22.16ff.: Because you have done this . . . I will indeed bless you, and I will multiply your descendants as the stars of heaven and as the sand which is on the seashore . . . and by you shall all the nations of the earth bless themselves, because you have obeyed my voice."

26.3f.: (The Lord said to Isaac) I will be with you, and will bless you; for to you and to your seed I will give all these lands, and I will fulfill the oath which I swore to Abraham your father. I will multiply your seed as the stars of heaven, and will give to your seed all these lands: and by your seed all the nations of the earth shall bless themselves . . .

26.24: Fear not, for I am with you and will bless you and multiply your descendants for my servant Abraham's sake.

28.3: (Isaac blessed Jacob and said) God Almighty bless you and make you fruitful and multiply you, that you may become a company of peoples. May he give you the blessing of Abraham, to you and to your seed with you, that you may take possession of the land of your sojournings which God gave to Abraham.

35.11f.: And God said to (Jacob) "I am God Almighty: be fruitful and multiply; a nation and company of nations shall come from you . . . the land which I gave to Abraham and Isaac I will give to you, and I will give the land to your descendants after you."

47.27: Thus Israel dwelt in the land of Egypt . . . and they gained possessions in it, and were fruitful and multiplied exceedingly.

48.3f.: Jacob said to Joseph, "God Almighty appeared to me . . . and said to me 'Behold, I will make you fruitful, and multiply you . . . and I will give you this land, to your seed after you . . .'"

Thus at key moments—Abraham's call, his circumcision, the offering of Isaac, the transitions from Abraham to Isaac and from Isaac to Jacob, and in the sojourn in Egypt—the narrative quietly makes the point that Abraham and his family inherit, in a measure, the role of Adam and Eve. The differences are not, however, insignificant. Except for (Gen.) 35.11f., echoed in 48.3f., the command ("be fruitful . . .") has turned into a promise ("I will make you fruitful . . ."). The word "exceedingly" is added in ch. 17. And, most importantly, possession of the land of Canaan, and supremacy over enemies, has taken the place of dominion over nature given in 1:28. We could sum up this aspect of Genesis by saying, Abraham's children are God's true humanity, and their homeland is the new Eden.[19]

---

19. N. T. Wright, "Adam, Israel and the Messiah," in *The Climax of the Covenant* (Minneapolis: Fortress, 1993), 21–23.

The Gospel and Israel

Abraham represents the new beginning for creation. Paul wrote that "from one [man] he (God) made all the nations to inhabit the whole earth" so that those nations would search for God and find him (Acts 17:26–27). By the time of Abraham, the nations were in fierce rebellion against the mandate given by God to Adam (Gen 11:4), so the call of Abraham included the declaration that the creational covenant blessing[20] would somehow be restored to the nations and families (cf. Gen 10:32) that acknowledged Abraham's blessing by God (Gen 12:1–3).

The overall purpose of God in calling Abraham was the blessing of the nations. Israel's role, as the primary descendent of Abraham, was to be a light to the nations (Isa 42:1, 6), and the Torah of Israel was to be understood as the law of God himself given in specific covenantal terms, with a view to the nations coming to Israel to discover the truth of Israel's God, with the result that shattered humanity may know glorious restoration (Isa 2:2–4). Describing the Torah in this way would explain why there is no particular distinction in the Torah between the so-called moral and ceremonial elements. Also we can see why some of the commandments are specifically for Israel and why later the new Christian church, though continuous with believing Israel, could reject certain items, or at least ignore them with a good conscience. As an example, Exodus 31:15–17 specifies that the institution of the Sabbath was "a sign forever between [the Lord] and the people of Israel." Imposition of Sabbath observance on Gentiles in the New Testament period, or on people today, is a failure to see the uniqueness of Israel's covenant relationship with the Lord. But this was not lost on Paul in Romans 14:5–6:

> Some judge one day to be better than another, while others judge all days to be alike. Let all be fully convinced in their own minds. Those who observe the day, observe it in honor of the Lord.

Likewise, neither Jesus nor the apostles were in conflict with the essential nature of the law concerning clean and unclean food when they declared all foods clean (Mark 7:20; Acts 10:9–15). Matthew 5:17–18 is important:

---

20. I understand "blessing" and "cursing" to be essentially covenant words, as exemplified in Deut 27–30. Dumbrell's argument (W. J. Dumbrell, *Covenant and Creation: A Theology of the Old Testament Covenants* [Grand Rapids: Baker, 1984], 11–46) that the covenant "established" with Noah was the confirmation of a prior covenant with the whole creation seems validated by the use of these words within the creation narrative and in the restoration of the creation mandate with Abraham.

The Place of Israel in Systematic Theology

> Do not think that I have come to abolish the law or the prophets; I have come not to abolish but to fulfill. For truly I tell you, until heaven and earth pass away, not one letter, not one stroke of a letter, will pass from the law until all is accomplished.

Though often taken to mean that the law and the prophets are eternally valid, I suspect that the opposite is the meaning. The law and the prophets are valid and applicable until they are filfiled (*plē̄rō̄sai*)! The law and the prophets are the written, unique testimony of Israel to the whole character of God. But that unique testimony has a particular purpose in view. Thus, Paul said that "Christ is the end [*telos*] of the law so that there may be righteousness for everyone who believes" (Rom 10:4). When Christ is believed as the one who takes away the sins of the world, whether that belief be by Jew or Gentile, then the *telos*, the end as the goal of Israel's law, will have come.

The place devoted to the nations in the Old Testament prophets should be noted here. On so many occasions the prophetic writings turn from dealing with Israel or Judah and address the nations. That is because the nations were always the focus of the plan of God. Equally, it was Israel's refusal to be part of that plan which was evidenced by its refusal to be the nation that testified, by its righteous living, to the truth of God. Far from being a tale about a large fish, the Book of Jonah is surely a record of Israel's resentment at God's concern for the nations and a demonstration of their refusal to be part of the stated solution, and a graphic declaration that God would indeed use them to fulfil his purpose.

Following the oracle concerning Babylon, Moab, Damascus, and others, and then Egypt and the judgement that would come on that nation, Isaiah has this to say:

> On that day Israel will be the third with Egypt and Assyria, a blessing in the midst of the earth, whom the Lord of hosts has blessed, saying, "Blessed be Egypt my people, and Assyria the work of my hands, and Israel my heritage." (Isa 19:24–25)

Far from the nations becoming part of Israel, Israel will be fully saved when it stands as a nation alongside other purified nations. Here the traditional enemies will be fully united.

ISRAEL AND JESUS

Paul's statement in Romans 9:5, mentioned above, that from Israel comes the Messiah, who is over all, God blessed forever, recalls Psalm 2, where the Anointed (Messiah) is the Son-King who is to receive the nations as his inheritance and the ends of the earth as his possession. This is what Adam was to do, to have dominion over all of creation—albeit a creation without rebellion or the pollutions of guilt. Thus, Jesus was born as "the king of the Jews" (Matt 2:2) and he was anointed as the beloved Son who would filfil all righteousness (Matt 3:15, 17). He came as Israel at last, "Out of Egypt I have called my son" (Matt 2:15), and he would indeed receive the nations, though not as the usurper's gift (Matt 4:8–10) but as the fruit of his triumph:

> And Jesus came and said to them, "All authority in heaven and on earth has been given to me. Go therefore and make disciples of all nations, baptizing them in the name of the Father and of the Son and of the Holy Spirit, and teaching them to obey everything that I have commanded you. And remember, I am with you always, to the end of the age." (Matt 28:18–20)

This was no missionary commission: it was the declaration that the purpose of God for creation was now established in the Last Adam, the one who had all authority in heaven and on earth, fully restored. Claiming the nations was everything that Israel had been set to do and now it was being done. There is a new Israel—and it is seen in all its restored purity on the day of Pentecost when first 120 and then 3,000 acknowledged that Jesus is Lord. Then from this new Israel, the word goes out to the nations, first to the Samaritans (Acts 8) and then to the Gentiles (Acts 10) and, after that, the kingdom of God is proclaimed and the things concerning the Lord Jesus Christ are taught boldly and without hindrance, even in Rome itself (Acts 28:31).

ISRAEL AT THE END OF ALL THINGS

How should we see Israel today? Given the way that God has worked salvation for the world, we could hardly be indifferent when there are ethnically Jewish men and women who do not know what it means to be part of the Israel of God. Redeemed humanity does not mean a homogeneous humanity, ethnically indistinct. Rather, the bride that is seen in Revelation

21 comprises God's "peoples" (21:3),[21] and as such includes all the nations of the earth (21:24) and "people will bring into [the holy city, the bride] the glory and honour of the nations" (21:26). This bride is radiant with the glory of God (Rev 21:11), once seen in Adam (Ps 8:5) and then in the worship of tabernacle and temple (Exod 40:34–35; 1 Kgs 8:10), then in Israel's Messiah (John 1:14). Now the glory is where it was intended. It fills the earth (Num 11:21)! And there is Israel, participating fully in the radiance because participating fully in her Messiah.

There is a place for Israel in systematic theology, but hardly in some limited eschatological role. It is the place of the privileged people, to whom "belongs the adoption, the glory, the covenants, the giving of the law, the worship, and the promises; to them belong the patriarchs, and from them, according to the flesh, comes the Messiah, who is over all, God blessed forever. Amen" (Rom 9:4–5).

And, by the abounding grace of Israel's Messiah, it is the place of a people who, having been provoked to jealousy for their inheritance through the preaching of the gospel, are now standing as heirs of God, fellow heirs of Christ and with all those who are in him. The bride of Christ is wonderfully, gloriously multi-ethnic.

---

21. See Bruce Metzger, *A Textual Commentary on the Greek New Testament* (London: UBS, 1971), 765.

3

How Jewish Is Israel in the New Testament?

—Dr. Stephen Voorwinde

The title of this chapter sounds like one of those redundant questions to which there must be an obvious answer: Is the pope a Catholic? Is the sky blue? Is water wet? Some readers may wonder whether there is really an issue here. Is this a question even worth considering? Does this question really deserve your precious time? At the outset let me say quite categorically that this is a question of the utmost significance. It is deeply theological, highly contemporary, and profoundly practical. At the same time it is also a question that we need to answer very precisely. Unless we do we could end up with a truncated view of the church; we will be misguided in our evangelism of Jewish people, and (perhaps most tragically) we leave ourselves open to repeating the mistakes of the past.

So how Jewish is *Israel* in the New Testament? I want to begin by citing the definition of Israel in Bauer's lexicon of the Greek New Testament. This lexicon is to New Testament Greek what the *Oxford English Dictionary* is to contemporary English. If you really want to know the meaning of a Greek word this will generally be regarded as the lexicon of choice. When it comes to the word "Israel" Bauer lists three categories of meaning:

1. The patriarch Jacob, who was also called Israel.
2. The people or nation of Israel.

3. In the transition between the second and third categories, the lexicon makes a very interesting and loaded statement: "Israel is the main self-designation of God's ancient people; from this as a starting-point it is also used of Christians as entitled to the term Israel."[1]

The quote is from the third English edition of Bauer's lexicon. When it came to the last category the first and second editions had a far bolder definition. They did not say that Israel referred to "Christians as entitled to the term Israel." They put it far more strongly than that: they claimed that Israel was "also used in a figurative sense of the Christians as the true nation of Israel."[2] Are Christians "the true nation of Israel" or are they merely "entitled to the term Israel"? The second alternative is to be welcomed as the more cautious definition. It would be more accurate to say that Christians are entitled to the term Israel than that they are the true nation of Israel.

Nevertheless, even the more cautious definition is open to challenge. Does the New Testament ever refer to Christians by the term Israel, and is an individual Christian ever called an Israelite in the New Testament? The name Israel is found sixty-eight times in the New Testament and the term Israelite occurs nine times. But in this total of seventy-seven occurrences do these terms ever refer to (Gentile) Christians? This chapter therefore will seek to question the validity of Bauer's third category. This may seem like a rather presumptuous thing to do. It is like questioning an entry in the *Oxford English Dictionary*. Sometimes this needs to be done. Otherwise dictionaries would become very hidebound affairs indeed. They thrive on scholarly criticism.

The best way to critique a dictionary is by re-examining the data on which a particular entry is based. So the ambitious task that lies before us is to examine the seventy-seven occurrences of Israel and Israelite in the New Testament. The more straightforward references to these terms are to be found in the Gospels, while the more nuanced and complex uses occur in Paul's writings. The rest of the New Testament writings occupy a midway

---

1. Frederick William Danker, ed., *A Greek-English Lexicon of the New Testament and Other Early Christian Literature* (3rd ed.; Chicago: University of Chicago Press, 2000), 481. This edition is based on Walter Bauer's *Griechisch-Deutsches Wörterbuch zu den Schriften des Neuen Testaments und der frühchristlichen Literatur* (6th ed.; ed. Kurt Aland and Barbara Aland, with Viktor Reichmann) and on previous English editions by William F. Arndt, F. Wilbur Gingrich, and F. W. Danker. Danker's 3rd edition is hereafter abbreviated by convention as BDAG. The previous editions are abbreviated BAG and BAGD.

2. BAG, 382; BAGD, 381.

position. Our discussion will therefore move progressively from the easier references to the more difficult.

1. MARK

This Gospel has two rather straightforward references to Israel:

In Mark 12:29 Jesus quotes the Shema from Deuteronomy 6:5: "Hear, O Israel: The LORD our God, the LORD is one."[3] Clearly the reference is to Old Testament Israel.

In Mark 15:32 the chief priests and the teachers of the law mock the crucified Jesus: "Let this Messiah, this king of Israel, come down now from the cross, that we may see and believe." One of the profound ironies of Mark's Gospel is that Jesus is called "king" only in chapter 15, in the context of the crucifixion. Whenever Gentiles, such as Pilate and the soldiers, refer to Jesus as a king, they call him "king of the Jews" (vv. 2, 9, 12, 18, 26). It is only the Jewish leaders who refer to him as the "king of Israel." So clearly here Israel refers to the Jewish people.

Although Mark uses the name Israel on only two occasions, he happens to pick up the two most common uses in the New Testament. It can refer to Old Testament Israel and also to the Jewish people of the first century AD. It would probably also be fair to say that the New Testament encourages us to see a continuity between the two groups.

2. MATTHEW

Matthew's twelve references to Israel are simply an extension of Marcan usage. The very first reference is again to Israel as the people of God. Matthew 2:6 quotes Micah's prophecy about Bethlehem: ". . . out of you will come a ruler who will shepherd my people Israel."

As the promised shepherd, Jesus takes this prophecy very literally. When he commissions the Twelve for their first mission trip he gives them very specific instructions: "Do not go among the Gentiles or enter any town of the Samaritans. Go rather to the lost sheep of Israel" (10:5–6). Their ministry is to be very focused and particularistic. Jesus reiterates this in his conversation with the Canaanite woman: "I was sent only to the lost sheep

---

3. Unless otherwise indicated, all Scripture quotations in this essay are taken from the NIV.

of Israel" (15:24). The language sounds like the Old Testament, where God says through the prophet Jeremiah, "My people have been lost sheep" (Jer 50:6). Jesus is essentially dealing with the same people, the people of God, the lost sheep of the house of Israel.

There are times in Matthew's Gospel when it is difficult to distinguish between Israel as God's Old Testament people and the Jews of Jesus' day. After an exorcism, for example, the crowd are amazed and exclaim, "Nothing like this has ever been seen in Israel" (Matt 9:33). Is this Old Testament Israel or the nation in Jesus' day? Either way their statement would be true.

The same ambiguity can be detected when Jesus astonishes another crowd, this time on the other side of the lake of Galilee: "The people were amazed when they saw the mute speaking, the crippled made well, the lame walking and the blind seeing. And they praised the God of Israel" (15:31).

Because Jesus' mission is consciously limited to the house of Israel, it is easy to understand his surprise at the faith of a Gentile centurion: "Truly I tell you, I have not found anyone in Israel with such great faith" (8:10).

The tragic irony of Matthew's Gospel is that Gentiles such as the centurion and the Canaanite woman are both commended for their great faith while, on the other hand, Jesus suffers the most from some of the very people to whom his mission was directed. Again the Jewish leaders mock him with bitter sarcasm as the king of Israel on the cross (27:42). Perhaps even more painful was the cruel betrayal by one of his own disciples: "Then what was spoken by Jeremiah the prophet was filfiled: 'They took the thirty pieces of silver, the price set on him by the people of Israel, and they used them to buy the potter's field, as the Lord commanded me'" (Matt 27:9–10; cf. Zech 11:12, 13; Jer 19:1–13; 32:6–9). In this context "the people of Israel" are actually the leaders—the chief priests and the elders, the very ones who were to mock him at the cross.

In all these references Matthew has been using the term Israel no differently from Mark. Israel is simply the people of God—either in its Old Testament incarnation or as Jesus' Jewish contemporaries. For Matthew it is one and the same people. Whether the focus is on the masses of lost sheep or on their leaders makes no difference. As with Mark, Israel is the nation, the people of God.

But Matthew also breaks new ground. After Herod dies, an angel of the Lord appears in a dream to Joseph in Egypt: "Get up," says the angel, "take the child and his mother and go to the land of Israel, for those who were trying to take the child's life are dead." Joseph obeys: "So he got up,

The Gospel and Israel

took the child and his mother and went to the land of Israel" (2:20–21). To the casual reader this may not seem unusual, but here Israel is used in a way that is unique to Matthew in the New Testament. He refers to "the land of Israel." Only Matthew of all the New Testament writers uses Israel in a geographical sense.[4] This was the standard way for Palestinian Jews to refer to their homeland and it also corresponds to the normal designation of the country in rabbinic literature.[5] Yet in the New Testament Matthew is the only writer to use the term in this way. Elsewhere the land is referred to by the individual provinces, such as Judea and Galilee.

The only other reference to Israel as the land would appear to be in 10:23, where Jesus tells his disciples, "You will not finish going through the towns of Israel before the Son of Man comes." Whatever precisely this prediction might mean, there is no mistaking the reference to Israel in a geographical sense. Again it needs to be said that this exhausts the New Testament references to Israel as the land. Apart from these few references in Matthew, there are no further references to the land of Israel. From now on, whatever else Israel may mean, it does not refer to the land.

We have now covered all of Matthew's references except one. Does this final reference go well beyond everything we have discovered so far? In 19:28 Jesus makes this astounding promise to his disciples: "Truly I tell you, at the renewal of all things, when the Son of Man sits on his glorious throne, you who have followed me will also sit on twelve thrones, judging the twelve tribes of Israel."

For our purposes the critical question has to do with the identity of "the twelve tribes of Israel." Are they physically and racially the twelve tribes of Israel? Or do they symbolise the entire church? In other words, are "the twelve tribes of Israel" to be understood ethnically or metaphorically? Does this verse provide support for Bauer's third category? The metaphorical use of Israel would be without precedent in Matthew's Gospel. This is also the only Gospel to make specific mention of the church (16:18; 18:17). To suddenly identify the church as Israel would therefore be out of character for Matthew.[6] Perhaps the best way to understand Jesus' promise is by

---

4. Horst Balz and Gerhard Schneider, eds., *Exegetical Dictionary of the New Testament* (Grand Rapids: Eerdmans, 1990–1992), 2:203 (hereafter abbreviated as *EDNT*).

5. Gerhard Kittel and Gerhard Friedrich, eds., *Theological Dictionary of the New Testament*, trans. and ed. Geoffrey W. Bromiley (Grand Rapids: Eerdmans, 1964–74), 3:384 (hereafter *TDNT*).

6. Robert H. Gundry, *Matthew: A Commentary on His Handbook for a Mixed Church under Persecution* (2nd ed.; Grand Rapids: Eerdmans, 1994), 393, argues as

adopting Don Carson's interpretation: "At the consummation the Twelve will judge the nation of Israel, presumably for its general rejection of Jesus Messiah."[7] So this may be an eschatological Israel, but it is still ethnic Israel. It is not the church.

In Matthew, therefore, Israel spans the whole gamut of the people or nation of Israel—from the Old Testament to the people in Jesus' day and beyond that to the consummation. Occasionally the word can also be used geographically. Israel is not only the people but may at times also refer to the land in which they live.

3. LUKE-ACTS

Matthew and Mark were both Jews. Now we come to the only Gentile writer in the New Testament—Luke, the beloved physician. Is it any different with him or does he maintain the pattern we have already discovered? It is interesting that he has a total of thirty-two references to Israel and Israelite in his two volumes. This is well more than any other writer, even more than Paul, who in all his letters has a total of only twenty occurrences. So Luke the Gentile writer refers to Israel more than any other writer in the New Testament (who, as far as we know, were all Jews!).

A. Luke's Gospel

In the Gospel there are eleven references to Israel, but more than half are found in the first two chapters, which is arguably the most Jewish section of the book:

---

follows: "Neither in Jesus' intention nor in Matthew's does 'Israel' mean the church (cf. the distinction made in 8:11, 12; 21:43; 22:7; 23:32–36; 27:25). Particular reference to the twelve tribes supports such a distinction."

7. D. A. Carson, "Matthew," in *The Expositor's Bible Commentary*, vol. 8, ed. Frank E. Gaebelein and J. D. Douglas (eds.), (Grand Rapids: Zondervan, 1984), 426. Cf. Donald A. Hagner, *Matthew 14–28* (WBC 33B; Dallas: Word, 1995), 565: "The twelve disciples, representing the true Israel, will thus be vindicated before unbelieving Israel by assuming authority over them—an authority to judge or rule over them delegated to the Twelve by the Son of Man himself." A more cautious interpretation is offered by Leon Morris, *The Gospel according to Matthew* (Grand Rapids: Eerdmans, 1992), 496: "Judging is sometimes used in the sense of ruling, and we cannot rule out such an understanding of the present passage. We can scarcely say more than that the Twelve would share in the activities of that glorious time, that they would enjoy kingly state, and that they would engage in some way in the ordering of the affairs of the twelve tribes."

The Gospel and Israel

The angel Gabriel prophesies of John the Baptist: "He will bring back many of the people of Israel to the Lord their God" (1:16).

Mary praises God because "He has helped his servant Israel" (1:54).

Zechariah praises "the Lord, the God of Israel" (1:68).

John the Baptist "lived in the wilderness until he appeared publicly to Israel" (1:80).

Simeon was a "righteous and devout" man "waiting for the consolation of Israel" (2:25). He called Jesus "a light for revelation to the Gentiles, and the glory of your people Israel" (2:32). Notice the contrast between the Gentiles and Israel at this point.

This contrast is again brought out when Jesus speaks in the synagogue at Nazareth in Luke 4:25–27:

> I assure you that there were many widows in Israel in Elijah's time, when the sky was shut for three and a half years and there was a severe famine throughout the land. Yet Elijah was not sent to any of them, but to a widow in Zarephath in the region of Sidon. And there were many in Israel with leprosy in the time of Elisha the prophet, yet not one of them was cleansed—only Naaman the Syrian.

The contrast continues when Jesus commends the Gentile centurion: "I tell you, I have not found such great faith even in Israel" (7:9). Again Israel is an ethnic entity, and this once more provides the background to his promise to his disciples that they will "sit on thrones, judging the twelve tribes of Israel" (Luke 22:30; cf. Matt 19:28).

Finally, after the resurrection on the way to Emmaus, Jesus has to listen to the complaints of some of his disappointed followers: ". . . but we had hoped that he was the one who was going to redeem Israel" (Luke 24:21).

So even in Luke all the references are to ethnic Israel in contrast to the Gentiles. Like Matthew he covers all the bases—Old Testament, contemporary, and eschatological. Yet the bottom line is still the same—Israel is Israel, not the church. But what about Acts? Here the church is born and the Gentile mission commences, but does the meaning of *Israel* change?

B. Acts

As with Luke there is a pattern to the references in Acts. In Luke the majority of occurrences were found in the very Jewish opening chapters. In Acts

How Jewish Is Israel in the New Testament?

it would be fair to say that the Jewish section of the book covers chapters 1–13. All but one of the sixteen references to Israel are found in this section.

At the outset we are reminded of the disciples' parochial vision when they ask the risen Jesus, "Lord, are you at this time going to restore the kingdom to Israel?" (1:6).

In his Pentecost sermon Peter addresses his audience as "the house of Israel" (2:36). Before the Sanhedrin he refers to "all the people of Israel" (4:10), while in the next chapter Luke calls this body "the Senate of the sons of Israel" (5:21 NASB).

When the Christians in Jerusalem are threatened by the Sanhedrin, they lift up their voices in prayer:

> Indeed Herod and Pontius Pilate met together with the Gentiles and the people of Israel in this city to conspire against your holy servant Jesus, whom you anointed. They did what your power and will had decided beforehand should happen. Now, Lord, consider their threats and enable your servants to speak your word with great boldness. (4:27–29)

Note again the contrast between the Gentiles and the people of Israel. It should also be noted that this prayer was answered. In the next chapter Peter and the other apostles boldly tell the Sanhedrin, "The God of our fathers raised Jesus from the dead—whom you had killed by hanging him on a tree. God exalted him to his own right hand as Prince and Saviour that he might give repentance and forgiveness of sins to Israel" (5:30–31).

The prayer for boldness is again answered in Stephen's majestic speech before the Sanhedrin. Three times he refers to Israel in the sense of God's Old Testament people (7:23, 37, 42).

When Paul is converted the Lord tells Ananias, "This man is my chosen instrument to carry my name before the Gentiles and their kings and before the people of Israel" (9:15). Again an explicit distinction is made between the Gentiles and Israel. Paul's mission was to be to both groups, whereas Peter reminds his audience at Cornelius' house that Jesus' ministry had been confined to Israel (10:36). We see Paul's broader ministry reflected in the opening line of his very first recorded sermon. When he addresses the synagogue at Pisidian Antioch he begins by saying, "Men of Israel[8] and you Gentiles who worship God, listen to me!" (13:16). There

---

8. "Men of Israel" translates Ἄνδρες Ἰσραηλῖται (literally "men Israelites"), an expression that also occurs in Acts 2:22; 3:12; 5:35; 21:28. In all cases Jews are addressing their fellow Jews.

The Gospel and Israel

are three further references to Israel in Paul's sermon and on each occasion Paul is referring to his fellow Jews, as he did in his opening line (13:16, 23, 24). He is consistently referring to Jews who lived either in Israel or the Diaspora in the first century AD. Paul is making a very clear distinction between Jews and Gentiles. It's a mixed gathering and he addresses his audience very precisely.

From here we move directly to the last chapter of Acts. After an adventurous sea voyage Paul at last arrives as a prisoner in Rome. One of the first groups he wants to meet is the Jewish leadership. When they have arrived he explains his situation: "It is because of the hope of Israel that I am bound with this chain" (28:20). That hope of Israel is the hope of the resurrection—a uniquely Jewish hope (cf. 26:22–23).

So even though Luke is a Gentile writer and the Book of Acts penetrates deeply into the Gentile world, he is always careful to use Israel in an ethnic sense.[9] It refers either to the Old Testament people of God or to the Jews of his own day. Gentiles are never called Israelites and Israel is never the church. The Gospel and Acts are share the same perspective.

4. THE GOSPEL OF JOHN

All the references in this Gospel have to do with Israel as a nation. Without exception all are found on the lips of Jewish speakers.

John the Baptist says about Jesus, ". . . the reason I came baptizing with water was that he might be revealed to Israel" (1:31).

Later in the chapter Jesus declares to Nathaniel, "Here is a true Israelite, in whom there is nothing false" (1:47). This is the only time that that the term Israelite is used anywhere in the Gospels. Nathaniel shows just what a true Israelite he is by responding, "Rabbi, you are the Son of God; you are the King of Israel" (1:49). He has recognised Jesus as the Messiah of Israel and as the fulfilment of God's promises.[10]

---

9. John F. Walvoord, "Is the Church the Israel of God?," *Bibliotheca Sacra* 101 (1944) 407, has rightly observed: "[T]he terms *Israel* and *Gentiles* continue to be used after the institution of the church at Pentecost and the terms are mutually exclusive. Both Gentiles and Israelites continue to exist after the church began, and while some of each came into the church, the Gentiles and Israelites continued as such. Israel as a nation is addressed again and again *after* the institution of the church (Acts 3:12; 4:8, 10; 5:31, 31, 35; 21:28 etc.)."

10. Cf. Colin Brown, ed., *The New International Dictionary of New Testament Theology* (3 vols.; Exeter: Paternoster, 1975–78), hereafter abbreviated as *NIDNTT*.

Next we find Jesus asking Nicodemus whether he is the teacher of Israel (3:10), and finally on Palm Sunday the crowd goes out to meet Jesus, shouting, "Blessed is the King of Israel" (12:13).

Although John is such a cosmic and universal Gospel, there is a sense in which it is also very parochial. Jesus is revealed to Israel and he is acknowledged as the king of Israel. The true Israelite is the one who confesses him as such. John's references are few and they have a uniform and consistent meaning. They always apply to ethnic Israel.

5. HEBREWS

The Epistle to the Hebrews uses Israel only three times. All three occurrences are rooted in the Old Testament and yet all three have somewhat different meanings. The first two references come from the longest Old Testament quotation in the New. In Hebrews 8:8–10 the author quotes from Jeremiah 31:8–10:

> But God found fault with the people and said: "The time is coming, declares the Lord, when I will make a new covenant with the house of Israel and with the house of Judah. It will not be like the covenant I made with their forefathers when I took them by the hand to lead them out of Egypt, because they did not remain faithful to my covenant, and I turned away from them, declares the Lord. This is the covenant I will make with the house of Israel after that time, declares the Lord. I will put my laws in their minds and write them on their hearts. I will be their God, and they will be my people."

Within these verses Israel is used in slightly different ways. First, the house of Israel is distinguished from the house of Judah (v. 8), and designates the northern kingdom, but then in v. 10 it is used more comprehensively to refer to both houses. The identification of this new covenant partner is crucial for our purposes. Even when it comes to the new covenant, the Lord makes the covenant with Israel. It doesn't say that he makes it with the church. This is not how Jeremiah prophesies it nor is this how the writer to the Hebrews understands the fulfilment. The new covenant is made with the house of Israel and the house of Judah. The first reference to this covenant in the New Testament is when Jesus institutes the Lord's Supper on the night before his death (Luke 22:20). Those with him at the time were his disciples—and they were all Jewish! So even the new covenant is

The Gospel and Israel

inaugurated in an exclusively Jewish context. It is still the covenant with Israel, a very Jewish covenant.

The only other reference is in Hebrews 11:22: "By faith Joseph, when he was dying, made mention of the exodus of the sons of Israel, and gave orders concerning his bones" (NASB). The "sons of Israel" should probably be understood here in a rather general sense.[11] The NIV simply calls them "the Israelites." Again it is a reference to the people of God in the Old Testament.

So the letter to the Hebrews continues the pattern. Israel refers to an ethnic group. It is not a metaphor for the church.

6. REVELATION

The Apocalypse is well known for its symbolism. In two of its three references to Israel that symbolism is clearly anchored in the Old Testament:

In his message to the church at Pergamum, Christ declares, "I have a few things against you, because you have there some who hold the teaching of Balaam, who kept teaching Balak to put a stumbling block before the sons of Israel, to eat things sacrificed to idols, and to commit acts of immorality" (Rev 2:14 NASB). The reference is to the tragic events that occurred at Baal-Peor as recorded in Numbers 25:1–2; 31:16.

On a brighter note, towards the end of Revelation there is a glowing description of the New Jerusalem. Once again the description draws on Old Testament imagery: "It had a great, high wall with twelve gates, and with twelve angels at the gates. On the gates were written the names of the twelve tribes of Israel" (Rev 21:12).

So far in Revelation Israel is Old Testament Israel. Can the same also be said in the third reference? In chapter 7 we meet a famous multitude of people. First an angel declares, "Do not harm the land or the sea or the trees until we put a seal on the foreheads of the servants of our God" (v. 3). In the next verse John recalls, "Then I heard the number of those who

---

11. According to *EDNT*, 2:203: "The NT has no independent interest in the use of 'Israel' as a personal name ... Already in the Hebrew explicit reference to the ancestor was largely lost and replaced by collective reference to the people." In the New Testament the members of the people of Israel are commonly referred to as "the sons of Israel" and "the house of Israel." In neither case does there seem to be a conscious reference to the patriarch Jacob. This observation may even apply in the case of the expression οἱ ἐξ Ἰσραήλ in Rom 9:6 which can simply be paraphrased as "those who are members of the people of Israel by birth."

were sealed: 144,000 from all the tribes of Israel" (v. 4). Within the context of chapter 7 it is appealing to identify the 144,000 in verses 1–8 with the church militant and the innumerable host in the remainder of the chapter with the church triumphant (vv. 9–17). Then both throngs would symbolise the church—first on earth and then in heaven. This would also imply that that the "144,000 from the tribes of Israel" is symbolic of the church. Admittedly this is a very attractive interpretation, but it is not the whole picture of what is happening in Revelation 7.

Richard Bauckham has very perceptively picked up some significant literary parallels between Revelation chapter 7 and chapter 5. In 5:5 John hears that victory has been won by the Lion of the tribe of Judah, the Root of David, but then in the next verse John sees the slaughtered Lamb, whose blood has ransomed a people from every tribe, people, language, and nation (v. 9). From this observation Bauckham concludes:

> By juxtaposing these images, John gives his Jewish Christian interpretation of Jewish messianic hopes. The conquering Davidic messiah is not repudiated, but his victory is shown to be by sacrifice, not military conflict, while the people he delivers are not only Israelites, but from all the nations. Moreover, the second image, the slaughtered Lamb, is just as scriptural as the first ... By juxtaposing the two scriptural images of the conquering messiah and the slaughtered Lamb, John builds the notion of a messiah who conquers by sacrificial death.[12]

Likewise in chapter 7 John hears the number of those who were sealed from all the tribes of Israel (v. 4), but he sees the countless multitude from all nations (v. 9). Again Bauckham draws a perceptive conclusion:

> Just as he has deliberately juxtaposed the contrasting images of the messiah in in 5:5–6, so he has deliberately juxtaposed contrasting images of the messiah's followers in 7:4–9 ... [T]he 144,000 are the Israelite army of the Lion of Judah, while the international multitude are the followers of the slaughtered Lamb. The purpose of the contrast is the same as in 5:5–6: to give a Christian interpretation of an element of Jewish messianic expectation.[13]

It would therefore be simplistic to say without qualification that the 144,000 are an image of the church. Rather John has taken Jewish hopes

12. Richard Bauckham, "The List of the Tribes in Revelation 7 Again," *JSNT* 42 (1991) 102–3.
13. Bauckham, "List," 103.

and transposed them to a higher key. The numbered multitude of Israel becomes the innumerable multitude of the nations.[14] So although the "144,000 from all the tribes of Israel" at first glance seem to symbolise the church, it can be argued that this is in fact indicative of a limited Jewish hope that in the light of Christ's redemptive work needs to be dramatically enlarged.

So Revelation consistently draws on Old Testament imagery. On each occasion Israel refers to the ancient people of God.

7. PAUL

Paul's usage is more complex than the other New Testament uses. To simplify matters the Pauline corpus will be handled in two parts: Romans and the rest. Romans is difficult; some of the remaining references in Paul are more difficult still.

A. Romans

Of Paul's twenty references to Israel (17x) and Israelite (3x), no less than fourteen are found in Romans—all of them in chapters 9–11. At the beginning of his discussion he refers to his fellow Jews for whom he has such heartfelt concern as Israelites (9:4). He is also careful to identify himself as an Israelite (10:1).[15] This makes Paul's discussion in these chapters all the more poignant. Those for whom Paul has such deep sorrow and anguish are his own flesh and blood, those of his own race (9:3). Here in a profoundly personal way he tackles one of the major objections to the doctrine of justification by faith that he has so carefully developed in chapters 1–5.[16]

---

14. Contra Christopher R. Smith, "The Portrayal of the Church as the New Israel in the Names and Order of the Tribes in Revelation 7.5–8," *JSNT* 39 (1990) 111–18.

15. The only other occasion on which he refers to himself in this way is in self-defence against the super-apostles who had infiltrated the church at Corinth: "Are they Hebrews? So am I. Are they Israelites? So am I. Are they Abraham's descendants? So am I" (2 Cor 11:22). "A sharp conceptual distinction between the three predicates is scarcely possible," writes H. Kuhli in *EDNT* 2:205, "rather, Paul describes his full membership in the people of God."

16. Cf. W. D. Davies, "Paul and the People of Israel," *NTS* 24 (1977) 13: "[T]he very validity or efficacy of the gospel which he preached was poignantly, even agonizingly, challenged for Paul by the refusal of his own people to accept it.... The failure of the mission to the Jews raised acutely the question of the faithfulness or reliability of the very

How can Paul's gospel be true if it was rejected by those for whom it was originally intended?[17] If Israel fails to believe, if Israel is not justified by faith, then haven't God's purposes also failed?[18]

Paul's response begins by making a fundamental distinction within Israel itself. Read literally, his assertion sounds like an epigram: "Not all those who are of Israel are Israel" (9:6).[19] In the Greek it is a verbless and therefore timeless statement. Here is a saying that has always been true, is still true, and will remain true until the end of history. Not all those who belong to Israel physically belong to Israel spiritually. Not all who are members of the people of Israel by birth are members of Israel by faith. Here Paul is not enlarging Israel, but reducing it. Spiritual Israel is the smaller circle within the larger circle of physical Israel. The context makes this clear. Not all the physical sons of Abraham were also the spiritual sons of Abraham. Ishmael and Esau are given as the earliest and clearest examples. Not all Israel is Israel. Those who are Israel by grace are found within those who are Israel by race. They are an *ecclesiola in ecclesia*. They are a smaller group, not a larger one, than the parent body.

This becomes clear in Paul's next reference to Israel: "And Isaiah cries out concerning Israel, 'Though the number of the sons of Israel be as the sand of the sea, it is the remnant that will be saved'" (9:27 NASB). Here spiritual Israel is defined as "an elect remnant within ethnic Israel."[20] In the references that follow, Israel is either the totality of the people or the remnant within the larger body. Again and again Paul is at pains to show that principle at work throughout the Old Testament and in his own day.

God who, Paul had claimed, justified even the ungodly. And so Paul devotes Rom. ix–xi to this question."

17. It is Israel's rejection of the gospel that Paul later describes as her "stumbling" (Rom 11:11), "transgression" (11:11, 12), "loss" (11:12) and "rejection" (11:15). See Terence L. Donaldson, "Jewish Christianity, Israel's Stumbling and the *Sonderweg* Reading of Paul," *JSNT* 29 (2006) 31. Donaldson further argues that this was the nature of Israel's failure rather than that it was "a failure to recognize what God was doing for the Gentiles in Christ" (33) or, more specifically, "Israel's rejection of Paul's Gentile mission" (39).

18. For a more detailed discussion of these chapters see my article, "Rethinking Israel: An Exposition of Romans 11:25-27," *Vox Reformata* 68 (2003) 4-48.

19. The word "descended" found in many English translations is not found in the Greek text. There is no conscious thought of the patriarch Jacob here. *Israel* is simply "an established term for the people" (*TDNT*, 3:383).

20. Thus W. Edward Glenny, "The 'People of God' in Romans 9:25-26," *Bibliotheca Sacra* 152 (1995) 46.

The Gospel and Israel

He laments the fact that "Israel, who pursued a law of righteousness, has not attained it" (9:31). It is a lament that is taken up again in the next chapter:

> Again I ask: Did Israel not understand? First, Moses says, "I will make you envious by those who are not a nation; I will make you angry by a nation that has no understanding." And Isaiah boldly says, "I was found by those who did not seek me; I revealed myself to those who did not ask for me." But concerning Israel he says, "All day long I have held out my hands to a disobedient and obstinate people." (10:19–21)

So Paul detects a pattern. What was true in his day was also true in Moses' day and again in Isaiah's day. What Paul is witnessing is nothing new. But if this is true, then it leads to the inevitable question that we find at the beginning of chapter 11:

> I ask then: Did God reject his people? By no means! I am an Israelite myself, a descendant of Abraham, from the tribe of Benjamin. God did not reject his people, whom he foreknew. Don't you know what the Scripture says in the passage about Elijah—how he appealed to God against Israel: "Lord, they have killed your prophets and torn down your altars; I am the only one left, and they are trying to kill me"? And what was God's answer to him? "I have reserved for myself seven thousand who have not bowed the knee to Baal." So too, at the present time there is a remnant chosen by grace. And if by grace, then it is no longer by works; if it were, grace would no longer be grace. But if by works, then it is no longer grace; if it were, grace would no longer be grace. What then? What Israel sought so earnestly it did not obtain, but the elect did. The others were hardened.

So there is Paul's answer. Did God reject his people? Has God's word failed? No! No! And a thousand times no!

And why not, Paul?

> Because there has always been a remnant, a remnant of grace. And I know. I can speak from experience, because I myself am a prime example of that remnant. Look at me. I am an Israelite. God has chosen me. I am a trophy of his grace.[21]

---

21. Cf. M. C. Mulder, "The Kingdom, Israel and the Church: Paul's Thoughts on the Relevance of God's Promises to Israel (Romans 9–11)," *In die Skriflig* 35 (2001) 297: "Salvation is purely dependent on God's merciful acting. This thought is stressed by quotations from the Old Testament as the continuing way of God's acting throughout history.

That would seem to be a logical end to Paul's argument: "There is still a remnant. There is still an *ecclesiola in ecclesia* as there always has been. That's how it was in the Old Testament and that's how it still is today. God's purposes haven't changed; they are the same as they have always been. Hence God's word has not failed. The principle that not all Israel is Israel is as true now as it ever was. I have proved my point. Case closed."

But this is not where Paul leaves it. This is not the end of his argument. God's faithfulness is not proved only by looking to the past (to the Old Testament) or even to the present (the believing remnant), but also by looking to the future.[22] There will come a time when the remnant is no longer a remnant, but when it can be described as "all Israel." This is what Paul looks forward to in Romans 11:25-26:

> I do not want you to be ignorant of this mystery, brothers, so that you may not be conceited: Israel has experienced a hardening in part until the full number of the Gentiles has come in. And so all Israel will be saved, as it is written: "The deliverer will come from Zion; he will turn godlessness away from Jacob. And this is my covenant with them when I take away their sins."

This is Paul's last reference to Israel in this discussion and it is the climax to everything that has gone before. Just as he has been speaking of ethnic Israel throughout these chapters, he is still speaking of ethnic Israel here. In fact, he specifically distinguishes Israel from the Gentiles in these verses. This is a glorious prophecy for the people of Israel.[23] This is a

---

Eventually this does not turn out to be a new soteriology after the coming of Jesus Christ. The same soteriology has already been present in the structure of the covenant in the Old Testament."

22. Thus Terence L. Donaldson, "'Riches for the Gentiles' (Rom 11:12): Israel's Rejection and Paul's Gentile Mission," *JBL* 112 (1993) 89: "Up to 11:10 Paul has defined Israel solely in terms of the faithful remnant (9:6b-9; 11:1-10); defended God's elective freedom to choose the children of promise from the Gentiles as well as from the Jews (9:10-29); and demonstrated the culpability of Israel for rejecting the gospel (9:30-10:21).... But from 11:1 the argument proceeds on the assumption that only if Paul can establish the eventual salvation of 'all Israel'—a category quite distinct from the present remnant—will he be able to affirm that 'God has not rejected his people' (cf. 11:1)."

23. Cf. Davies, "Paul and Israel," 34: "Paul recognizes that the role of the Jewish people in the future, as in the past, is not comprehensible apart from the mysterious purpose of God, which is full of grace. For him the existence and continuance of Israel up to the limit of the historical process is grounded in the mysterious divine purpose and is, as such, a source of ultimate blessing. For him, there is no 'solution' to the Jewish question until we are at the very limit of history and at the threshold of the age to come, when God will be all in all and the distinctions of this world even between Jew and

The Gospel and Israel

wonderful promise. "All Israel will be saved." This is a reference to Jewish people. "All Israel" is not a metaphor for the church.[24] It does not refer to Gentiles. Rather Paul gives us every reason to believe that in the future his own people the Jews will come to faith in Christ in large numbers, so much so that it can be said that "all Israel will be saved." There is no suggestion that this is a country or a nation-state any more than would have been the case in Paul's own day, but it does suggest very clearly that many, many of Paul's fellow Jews will be saved.

B. Other Pauline References

At this point it may seem that we have reached the pinnacle of Paul's pronouncements about Israel. What can be more spectacular and more glorious than the heights that Paul has scaled in Romans 11? What better prospect, what richer promise can there be than all Israel being saved? Well there is more. We have come a long way, but we not quite reached our destination.

Our first stop is 1 Corinthians 10:18: "Consider the people of Israel: Do not those who eat the sacrifices participate in the altar?" More literally it reads, "Consider Israel according to the flesh." The reference is to the Old Testament practice of the priests being allowed to eat the sacrifices made at the tabernacle (Lev 7:6, 14–15). So "Israel according to the flesh" is Old Testament Israel, the people who observed the ceremonial laws of Moses. But if there was an "Israel according to the flesh," doesn't that imply that there is now also an "Israel according to the Spirit"? Doesn't the "fleshly

---

Gentile transcended and even Christ himself made subordinate to the Father. Till that end comes, even when taken up into the life in Christ, Israel remains identifiably Israel."

24. Cf. Donaldson, "*Sonderweg* Reading," 51–52: "With most commentators I take Rom. 11.25–26 as a reference to ethnic Israel and not to the church as a redefined 'Israel,' and to an event at the end of the age and not to an ongoing process in the present. Thus the existence of the remnant in the present stands as a sign that in the future . . . ethnic Israel as a corporate entity will takes [sic] its proper place in the salvation of God." Contra Eckhard J. Schnabel, "Israel, the People of God and the Nations," *JETS* 45 (2002) 55–56: " . . . the phrase 'all Israel' can hardly mean 'all Jews'—no matter whether this would refer to all Israelites and all Jews who live at the time of the Parousia. The argument that the term 'Israel' in v. 26a has a different *referent* than in v. 25b cannot be dismissed easily: right from the beginning of his argument Paul worked with a programmatic distinction between two 'Israels,' and since 2:25 he systematically transferred privileges and attributes of 'Israel' to the Messiah and his people. It is not at all impossible that his readers who have followed his argument so far would understand the phrase 'all Israel' in 11:26b as (polemic) redefinition of Israel."

Israel" of the Old Testament correspond to the "spiritual Israel" of the New? Isn't physical Israel the Old Testament nation, while spiritual Israel is the New Testament church? These equations seem so easy to make, and yet the answer to all of these questions must always be an emphatic "No!" Nowhere does the New Testament speak of an "Israel according to the Spirit."[25] Nowhere does the New Testament suggest that the church is the spiritual Israel. Here we need to read Paul with the utmost caution and reserve. Here in 1 Corinthians he is simply drawing an illustration from the Old Testament about eating sacrifices. He is not telling the Corinthians that they are the spiritual Israel.[26] We must be careful not to put words in Paul's mouth at this point.

Again in 2 Corinthians, Paul uses Israel to refer to the Old Testament people of God:

> But if the ministry of death, in letters engraved on stones, came with glory, so that the sons of Israel could not look intently at the face of Moses because of the glory of his face, fading as it was, how shall the ministry of the Spirit fail to be even more with glory? ... Having therefore such a hope, we use great boldness in our speech, and are not as Moses, who used to put a veil over his face that the sons of Israel might not look intently at the end of what was fading away. (3:7-8, 12-13 NASB)

The "sons of Israel" in this context are simply the contemporaries of Moses, as was "Israel according to the flesh" in the previous reference.

The next reference is in Ephesians 2:11-12:

> Therefore, remember that formerly you who are Gentiles by birth and called "uncircumcised" by those who call themselves "the circumcision" (that done in the body by the hands of men)—remember that at that time you were separate from Christ, excluded

---

25. See *TDNT*, 3:387: "... there is no specific contrast between this Ἰσραὴλ κατὰ σάρκα and an Ἰσραὴλ κατὰ πνεῦμα. That there can be no transfer of the title to the new community at the expense of the old is shown particularly clearly by the image of the olive-tree in R. 11:17ff.; Israel is the one community of God into which Gentiles are now engrafted."

26. See *EDNT*, 2:204: "Despite the early demonstrable Christian self-understanding as the legal successor of Israel, the NT exercises extraordinary reserve in using the designation Ἰσραὴλ with respect to the Church or Christians. Thus when one observes the beginning of the usurpation of the name by Christians in the reference to the Israel according to the flesh (1 Cor 10:18), even this is not conclusive, for Ἰσραὴλ κατὰ σάρκα does not demand a correlative Ἰσραὴλ κατὰ πνεῦμα any more than numerous κατὰ σάρκα phrases."

The Gospel and Israel

from citizenship in Israel and foreigners to the covenants of the promise, without hope and without God in the world.

The implications of these verses are far-reaching. A huge reversal has taken place:

- These believing Gentiles who were once separate from Christ are now in Christ.
- Those who were excluded from citizenship in Israel are now included in citizenship in Israel.
- Those who were foreigners to the covenants of promise are now partakers of those covenants.
- Those who were without hope now have hope.
- Those who were without God now belong to God.

Again these words need to be read carefully. These Christian Gentiles are not the new Israel. They have not replaced Israel. Rather they are now included in citizenship in Israel. The same word is used of Roman citizenship (Acts 22:28). Just as in the first century non-Romans could become Romans, so now, through faith in Christ, Gentiles could belong to Israel.[27]

Compared to these alienated Gentiles, Paul is virtually their polar opposite. He had all the religious privileges he could have wished for. In Philippians 3:5 he describes himself as "circumcised on the eighth day, of the people of Israel, of the tribe of Benjamin, a Hebrew of Hebrews; in regard to the law, a Pharisee." He had the purest Jewish pedigree that was possible in his day (cf. 2 Cor 11:22).[28]

What we have seen in this last verse is true in every verse that we have examined so far in the New Testament. Every reference to Israel is ethnic.

---

27. David J. Williams, *Paul's Metaphors: Their Context and Character* (Peabody, MA: Hendrickson, 1999), 151, further explains: "Paul is referring not to their standing with the Jews but to their status with God, made possible by Christ's death for their sins (2:13). It is a sociopolitical metaphor of their salvation."

28. Cf. *NIDNTT*, 2:310: "Paul emphasized in 2 Cor. 11:22 and Phil. 3:5 his Heb.-speaking origins and affiliations as something positive." F. F. Bruce, *Paul: Apostle of the Free Spirit* (rev. ed.; Carlisle: Paternoster, 1992), 43, further observes: "It appears, then, that while Paul was born into a Jewish family which enjoyed citizen rights in a Greek-speaking city, Aramaic and not Greek was the language spoken in the home and perhaps also in the synagogue which they attended. Unlike many Jews resident in Anatolia, this family was strictly observant of the Jewish way of life and maintained its links with the home country." It is significant that even as the apostle to the Gentiles Paul continued to identify himself in terms of his Jewish heritage.

How Jewish Is Israel in the New Testament?

Whether it be Old Testament Israel or Israel in the first century AD or even eschatological Israel, without exception so far the meaning has always been ethnic. Although at times it seems to come close, the New Testament never calls the church "Israel." It is never referred to as "the new Israel" or "the true Israel," nor even as "spiritual Israel." Nor is a Gentile Christian ever called an "Israelite."[29] The terms Israel and Israelite have always been reserved for a particular ethnic group of people—at least up till now.

The last reference to be discussed is the most controversial and difficult of them all: "Peace and mercy to all who follow this rule, even to the Israel of God" (Gal 6:16). In this verse who is "the Israel of God"? Surely it is "all who follow this rule" in the first part of the verse. And what is the rule that they are following? We are told in the preceding verse: "Neither circumcision nor uncircumcision means anything; what counts is a new creation" (6:15).

So that's the rule. There is no distinction between Jew and Gentile. What is important is "a new creation." All who follow this rule are "the Israel of God." So isn't that "Israel of God," that "new creation," the church—where all distinctions between Jews and Gentiles have been abolished? Isn't that Paul's whole point in his letter to the Galatians?[30]

Well, yes, but things are not quite so simple. The NIV is not very literal at this point. Here are some more literal translations:

> "And those who will walk by this rule, peace and mercy be upon them, *and* upon the Israel of God" (NASB, italics added).

> "And as many as walk according to this rule, peace be on them, and mercy, *and* upon the Israel of God" (KJV, italics added).

---

29. Thus *NIDNTT* 2:310, "Each time it refers to Jews as members of the people of God."

30. Cf. Andreas J. Köstenberger, "The Identity of the ΙΣΡΑΗΛ ΤΟΥ ΘΕΟΥ (Israel of God) in Galatians 6:16," *Faith and Mission* 19 (2001) 4: "Paul's sustained anti-Judaizing polemic renders a sudden shift in his argument in Gal. 6:16b (e.g. in the form of pronouncing a blessing on literal Israel) implausible." He further argues that "all the views that take Gal. 6:16 as a reference to Jews and not to Gentiles, while supportable by Paul's usage elsewhere, are rendered improbable by the context of the Galatian epistle itself" (15). Thus also G. K. Beale, "Peace and Mercy upon the Israel of God: The Old Testament Background of Galatians 6, 16b," *Biblica* 80 (1999) 205: "Those who have identified 'the Israel of God' with the entire Galatian church (Jewish and Gentile believers) have usually done so because of the epistle's main theme of unity between believers of different ethnic groups."

A key difference is between "even" (NIV) and "and" (KJV, NASB). At first sight it may seem minor, but the difference is crucial. Are those "who walk by this rule" identical to "the Israel of God" or are they different? The NIV suggests that they are one and the same. The other two translations suggest that somehow they are different. In fact a comparison of twelve major English translations and paraphrases indicates that eight see the two groups as different (ESV, LB, NEB, NRSV, RV, TEV). Only three agree with the NIV (JB, RSV, Phillips). So it would appear that a significant majority of English versions recognise some distinction between "those who walk by this rule" and "the Israel of God."

As a result, this verse has become a battleground between competing Israelologies—and it all hinges on the little word "and." Does it equate or does it merely connect?[31] Those whose theology says that the church is now the true Israel argue that "and" equates the two groups.[32] Those whose theology tells them that Israel and the church are distinct will argue that "and" merely connects.[33]

---

31. Greek Grammars are remarkably reticent at this point and the few that do discuss it are very tentative in their conclusions. Maximilian Zerwick, *Biblical Greek Illustrated by Examples* (Rome: Scripta Pontificii Instituti Biblici, 1963), 154, admits that καί can mean "that is" but places question marks beside this meaning in the case of Gal 6:16. Likewise Max Zerwick and Mary Grosvenor, *A Grammatical Analysis of the Greek New Testament* (rev. ed.; Rome: Biblical Institute Press, 1981), 577, in their notes on Gal 6:16 are hesitant to come to a firm conclusion: "καί (3rd time) may stand for *that is*."

32. This has generally been the view held among covenant theologians. For example, Herman Ridderbos, *The Epistle of Paul to the Churches of Galatia*, trans. Henry Zylstra (Grand Rapids: Eerdmans, 1956), 227, insists that the "*Israel of God* does not refer to the empirical, national Israel . . . neither only to the believing part of national Israel, but to all the believers as the new Israel." This is also the conclusion drawn by O. Palmer Robertson, *The Israel of God Yesterday, Today and Tomorrow* (Phillipsburg: Presbyterian and Reformed, 2000), 43: "The only explanation of Paul's phrase 'the Israel of God' that satisfies the context as well as the grammar of the passage also begins by understanding the Greek conjunction *kai* as epexegetical of 'all those who walk according to this canon.' These people agree that no distinction is to be made between Jew and Gentile when it comes to identifying the people of God."

33. See such Dispensationalist writers as Arnold Fruchtenbaum, "Israel Present," *CTSJ* 5 (1999) 40; Stanley Toussaint, "The Church and Israel," *CTJ* 2 (1998) 350–74; John F. Walvoord, "Will Israel Continue as a Nation?," *Bibliotheca Sacra* 109 (1952) 147; Walvoord, "Is the Church the Israel of God?" 413: "The use of καί is difficult to explain apart from the intention of the writer to set off the 'Israel of God' from those considered in the first half of the verse. It is rather another indication that Gentile and Jewish believers are on the same level as καί is used principally to link coordinate parts of a sentence. In any case, the argument of those who would destroy Israel's national hope based upon this verse is not founded on sound exegesis. The passage does not state explicitly, even

How Jewish Is Israel in the New Testament?

Not only do conflicting theologies vie for the correct interpretation of this verse, there are also two important hermeneutical principles that seem to clash at this point. As we have seen, of the seventy-seven occurrences of Israel and Israel*ite*, seventy-six can be taken in a literal, ethnic sense. This leaves Galatians 6:16 as the last man standing. Could this be the only case where Israel is metaphorical? Is it only here that it could refer to non-Jews? That would make it a rare exception indeed. The other hermeneutical principle is context. The overall context in Galatians suggests that there is no distinction between Jewish and Gentile believers. It has been eradicated. Circumcision is irrelevant. Richard Longenecker argues that "in a letter where Paul is concerned to treat as indifferent the distinctions that separate Jewish and Gentile Christians and to argue for the equality of Gentile believers with Jewish believers, it is difficult to see him at the very end of that letter pronouncing a benediction (or benedictions) that would serve to separate groups within his churches."[34]

So which way do we go? Do we follow the immediate context of Galatians, which erases distinctions between Christians? Or do we take the wider context of the New Testament as a whole, where Israel is never used metaphorically? This is one tough exegetical decision, and equally competent and godly expositors have come down on either side.[35] This is really a hard chestnut and very difficult to crack.

---

if strained to accommodate their view, that the 'Israel of God' and the 'new creation' are identical."

34. Longenecker, *Galatians* (WBC 41; Dallas: Word, 1990), 298.

35. Michael Marlowe in his December 2004 internet article "The Israel of God (Galatians 6:16)" (http://www.bible-researcher.com/gal6-16.html), has rendered a valuable service by listing in his first footnote the major expositors on both sides of this debate: "H.A.W. Meyer in his *Critical and Exegetical Handbook to the Epistle to the Galatians* (5th German edition, 1870), lists the following commentators as supporting this view [i.e. that 'The Israel of God' was understood as a name for the Church]: Chrysostom, Theodoret, Luther, Calvin, Pareus, Cornelius a Lipide, Calovius, Baumgarten, Koppe, Rosenmüller, Borger, Winer, Paulus, Olhausen, Baumgarten-Crusius, and Wieseler. Meyer himself favors this view. To these names, the American editor of the English translation of his commentary (1884) adds Alford and Lightfoot. Andreas J. Köstenberger (who favors this view in 'The Identity of the *Israel tou theou* (Israel of God) in Galatians 6:16,' *Faith & Mission* 19/1 [2001]: 3-24) adds the names of Justin Martyr, Beale, Dahl, D. Guthrie, Lietzmann, Luz, Longenecker, Ray, Ridderbos, and Stott. But not all of these are commentators. For commentators favoring the view that the phrase refers to Jewish Christians, Meyer lists Ambrosiaster, Beza, Grotius, Estius, Schoettgen, Bengel, Räckert, Matthies, Schott, de Wette, Ewald, and Reithmayr; and the American editor adds Ellicott and Eadie. G. Schrenk (who favors this view in 'Was bedeutet 'Israel Gottes'?' *Judaica* 5 [1949]: 81-94) adds to these Pelagius, B. Weiss, Hofmann, Zahn, Schlatter, Bousset, and

The Gospel and Israel

So before making a decision, let me make one further observation. Back in verse 11 Paul says, "See what large letters I use as I write to you with my own hand." From this comment it is fair to assume that the last paragraph of Galatians was in Paul's own handwriting. The rest of the letter was probably dictated to a secretary.[36] Paul's personal note turns out to be a summary of the main message of the epistle as a whole. It is not as though the entire letter is free of distinctions between Jews and Gentiles, but such distinctions are pragmatic rather than principal.

Back in chapter 2 mission fields were allocated to the various church leaders:

> God, who was at work in the ministry of Peter as an apostle to the Jews, was also at work in my ministry as an apostle to the Gentiles. James, Peter and John, those reputed to be pillars, gave me and Barnabas the right hand of fellowship when they recognized the grace given to me. They agreed that we should go to the Gentiles, and they to the Jews. (vv. 8–9)

So when Paul mentions "the Israel of God" at the end of the letter, he is simply casting his mind back to the Jewish church. Although he has largely been addressing Gentiles, he hasn't forgotten Peter and the other apostles and their mission to the Jews.[37] When Paul wrote Galatians, Christianity was still predominantly a Jewish movement with Jerusalem as the mother

---

Burton. Köstenberger lists also Schrenk, Robinson, Mussner, Bruce, Davies, Richardson, Betz, Walvoord, S. L. Johnson, and 'other dispensationalists' as favoring this view. For a survey of commentators and an argument in favor of the latter view see S. Lewis Johnson, Jr., 'Paul and "The Israel of God": An Exegetical and Eschatological Case-Study,' in *Essays in Honor of J. Dwight Pentecost* (ed. Stan Toussaint and Charles Dyer; Chicago: Moody, 1986), pp. 183–94."

36. Cf. John R. W. Stott, *Only One Way: The Message of Galatians* (Leicester: InterVarsity, 1976), 176: "Paul has now reached the end of his letter. So far he has been dictating to an amanuensis, but now, as his custom was, he takes the pen from his secretary's hand, in order to add a personal post-script." See also 1 Cor 16:21; Col 4:18; 2 Thess 3:17.

37. Cf. Davies, "Paul and the People of Israel," 10: "[T]here is even in the uncompromising epistle to the Galatians an insinuating ambiguity. Nowhere in it does Paul refer to a new Israel.... This verse, written in Paul's own hand and probably summing up his position (and recalling the *Shemoneh Esreh*), ends with a prayer for and a declaration of peace and mercy on the Israel of God—which may refer to the Jewish people as whole." This perspective raises the possibility that "the Israel of God" in Gal 6:16 is equivalent to "all Israel" in Rom 11:26. *NIDNTT*, 2:315, summarises Paul's usage: "Israel (17 times) stands for either the historic people or the eschatological whole Israel but significantly not for Paul's own community."

How Jewish Is Israel in the New Testament?

church.[38] Subsequent events were to show just how much Jewish believers were to need the peace and mercy of God.[39] That Paul should direct a benediction to them was therefore wholly appropriate.

Israel in the New Testament is somewhat like an ornamental snowman made of white stone. It never melts into metaphor. It is no more metaphorical than Israel was in the Old Testament. Even the noonday warmth of God's revelation in Christ has not melted Israel into a metaphor for the church. Although Gentiles were becoming believers in great numbers they are never called Israelites in the New Testament and the church is never called Israel. Throughout the New Testament both Israel and Israelite stubbornly and consistently retain their ethnic identity. No one can appeal to Galatians 6:16 in a last desperate attempt to say otherwise![40]

IMPLICATIONS

These conclusions have far-reaching implications. Here we touch on just three—theological, prophetic, and evangelistic.

A. Theological

If the New Testament is always careful to use the term Israel in its ethnic sense, then strictly speaking it would be incorrect and even unbiblical to speak of the church as "the new Israel" and "the true Israel" or even as "spiritual Israel." As close as the New Testament comes to using this kind of terminology, it exercises great reserve and stops short of making such an

---

38. See Richard Bauckham, "James at the Centre," *Society for the Study of Early Christianity Newsletter* 39 (February 2001) 3: ". . . while Peter and Paul, the great missionary apostles, represent the centrifugal movement of Christianity out from the centre, James, the widely revered head of the mother church in Jerusalem, represents the still centre and centripetal attraction of the early Christian movement."

39. Beale, "Old Testament Background," has argued that the "peace and mercy" combination can be traced to Isa 54:10. The connection is, however, a conscious allusion at best. It does not necessarily follow, as Beale concludes from the new creation context in Isaiah 54, that "the Israel of God" also applies to Gentiles.

40. Walvoord, "Will Israel Continue?," 146, has correctly observed: "It has been alleged on the basis of this passage that the church as such is specifically called 'the Israel of God.' To this is opposed the fact that everywhere else in the Scriptures the term Israel is applied only to those who are the natural seed of Abraham and Isaac, never to Gentiles."

The Gospel and Israel

identification.⁴¹ Some of the early church fathers were not always as cautious, so this kind of language begins emerging as early as the second century. Justin Martyr, for example, in his dialogue with Trypho, a Jew, makes this claim: "As, therefore, Christ is the Israel and the Jacob, even so we, who have been quarried out from the bowels of Christ, are the true Israelite race."⁴² In the light of Scripture, however, it must be said that the claim is overstated. This lack of caution was to have serious ramifications. Socially, it amounted to an early case of "identity theft" that made life difficult for Jews when the Roman Empire was Christianised.⁴³ Doctrinally, it spawned a replacement theology⁴⁴ that has been very influential to our own day. This very common view suggests that in the purposes of God the church has simply replaced Israel and that therefore Israel, in the sense of ethnic Israel, has become theologically irrelevant.

Yet a careful reading of the New Testament does not suggest a replacement theology but an engrafting theology. The church does not replace

---

41. Davies, "Paul and the People of Israel," 10, draws a nuanced and significant conclusion from Paul's discussion in Romans 9–11: "Paul recognizes that it is the Gentiles who are now ready to accept the gospel and are being incorporated into 'Israel,' while the Jewish people itself is being disobedient. . . . But it cannot be said that the Jewish people as a totality has been disobedient and has, therefore, been replaced as the people of God by a Gentile community, the Church." Further careful distinctions have been made by Michael Bachmann, "*Verus Israel*: Ein Vorschlag zu einer 'mengentheoretischen' Neubeschreibung der betreffenden paulinischen Terminologie," *NTS* 48 (2002) 500–512. In the Pauline corpus, Bachman discovers a semantic field where terms are used in highly nuanced yet precise ways:[BL a-e]

Jew, circumcision and *seed of Abraham* can be used of both believing and unbelieving Jews, as well as of Gentile Christians;

sons, children and *heirs of God* are used of believing Jews and Gentiles (and perhaps by extension of unbelieving Jews);

people of God and *my people* are used of unbelieving and believing Jews (and perhaps by extension of believing Gentiles);

Israelite is used mainly of Jewish Christians—never of Gentile Christians;

Israel is used of ethnic Israel: whether believers or unbelievers—never of Gentile Christians (not even in Rom 11:26 or Gal 6:16!).

42. Alexander Roberts and James Donaldson, eds., *The Ante-Nicene Fathers: Translations of the Writings of the Fathers down to A.D. 325* (Grand Rapids: Eerdmans, 1956) 1:267.

43. See Stephen Center, "The Jews under Roman Rule in the Fourth Century," *Society for the Study of Early Christianity Newsletter* 42 (February 2002) 3–7.

44. Donaldson, "Riches for the Gentiles," 82, has noted: "By the latter half of the second century CE, displacement approaches to the relationship between the church and Israel were well established within the Christian self-understanding."

Israel, but has become engrafted into Israel. This is precisely the point of Paul's olive tree[45] image in Romans 11:16-24:

> If some of the branches have been broken off, and you, though a wild olive shoot, have been grafted in among the others and now share in the nourishing sap from the olive root, do not boast over those branches. If you do, consider this: You do not support the root, but the root supports you. You will say then, "Branches were broken off so that I could be grafted in." Granted. But they were broken off because of unbelief, and you stand by faith. Do not be arrogant, but be afraid. For if God did not spare the natural branches, he will not spare you either. Consider therefore the kindness and sternness of God: sternness to those who fell, but kindness to you, provided that you continue in his kindness. Otherwise, you also will be cut off. And if they do not persist in unbelief, they will be grafted in, for God is able to graft them in again. After all, if you were cut out of an olive tree that is wild by nature, and contrary to nature were grafted into a cultivated olive tree, how much more readily will these, the natural branches, be grafted into their own olive tree!

Just as in Ephesians 2 Gentiles are included into Israel, here they are engrafted into Israel. The image is a very powerful one, even though at first it seems wrongheaded. Naturally one would expect cultivated olive shoots to be grafted into a wild olive tree. Horticulturally this is standard practice. So is Paul's illustration true to life? There is evidence that it is. John Stott quotes Sir William Ramsey, who describes "exceptional circumstances [where] it is customary to reinvigorate an olive tree which is ceasing to bear fruit by grafting it with the shoot of the wild olive tree, so that the sap of this tree ennobles this wild shoot and the tree now again begins to bear fruit."[46] The illustration is therefore remarkably apt and genuinely indicative of the situation in Paul's day. Gentile Christians were ennobled by being grafted into Israel, and Israel was reinvigorated by the wild shoots

---

45. This image is probably dependent on OT conceptions of Israel as an olive tree (*EDNT*, 1:425); see Jer 11:16-19; Hos 14:6-7. From this background some commentators have argued that Paul's application of the metaphor extends beyond ethnic Israel to the people of God as composed of both Jews and Gentiles. See Thomas R. Schreiner, *Romans* (Grand Rapids: Baker, 1998), 605. Although it is quite possible that Paul's metaphor has outgrown its OT counterpart, the fact remains that the Gentiles in his image are merely branches. Their root and sustenance is found in ethnic Israel.

46. John R. W. Stott, *The Message of Romans: God's Good News for the World* (Leicester: InterVarsity, 1994), 300.

from the Gentiles. These Gentiles do not become the new Israel, but they draw their root and their sap from the olive tree that is Israel. They become sons of the patriarch Abraham. They are spiritually nourished by Israel's Old Testament prophets. They are saved by the Jewish Messiah Jesus. Such are the blessings of being grafted into the olive tree that is Israel. Christians become part of Israel.

B. Prophetic

There is still more to Paul's image than Gentiles being grafted into the olive tree. At the end of his allegory Paul raises one final possibility:

> Verse 24: "After all, if you were cut out of an olive tree that is wild by nature, and contrary to nature were grafted into a cultivated olive tree, how much more readily will these, the natural branches, be grafted into their own olive tree!"

Within the context of Romans 11 there is every suggestion that this possibility will one day be realised. Both before and after Paul uses the olive tree illustration he predicts great spiritual blessings for ethnic Israel:

> Verse 12: "But if their transgression means riches for the world, and their loss means riches for the Gentiles, how much greater riches will their fullness bring!"

> Verse 15: "For if their rejection is the reconciliation of the world, what will their acceptance be but life from the dead?"

> Verse 26: "And so all Israel will be saved."

Ethnic Israel is not theologically irrelevant. The hope that Paul holds out for Jewish restoration (vv. 23–24) will one day be realised "when the full number of the Gentiles comes in" (v. 25). It is then that "all Israel will be saved" (v. 26). This glorious future for the majority of the Jews will bring untold blessings to the nations. From verses 12 and 15 we learn that the fullness and acceptance of the Jews will bring greater riches and life from the dead. Whether we understand these blessings as a worldwide spiritual awakening or as the final resurrection at the end, it is clear that God is not finished with the Jews. In Paul's day those Jews included both Palestinian and Diaspora Jews. In our day too there is still a worldwide Jewish community. We are not here speaking of the nation or the political state of Israel. Rather we have every reason to hope that at some future time Jewish people will turn to Christ in large numbers. When they do, it will bring such riches and blessings to the world that Paul's Gentile mission will look pale in comparison.[47]

C. Evangelistic

If "greater riches" and "life from the dead" will attend the salvation of all Israel, then the conversion of the Jews is worth working and praying for! What could be a more worthwhile evangelistic enterprise than a venture like Christian Witness to Israel? In private correspondence with me back in 2003, Paul Morris of CWI Australia told me that he firmly believed on the basis of Romans 11 "that there will be a future return of the Jews to Messiah Jesus in great numbers." Then on a personal note he added, "I came to this understanding as I struggled with the emphasis in God's Word on the worldwide impact of the Gospel. My longing for the salvation of the nations led me to see the importance of Jewish evangelism because their salvation will be the key to abundant blessing worldwide." What a prospect!

This is a vision that the church today sorely needs to recapture. It is there in our heritage but we need to rediscover it. The Larger Westminster Catechism has a section on the Lord's Prayer. In Q. 191 it asks, "What do we pray for in the second petition?" In part, it answers as follows: "We pray, that the kingdom of sin and Satan may be destroyed, the gospel propagated throughout the world, the Jews called [and] the fullness of the Gentiles brought in."[48] Likewise in the Westminster Assembly's Directory for Public Worship churches are asked "to pray for the propagation of the gospel and kingdom of Christ to all nations; for the conversion of the Jews [and] the fullness of the Gentiles."[49]

---

47. Cf. Robert Vasholz, "The Character of Israel's Return in the Light of the Abrahamic and Mosaic Covenants," *Trinity Journal* 25 (2004) 58: "Without question, the salvation of 'all Israel' can only bring worldwide benefits beyond imagination. The glorious promises made to Israel in the OT serve merely as a hint of the glories to come. Wonderful opportunities forfeited by Israel in the past are but shadows compared with those that will be offered on a much grander scale in the future in comparison to natural and earthly descriptions of blessings in the ancient world. I would not even venture to describe what lies ahead lest my faltering words detract from that glory."

48. *The Confession of Faith; the Larger and Shorter Catechisms, with the Scripture-Proofs at Large: Together with The Sum of Saving Knowledge* (Belfast: Graham and Heslip, 1933), 216.

49. *Confession of Faith and Catechisms*, 290.

These requirements of yesteryear serve as both a challenge and a rebuke to the church today. Even more recent events stand as solemn reminders of the church's duty. During the Second World War there were pastors in occupied Europe who faced arrest and imprisonment (and worse!) if they dared to pray publicly for the Jews. Today we have every liberty to pray for the Jewish people. How often do we avail ourselves of the opportunity? How often in the worship services in our churches is there prayer for the Jews?

CONCLUSION

So "how Jewish is *Israel* in the New Testament?" At first it sounds like such a redundant question, but it turns out to be quite a loaded question. If we take it seriously it should impact us in a number of key areas:

- Theologically, it should serve to remind us that the church in the New Testament is included in Israel and it is grafted into Israel. It does not replace Israel.

- Prophetically, Israel is not irrelevant. There is still the bright prospect that a majority of Jews will yet believe the gospel and come to Christ.

- Evangelistically, it means that our witness to Jewish people is strategically important. Jewish evangelism is the key to worldwide blessing and desperately deserves our private and public prayers.

Finally, Bauer's dictionary could do with a little revision. In the New Testament Israel never unambiguously refers to the patriarch Jacob and it is never "used of Christians as entitled to the term Israel."[50] So of Bauer's three categories only one is left standing: Israel "can refer to the people or nation of Israel."[51] This is the only meaning it carries in the New Testament. It is always ethnic and literal, never metaphorical.

50. BDAG, 481.
51. BDAG, 481.

4

Luther and the Jews

—Dr. Mark D. Thompson

THE DIFFICULT CHARGE

SINCE THE HOLOCAUST, IT has been impossible to speak about Luther without facing squarely his harsh words against the Jews. For more than seventy years now, there have been those who find tracing a link between the archetypical German and the moment of Germany's greatest shame and guilt both irresistible and productive. Perhaps the classic example is one of the earliest: Peter F. Wiener's *Martin Luther: Hitler's Spiritual Ancestor*.[1] According to Wiener, Luther's ferocity in the sixteenth century bore its inevitable fruit in the twentieth. He bred it into the German nation. He bound Protestantism so tightly to anti-Semitism at its very roots that it should come as no surprise that the national German church was silent as the Final Solution was proposed.

Of course there have always been those who see things differently. Far from being responsible for the Holocaust, Luther's theology, rightly understood, was its real answer. And so in 1945 Gordon Rupp published his response to Wiener: *Martin Luther: Hitler's Cause or Cure?*[2] On his view, it is critical to remember that hatred and fear so often arise from our insecurity before each other and, more importantly, our insecurity before God. Yet Lu-

---

1. P. F. Wiener, *Martin Luther: Hitler's Spiritual Ancestor* (London: Hutchinson, 1945). A new edition of this work was published in 1999 by American Atheist Press.

2. E. G. Rupp, *Martin Luther: Hitler's Cause or Cure* (London: Lutterworth, 1945).

The Gospel and Israel

ther's wonderful discovery of justification by faith led to a new confidence before God that carried with it a new understanding of Christian freedom. Freed from fear, from the need to prove oneself and other forms of self-interest, the Christian lives "in Christ through faith [and] in his neighbour through love."[3] And so, even in the midst of Luther's ferocious and at points highly offensive language, he would insist that the principal motivation in all our relationships should be disinterested Christian love. In his very last sermon, he made clear that this extends even towards the Jews: "still we want to practice Christian love toward them and pray that they convert."[4] As Rupp and many others have argued, Hitler and his henchmen may have wanted to claim Luther for themselves, but they did not understand this truth that lay at the heart of all he did and wrote.

There may, in fact, be little to be gained from adopting either of these positions on the relationship between Luther's advocacy of "sharp mercy" towards the Jews and the almost impenetrable darkness of the Nazi holocaust. On the one hand, approaches such as that of Wiener regularly fail to give due weight to other ferocious writing against the Jews in this same period, for instance, the work of Luther's infamous opponent Johann Eck of Ingolstadt, who published his *Refutation of a Jew Book* in 1541—a full two years before Luther's *On the Jews and Their Lies* appeared.[5] Nor do they take seriously enough a long history of action against the Jews in Europe, for example, their expulsion from England in 1290, from France in 1394, and from a newly united Spain in 1492.[6] Luther's anger at the Jews and his suggestion that as a last resort they should be driven out of Germany was hardly a novelty in the sixteenth century.

---

3. M. Luther, "The Freedom of a Christian" (1520), in *Luther's Works*, eds. J. Pelikan and H. T. Lehmann, 55 vols. (St. Louis/Philadelphia: Concordia/Fortress, 1955-86), 31:371 (hereafter *LW*).

4. "Noch wollen wir die Christliche lieve an jnen uben und vor sie bitten, das sie sich bekeren." Martin Luther, "Eine vermanung wider die Juden" (February 15, 1546), *WA* 51:195.39-40. Perhaps because they are largely critical of the Jews, the last two pages of the German original of this sermon (pp. 195-96 in the Weimar edition) were not translated as part of the sermon in the standard English collection (*LW* 51:383-92).

5. J. Eck, *Ains Juden büechlins verlegung: darin ain Christgantzer Christenhait zu schmach will es geschehe den Juden vnrecht in bezichtigung der Christen kinder mordt* (Ingolstadt, 1541).

6. Still the most detailed study of Jewish-Christian relations in this period is S. W. Baron, *A Social and Religious History of the Jews: XIII Inquisition, Renaissance, and Reformation* (New York: Columbia University Press, 1969).

Luther and the Jews

On the other hand, apologists for Luther sometimes engage in special pleading and gloss over both the ferocity of his language and the similarity between some of what he proposed in 1543 and the early stages of the Nazi program in the 1930s. Diarmaid MacCulloch's challenge to such writing is only slightly exaggerated. He writes, "Luther's writing of 1543 is a blueprint for the Nazi's Kristallnacht of 1938."[7] Any fair-minded observer must admit that the similarities are certainly striking, even if Luther was not advocating mob violence or the murder of Jewish men and women. Furthermore, even the most ardent supporter of Luther must cringe, as his contemporaries Melanchthon and Osiander did, at the severity of his language.[8]

The simple fact is that the association of Luther and anti-Semitism has become conventional. The connection is made so often that no serious study of Luther can avoid the topic. As Heiko Oberman, one of the most significant of Luther's biographers in the last fifty years, put it:

> The Third Reich and in its wake the whole Western world capitalized upon Luther, the fierce Jew-baiter. Any attempt to deal with the Reformer runs up against this obstacle. No description of Luther's campaign against the Jews, however objective and erudite it may be, escapes the horror: we live in the post-Holocaust era.[9]

And there's the rub, as Shakespeare would put it. For anachronism works in both directions: Luther is, and must remain, a sixteenth=century European man, while we cannot help but view all we see from the vantage point of the twenty-first century on this side of the Shoah. Even when we try to put ourselves in Luther's shoes, to view the world as he and his contemporaries did, we cannot quite do it. We are still scandalised by the words. We can't pretend they don't echo the thud of jackboots. But we must not turn Luther into a post-Enlightenment, post–World War II Antipodean

---

7. D. MacCulloch, *Reformation: Europe's House Divided* (London: Penguin, 2003), 690.

8. For the reaction of Melanchthon, Osiander and other contemporaries to Luther's 1543 tract, see R. Lewin, *Luthers Stellung zu den Juden: Ein Beitrag zur Geschichte der Juden in Deutschland während des Reformationszeitalters* (Berlin: Trowitzch & Sohn, 1911), 97–98.

9. H. A. Oberman, *Luther: Man Between God and the Devil* (New Haven, CT: Yale University Press, 1982), 292. In support of Oberman's observation, we might quote from one of Hitler's early speeches (cited in the prefatory pages of Weiner's work): "I do insist on the certainty that sooner or later—once we hold power—Christianity will be overcome and the German church, without a pope and without the Bible, and Luther, if he could be with us, would give us his blessing." N. H. Baynes, ed., *The Speeches of Adolf Hitler, April 1922–August 1939* (London: Oxford University Press, 1942), 369.

either. He wouldn't understand the contemporary call to tolerance. Any attempt by Christians to grant the integrity of Jewish thought and practice would make no sense to him. He certainly would never have expected a modern Jewish state. So the historian is as historically located as the object of his or her study. And perhaps in the case of this object in particular—Luther's sixteenth-century engagement with Jewish thought and life—realizing that is a very important first step.

Our task here is to attempt to understand Luther's stance towards the Jews on his terms as much as we are able. This will mean attending to Luther's fierce and offensive words from 1543 in their own context, suspending any desire to condemn or vindicate him. It will mean taking seriously what he actually wrote and how it compares to other things he wrote, for instance, about unbelief and corruption at Rome or about the threat of anarchy emerging from the Peasants' Revolt. It will be important to take particular note of the catalyst for his various writings about the Jews and the sources from which he gained his information. Perhaps most importantly of all, it will involve understanding Luther's larger agenda—what was the critical and non-negotiable core of his ministry and his life.

LUTHER'S LARGER AGENDA

Martin Luther's enduring passion was the gospel of Jesus Christ. He knew himself to be a sinner saved by grace on the basis of Jesus' powerful death and resurrection. He also understood that embracing this gospel of salvation in Christ was not simply an important first stage of the Christian life: the gospel remains the critical reality that shapes the everyday experience of the Christian. Struggling with sin and temptation throughout our lives, attacked and accused by the Satan himself, Christians are nevertheless secure in the hands of God: the Christian is both sinner and righteous at one and the same time (*simul iustus et peccator*).[10] The tension this dual reality creates for the Christian will only be resolved when the last days themselves come to an end.

Luther's framework of thinking was powerfully eschatological and at points even apocalyptic. The Christian is caught in the midst of the great cosmic struggle which was first glimpsed in the Garden of Eden but came right out into the open only when the Word became flesh: "the light shines in the darkness and the darkness has not overcome it" (John 1:5). Luther

---

10. M. Luther, *Lectures on Romans* (1515–16), in WA 56:269–70 = LW 25:258.

knew well he lived in the last days, when this struggle was destined to be most intense. The rise of the papacy as antichrist was to him a signal that the end was close, demanding emergency measures so that as many men and women as possible could be rescued.[11] Of course, God's ultimate victory is not in doubt for a moment. He will rescue men and women of faith. However, in the meantime, Satan will employ any strategy, enlist any ally, in his frantic attempts to silence the gospel and arrest its progress. To quote Oberman again,

> According to Luther's prediction, the Devil would not "tolerate" the rediscovery of the Gospel; he would rebel with all his might, and muster all his forces against it. God's Reformation would be preceded by a counterreformation, and the Devil's progress would mark the Last Days. For where God is at work—in man and in human history—the Devil, the spirit of negation, is never far away.[12]

Luther had learned of God's wonderful provision for sinners like him and its cosmic context through his study of the Scriptures. Johann von Staupitz had set him on that path, ensuring that the conscience-stricken monk who kept coming to confess before him should be given the important task of memorizing the Scriptures in the Erfurt cloister. Later he would become lecturer in Bible at the new University of Wittenberg. Luther would spend his entire life studying and expounding the Scriptures, consistently exposing the misreading of the Scriptures that lay behind the Catholic sacramental system and other opposition to the gospel he now proclaimed in the name of Christ.

It should come as no surprise that honouring the Scriptures and the Lord witnessed to by the Scriptures was Luther's paramount concern throughout his life. After all, it was through his study of the Bible that he came to understand the true dimensions of what had been done for him in the cross of Christ. It was through his study of the Bible that he was liberated from the cycle or religious effort and despair. Through his study of the Bible he found the only true answer to the spiritual trials that plagued him all his

---

11. Oberman, *Luther*, 70–72. Oberman observes that Luther's identification of papal practice as a sign of the Last Days bred in Luther a "sense of urgency in preaching the Gospel. This urgency breeds impatience, and impatience an uncompromising stance against all opposition" (71).

12. Ibid., 12; cf. 104–6. Luther's understood "God's Reformation" to be that final act of bringing all things to their proper order through the final judgment.

The Gospel and Israel

life—his *Anfechtungen*.[13] The entire reform program that Luther initiated, beginning with the reform of the university curriculum at Wittenberg, but extending to the reform of the church throughout Europe, arose from his determination to take with utmost seriousness the teaching of Scripture.

These are all-important observations for understanding what was happening when Luther wrote against the Jews. For him, the Scriptures are honoured when their intention of "driving home" Christ is taken seriously. To make use of the Scriptures with some other intention was to abuse them. And Luther made clear his attitude to anyone who dishonoured Christ by manipulating or evading the clear teaching of Scripture. As he said in March 1519, "I cannot help loving those about whom I hear that they love the Holy Scriptures, and hating those who distort and despise them."[14] Martin Brecht was undoubtedly right to say "Luther's theological controversies were always a struggle over the interpretation of the Bible."[15] His early debates with Catholic theologians kept returning to the text of Scripture. His dispute with Erasmus involved both Erasmus' method of dealing with the Bible (his distaste for assertions and his claim that parts were obscure) and his exegetical conclusions on important passages to do with the human will. Luther argued with Zwingli, extensively and repeatedly, over the way the latter treated the Bible, in particular the words of institution from the Last Supper narrative. The same basic preoccupation is discernible in the particular controversies that concern us. Luther's writings about the Jews are dominated by extended discussions of key biblical texts, Messianic texts (in particular Gen 49:10; 2 Sam 23: Hag 2:6-9; and Dan 9:24) and texts used by Jews to point to their continued privileged status (e.g., Gen. 12, 17; Ps 147). Explaining Scripture clearly and showing where others had erred in their reading of Scripture was his responsibility as a doctor of the church.[16]

---

13. This word, which is variously translated, is the word Luther habitually used to describe the intense spiritual struggles he experienced and understood to be the devil's attempts to bring him low.

14. M. Luther, *Operationes in Psalmos* (1519), in WA 5:22.11-13 = LW 14:284.

15. M. Brecht, *Martin Luther: The Preservation of the Church 1532-1546*, trans. James L. Schaaf (Philadelphia: Fortress, 1993), 336.

16. Luther took very seriously his vocation as a doctor of the church: something forced upon him rather than sought by him. Studies of his *Doktoratsbewußtein* include B. A. Gerrish, "Doctor Martin Luther: Subjectivity and Doctrine in the Lutheran Reformation," in *Seven-Headed Luther: Essays in Commemoration of a Quincentenary 1483-1983*, ed. P. N. Brooks (Oxford: Clarendon, 1983), 2-24; and H. Steinlein, *Luthers Doktorat: zum 400 jährigen Jubiläum desselben, 1912* (Leipzig: Deichert, 1912).

As I have already suggested, behind this passionate attachment to Scripture, and to a careful and appropriate reading of Scripture, lay Luther's absolute devotion to Jesus Christ, the only hope of men and women in the last days. Luther knew he owed everything to Christ. Once again it was Staupitz who had pointed him in this direction. Through Staupitz, Luther learnt to look to Christ when confronted with the reality of God's wrath rather than be drawn into despair by his own wretched state or his inadequate performance of penitential acts.[17] Christ has done all that is necessary and the Christian belonged body and soul to his Saviour. In the midst of his struggle with spiritual despair, Luther would often repeat the prayer of Psalm 119:94—"I am yours; save me."[18]

Devotion to Christ meant defending the honour of Christ against all assault. The evil one's war against the gospel is waged through lies, deceit, and heresy. He does not want others to bow the knee to Christ, just as he refuses to bow the knee himself. Most of the time the assault upon Christ is indirect, through an attack upon the church and each Christian man or woman. However, in his desperation, the devil's attacks can be expected to become more and more deranged and the open slander of Christ become a chief weapon. He will employ various mouthpieces to do this dirty work, from the papacy itself, to unstable heretics, and even further afield to the Jew and the Turk. Luther stood ready to challenge and rebuke all who allowed themselves to be used by the devil in this way.

In reality, Luther's devotion to Christ and his commitment to the Scriptures were one and the same. Luther was convinced that all of Scripture must be understood in the light of Christ, and as a testimony to Christ. In the year before he died, he wrote once more against the papacy, drawing a direct link from the institution to the schemes of the Satan to undermine the proclamation of the gospel. Expounding Peter's confession at Caesarea-Philippi, he wrote,

> In these few words of Peter, which he confesses with all the other disciples (for they are all represented in Peter's reply), is included the whole of the gospel, indeed all of Holy Scripture. For what else does Scripture intend from beginning to end, except that the Messiah, the Son of God, should come and through his sacrifice, "like that of a lamb without blemish," bear and take away the sin of

---

17. Oberman, *Luther*, 181–82.

18. It is sometimes suggested that Luther adopted this practice on the advice of Staupitz (Oberman, *Luther*, 182).

the world and thus deliver from eternal death to eternal salvation? Holy Scripture was written for the sake of the Messiah and Son of God, and for His sake everything that happened took place.[19]

Twenty years earlier he had put it succinctly in a question to Erasmus in 1525: "Take Christ out of the Scriptures and what will you find left in them?"[20]

With Luther's larger agenda, which remained consistent throughout his teaching career, as the proper context of our investigation—an agenda which already hints at the shape and motivation of Luther's writing against the Jews—I propose now to examine what he actually said on the subject from his early days as a member of the theology faculty at Wittenberg till the last days of his life in Eisleben in 1546.

THE EARLIEST MENTIONS

Luther spoke of the Jews in one of the first pieces of his writing that has survived, his first letter to Georg Spalatin, the secretary at the court of the Saxon Elector, who would become a lasting friend.[21] The issue at hand was the Reuchlin affair, the prosecution of the renowned Hebraist Johannes Reuchlin (who was, incidentally, Philip Melanchthon's great-uncle) by the Roman Inquisition, for positive comments he had made about Jewish religious literature. In 1510, Reuchlin had objected to the banning and burning of Jewish literature, which had recently been advocated by the university in Cologne. By September 1513, the Inquisition's legal process had begun. It would only end when Reuchlin was condemned by the pope in 1520.[22] Luther wrote to Spalatin with his opinion on the matter, amongst other things rejecting any suggestion that "burning, banning and such mere external things" could bring about a change in the Jewish opposition to Christ. He was concerned for real conversions, which could only come from within as a work of God.

19. M. Luther, *Against the Roman Papacy, an Institution of the Devil* (1545), in *WA* 54:247.25–33 = *LW* 41:313–14. Note that the last two lines of the original paragraph have been omitted in the standard English translation.

20. M. Luther, *The Bondage of the Will* (1525), in *WA* 18:606.29 = *LW* 33:26.

21. This first letter from Luther to Spalatin is not included in the collection in *LW*. It can be found in Latin in *WABr* 1:23–24.

22. M. Brecht, *Martin Luther: His Road to Reformation 1483–1521*, trans. J. L. Schaaf (Philadelphia: Fortress, 1985), 162–63.

At this very early stage, Luther still was hopeful that some Jews would indeed come to Christ. Apart from that there would be no hope for them. But he was not prepared to endorse the measures many others had been calling for. It would take almost thirty years for Luther's attitude to change.

Two years later, Luther was lecturing on Romans 9–11. Faithfulness to the text meant he could not avoid the issue of the future of the Jews. Once again, it is clear that Luther had no interest in arguing for a special status for the Jews by virtue of physical descent. Their future, he made clear, is dependent upon whether they will turn to Christ or not. While he accepted the traditional understanding that there would be a massive return to faith on the part of the Jews on the last day, he recognised that this was pushing a little further than the text itself: "no one would seem to be convinced of this purely on the basis of the text," he told his students.[23]

THE JEWISH JESUS

The first substantial treatment of the condition of the Jews and how Christians should respond to them is found in Luther's treatise from 1523, *That Jesus Christ was Born a Jew*.[24] The immediate stimulus for this piece was a series of charges about Luther and his teaching, which had been put about by Luther's Catholic opponents and which had received an airing at the Diet of Nuremberg in 1522. It was claimed he had denied the virgin birth of Jesus by his insistence that Jesus was born of the seed of Abraham. The report was clearly malicious, but Luther could not afford to let it go unchallenged.

The little tract he produced had two main parts: a defence of Jesus' miraculous and yet Jewish birth, and a presentation of the case for Jesus' messiahship from the passages that were standard fare in apologetic texts circulating at the time. Luther wanted everyone to know why he was writing on this subject:

> Since for the sake of others, however, I am compelled to answer these lies, I thought I would also write something useful in addition, so that I do not vainly steal the reader's time with such dirty rotten business. Therefore, I will cite from Scripture the reasons

---

23. M. Luther, *Lectures on Romans* (1515–6), in *WA* 56:436 = *LW* 25:429.
24. M. Luther, *That Jesus Christ Was Born a Jew* (1523), in *WA* 11:314–36 = *LW* 45:199–229.

that move me to believe that Christ was a Jew born of a virgin, that I might perhaps also win some Jews to the Christian faith.[25]

Luther still hoped to see Jews become Christians. He had actually had some contact with a converted Jew, Jacob Gipher, who had taken the name Bernard. Luther would remain in contact with him over many years, and in fact Luther and Melanchthon would look after Bernard's children when he had to leave Wittenberg in search of work.[26] Perhaps Bernard was the primary source for Luther's optimism that the emergence of evangelical theology would mark a new era in Jewish evangelism. "I have myself heard from pious baptized Jews," he wrote, "that if they had not in our day heard the gospel they would have remained Jews under the cloak of Christianity for the rest of their days."[27]

It was not only the Catholic subversion of the gospel that had made the effective evangelisation of the Jews difficult, according to Luther; this had been compounded by the way Catholic authorities had treated the Jews. Inhumane treatment and forced conformity to Catholic practices had kept them from hearing the word of life. In Luther's words:

> They have dealt with the Jews as if they were dogs rather than human beings; they have done little else than deride them and seize their property. When they baptize them they show them nothing of Christian doctrine or life, but only subject them to popishness and monkery.[28]

He goes on to draw the unhappy conclusion:

> If the apostles, who also were Jews, had dealt with us Gentiles as we Gentiles deal with the Jews, there would never have been a Christian among the Gentiles.[29]

What is most interesting at this point is how Luther stands against the prevailing cultural trends to challenge the inhumane treatment of Jewish people. The expulsions had been happening across Europe for centuries. From time to time, violence had broken out against Jewish communities. Yet Luther argued for something different, not out of some sense that

---

25. Ibid., *LW* 45:199–200.

26. D. Wilson, *Out of the Storm: The Life and Legacy of Martin Luther* (London: Hutchinson, 2007), 316.

27. M. Luther, *That Jesus Christ Was Born a Jew* (1523), in *LW* 45:200.

28. Ibid.

29. Ibid.

everybody deserved the right to respect, tolerance and a life without fear, but rather for more obviously Christian motives: "Since they [the apostles] dealt with us Gentiles in such brotherly fashion, we in our turn ought to treat the Jews in a brotherly manner in order that we might convert some of them."[30] Apart from the hope that some might turn to Christ, the Jews stand in great peril. Luther's concern was that the spiritual debt we Gentiles owed to the Jews might be repaid with compassion and a clear proclamation of the gospel. Far from lording it over the dispersed Jewish people, we should remember that "we are but Gentiles, while the Jews are of the lineage of Christ. We are aliens and in-laws; they are blood relatives, cousins, and brothers of our Lord."[31]

The first major section of this tract is Luther's treatment of those passages from the Old Testament that promise the deliverer to come in such a way that clearly points to the Christian proclamation of the virgin birth. Luther begins with Genesis 3:15, the protoevangelium, which promises victory through the seed of the woman. This seed, Luther insists, "is a natural son of the woman, derived from the woman, however, not in the normal way but through a special act of God." It was envisaged from the beginning that he would be "the seed only of a woman and not of a man."[32] He then turns to Genesis 22:18 and the promise of blessing through Abraham's seed. For this promise to be filfiled, Luther argues, the seed to come must be Abraham's flesh and blood. And yet the promise also points to this blessed seed blessing others, and for this reason he could not be begotten by man.[33] The third passage he touches upon briefly is 2 Samuel 7:12–14, where he points out that the promise cannot refer to Solomon but must in its entirety refer to Christ.[34] Finally, he turns to Isaiah 7:14. Here God's promised sign must be something remarkable and marvellous rather than something indistinguishable from "the ordinary course of nature." How else would it be recognised as a sign? There is nothing noteworthy in a woman who is no longer a virgin giving birth to a child. So whatever the ambiguities associated with the vocabulary used, the sense of the entire passage points in the direction of the virgin birth.[35] With his exposition of these four passages,

30. Ibid., 200–201.
31. Ibid., 201.
32. Ibid., 202.
33. Ibid., 203.
34. Ibid., 206.
35. Ibid., 206–13.

The Gospel and Israel

Luther believes he has sufficiently answered the attempts by his opponents to publicly malign him by charging him with denying Mary's virginity.

Luther introduces the second major section of this treatise by explaining his desire "to do a service to the Jews on the chance that we might bring some of them back to their own true faith, the one which their fathers held."[36] His intention, as we have already noted, was not merely to defend himself against the lies that had been told about him: he wanted to evangelise the Jews as well. Here Luther picks up two standard messianic texts from the Old Testament and seeks to persuade his Jewish readers that they only really make sense when they are referred to Jesus. Genesis 49:10–12, the promise to Judah and his descendants with its enigmatic reference to "until Shiloh comes," gives Luther an opportunity to point out that for nearly 1,500 years there has been no kingdom or ruler from Judah. Shiloh has come just as the Jewish kingdom passed from history and now the nations flock to him. His eternal kingdom has a different quality from everything that preceded it. Through the gospel and the forgiveness of sins he rules his people in a spiritual kingdom. Daniel 9 and the prophecy of the seventy weeks fits very neatly, according to Luther, with the timing of Jesus' life and ministry. He came between the rebuilding of Jerusalem under Nehemiah and its final destruction under Emperor Titus in AD 70. Contrary to some rabbinic Jewish interpretation, this prophecy cannot refer to Cyrus since the one who is to come will seal the forgiveness of sins and atone for our iniquity, and that was hardly on Cyrus' agenda. Luther merely cites two other texts, Haggai 2:9 and Zechariah 8:23, but considers he has done enough to begin to mount his case.

Luther's conclusion in 1523 was that proper treatment and proper instruction of the Jews might well see many come to faith in Jesus. He repeatedly stressed the need to deal gently with them.

> For they have been led astray so long and so far that one must deal gently with them, as people who have been all too strongly indoctrinated to believe that God cannot be man. Therefore I would request that one deal gently with them and instruct them from Scripture, then some of them may come along [. . .] If we really want to help them, we must be guided in our dealings with them not by papal law but by the law of Christian love.[37]

---

36. Ibid., 213.
37. Ibid., 229.

Even at this early stage, Luther did not believe that the results would necessarily be overwhelming. The indoctrination might prove too strong. The gospel might be resisted. Mass conversions might not yet be the order of the day. But in Luther's words, "If some of them should prove stiff-necked, what of it? After all, we ourselves are not all good Christians either."[38] The point was hardly disputable.

LUTHER'S HOPES DASHED

Luther had hoped that the advent of evangelical theology after centuries of Catholic obfuscation would see a new influx of Jews into the kingdom of Christ. By example and by clear proclamation, Christians would commend the gospel so that sincere and fair-minded Jews could no longer resist the call to return to the faith of the Jewish apostles. As late as January 1533, he expressed the belief that "many Jews will be converted if they hear our preaching and our interpretation of the Old Testament."[39] But in the years that followed, no such significant movement among the Jews emerged. Luther occasionally came across a converted Jew and was delighted to meet them and rejoice with them. He kept the channels of communication open with Jews inquiring about the Christian faith. But as the 1520s merged into the 1530s, Luther became more and more disillusioned.

This disillusionment gave way to anger as Luther learned how his efforts to reach Jews for Christ had been turned on their head. He had advocated a gentle dealing with the Jews, allowing them to live amongst Christians, with believers taking all opportunities to demonstrate Christian love to them and share the Christian gospel with them. But Luther began to hear how some Jewish apologists interpreted this as weakness. Reports began to reach him of evangelistic efforts in the opposite direction: Jews seeking to turn Christians from Christ and towards the Jewish law. This, it need hardly be said, was not at all what he intended. In the light of his eschatological perspective, this could only be seen as yet another of the devil's strategies. The evidence makes clear that Luther didn't abandon his desire to see Jews saved in the light of this new development. Rather, throughout the 1530s he began to re-evaluate his strategy for bringing them to repentance and faith.

---

38. Ibid., 229.
39. M. Luther, *Table Talk # 2912a* (January 26–29, 1533), in *WATr* 3:76.23–24.

The Gospel and Israel

In August 1536, the Saxon elector John Frederick banished all Jews from his territories. In one sense this simply took existing state policy a step further: Jews had been forbidden from taking up permanent residence in electoral Saxony since 1432. Why this additional step was taken is not quite clear. Some have implicated Luther, since he is known to have met with the elector in Wittenberg on July 23–24. However, apart from knowledge that they met, there is no evidence that Luther suggested or encouraged this. Not long after, though, Luther spoke at table about how he had been visited by Jews who had heard of his interest in the Hebrew language and apparently hoped soon to make him into a proselyte. While Luther gave them the letter of introduction they were seeking, he included in it a reference to Christ, which kept them from using it.[40]

Eight months after John Frederick's mandate (April 26, 1537), Wolfgang Capito, himself a Hebrew scholar in Strasbourg, wrote to Luther urging him to intervene on behalf of a prominent Jewish leader, Josel von Rosheim. Josel had been appealing to the elector to rescind the mandate and Capito was seeking Luther's support for the cause.[41] Luther responded directly to Josel in June. He refused to intervene, largely because every effort he had made to reach the Jews with the gospel had been rebuffed and misused. The behaviour of the Jews more generally had itself undermined any influence others might have on their behalf with the authorities. And yet Luther had not yet finally turned his back on the Jews. "My opinion was, and still is," Luther wrote, "that one should treat the Jews in a kindly manner, that God may perhaps look graciously upon them and bring them to their Messiah—but not so that through my good will and influence they might be strengthened in their error and become still more bothersome." The letter concludes, "For the sake of the crucified Jew, whom no one shall take from me, I would gladly do my best for all you Jews, except you abuse my good will out of your stubbornness."[42]

Around the same time, Luther spoke at table about the news that was reaching him from Moravia. "In Moravia," he told those gathered, Jews "have circumcised many Christians and call them by the new name of Sabbatarians."[43] This was just one such report. Luther began to conclude

---

40. M. Luther, *Table Talk #3512* (December 1536), in *WATr* 3:370.9–21. See Brecht, *Preservation*, 336–37.
41. *WABr* 8:77–78.
42. Ibid., 89.9—90.2; 91.57–59.
43. M. Luther, *Table Talk #3597* (May–June 1537), in *WATr* 3:442.5–7 = *LW* 54:239.

that he had misjudged the situation in his earliest writing about the Jews. His hope of significant conversions from among them was replaced with an increasing conviction that their stubborn rejection of their Messiah was incurable. Worse than this, they were now proving to be a danger to the faith of some who belong to Christ. Given Luther's lifelong habit of confronting all challenges to Christian faith and teaching, it was to be expected that before long he would write more extensively against what he would later label "the Jews and their lies."

AGAINST THE SABBATARIANS

Sometime late in 1537, Luther received a letter from Wolfgang Schlick of Falkenau. It brought further news about the Jewish advance in Bohemia and Moravia. The letter, it would seem, is now lost. However, the little booklet Luther wrote in response, in March 1538, begins with Luther's summary of what he had been told:

> You informed me that the Jews are making inroads at various places throughout the country with their venom and their doctrine, and that they have already induced some Christians to let themselves be circumcised and to believe that the Messiah or Christ has not yet appeared, and that the law of the Jews must prevail forever, that it must also be adopted by all the Gentiles, etc.[44]

This booklet has two parts: the first dealing with the judgement the Jews are experiencing because they have rejected the Messiah, and the second dealing with the bankruptcy of the Jewish appeal to the law. Luther is clearly arming Schlick and others with the arguments from Scripture which he believes most effectively counter Jewish claims. Luther places his argument right up front in the first half of the work:

> The Jews have been living away from Jerusalem, in exile, for fifteen hundred years, bereft of temple, divine service, priesthood, and kingdom. Thus their law has been lying in the ashes with Jerusalem and the entire Jewish kingdom all this time.[45]

All the claims of privilege and a special standing before God falter at this point. The Jews are, very demonstrably, under the judgement of God. No king descended from David sits on the throne in Jerusalem; there is no

44. M. Luther, *Against the Sabbatarians* (1538) *LW* 47, 65.
45. Ibid., 66.

The Gospel and Israel

temple there, no sacrifices, no law and no promise of a return. The situation now is much more dire than that during the Babylonian exile, for at that time God had sent prophets to fortify their faith and assure them when this captivity would end. But there has been no new word from God for a millennium and a half. Even the Jews themselves must admit there is something wrong.

Luther wanted to insist on the obvious question:

> Now you must ask them the nature and name of the sin that caused God to punish them so cruelly, obliging them to live in exile so long, without priestly and princely, that is, Mosaic, office and government, without the sacrifices and the other regulations of the law, and particularly without Jerusalem [. . .] you must ask what is wrong, for God cannot lie or deceive [. . .] you must press them hard to name the sin.[46]

Abraham had sinned and yet was forgiven; so was David. Yet now the judgement goes on and on. The first of the Ten Commandments envisages the anger of God extending to the third and fourth generation. But this exile has lasted 1,500 years with no indication that there is an end in sight. The sin this time around must be heinous indeed. And so it is, Luther argues:

> The Messiah has come and God's promise has been kept and fulfilled. They, however, did not accept or believe this but constantly gave God the lie with their own unbelief etc.[47]

It is the Jewish rejection of the Messiah who has come that has brought them to this end. After all they had been given, after the promises and prophetic words, unbelief on this scale cannot but place them under judgement.

In the second part of the booklet, Luther confronts the Jewish insistence on the law. If the Jewish law is eternal and all must come to obey it, then why don't they keep it all themselves? Why don't they keep the parts of the law associated with the temple, the priesthood, the kingship? Surely if the law remains valid and compelling then all of it remains valid and compelling. And yet the temple lies in ruins and there is no Jewish king of David's line ruling in Jerusalem. Their trumpeting of the law is incoherent. Not even they can keep their law.

---

46. Ibid., 66, 67.
47. Ibid., 73.

When it comes to circumcision there is an additional problem. Throughout the Hebrew Scriptures—our Old Testament—it is clear that God accepts Gentiles as his own without circumcision. When Joseph ruled in Egypt and Pharaoh and the whole land prospered, the Egyptians were not compelled to be circumcised. When Jonah called on Nineveh to repent, there is not the slightest indication that the broken people of that city submitted to circumcision or were asked to do so. Similarly with King Nebuchadnezzar and Darius and Cyrus. What about Job? If these true believers were not compelled to be circumcised, why should we?[48]

Luther takes on Sabbath observance as well. What the Sabbath provides is an opportunity to hear God's word or teach it and so to sanctify both the day and ourselves. The issue is sanctifying the day rather than celebrating a particular day. "The Jews [. . .] lay greater emphasis on the celebrating than on the sanctifying," Luther says. But the seventh day as such "does not concern us Gentiles." Instead Luther insists, "by the very nature of things one must [. . .] rest, celebrate, and keep the Sabbath on whatever day or at whatever hour God's word is preached."[49]

Clearly Luther's tone has changed since his first treatise on the Jews back in 1523. He is more pessimistic about them now. They stand under judgement and only by illusion and deception are they able to convince men and women to leave the gospel and cling to a law they themselves cannot keep. The antidote is and can only be an appeal to the clear teaching of Scripture. Like *That Jesus Christ Was Born a Jew* twenty-five years before, this booklet is dominated by expositions of biblical passages.

In the months that followed the publication of this tract, we know that Luther was reading anti-Jewish propaganda. Some of the polemical works prepared by ex-Jews became a particular interest. He first became acquainted with Anthony Margaritha's *The Whole Jewish Faith*, which had been published in 1530.[50] It convinced him afresh of the legalistic and anti-evangelical character of Jewish religion. More scurrilous publications suggested other nefarious Jewish activities. Urban legends—of Jews abducting women and children, of murder and dark rituals—were repeated in the Luther household. Letters to his wife Katie during his last journey from

---

48. Ibid., 85–87.
49. Ibid., 92, 93.
50. Brecht, *Preservation*, 339; M. Luther, *Table Talk #5504* (1542), in *LW* 54:436.

home in 1546 hint that she habitually made reference to the designs of the Jews when there were mishaps in the family of one kind or another.[51]

In 1539, the elector modified his mandate of 1536 and allowed Jews to travel through his territories. We know from later comments that Luther viewed such moves with concern.[52] In that same year, Martin Bucer produced his critique, *On the Jews*, in which he produced a set of proposals for dealing with these "implacable foes of the true faith." He called on no new synagogues to be built, measures to ensure Jews refrained from insulting Christ and Christians, and to compel them to attend Christian sermons. What is more, they were to be barred from all business activity and be assigned menial tasks.[53] The similarity between these proposals and some which Luther himself would later put forward is not often noted. However, Bucer's language, as always, was more measured than Luther's.

Johann Eck, Luther's old opponent from the Leipzig Disputation of 1519, wrote on the same subject in 1541 with a work entitled *Refutation of a Jew Book*. The "Jew Book" Eck had in mind was in fact the work of Andreas Osiander, Lutheran pastor, theologian, and uncle of Margaret Cranmer, the wife of Archbishop Thomas Cranmer of England. Osiander had defended the Jews against various preposterous charges and for his trouble was labelled a Jewish sympathiser. The venomous style of Eck's work is evident in his description of the Jews as "cunning, false, perjured, thievish, vindictive, and traitorous."[54]

It is not entirely clear how familiar Luther was with the work of Bucer and Eck on this topic. He may indeed have read them as part of the feverish research program he embarked upon in 1542. At the very least, they show the breadth of interest in this topic in the German-speaking lands during this period. This was far more than Luther's personal obsession. We do know that Luther received and read the rabbinic work that attacked his *Against the Sabbatarians*. There is some evidence that it was sent to him by

---

51. *WABr* 11:275-76 = *LW* 50:290-91.

52. E.g. M. Luther, *Table Talk* #5475 (1542), in *LW* 54:426.

53. Bucer had been involved in a commission set up to investigate the viability of Jews living alongside Christians and in this context had clashed with Philip of Hesse over the issue. In response to published comments by Philip, Bucer published a brief open letter *Von den Juden*, on May 10, 1539. A copy is kept in the Bayrische Staatsbibliothek, Munich. See S. Rowan, "Luther, Bucer and Eck on the Jews," *Sixteenth Century Journal* 16/1 (1985) 79-90.

54. See Bertram's informative introduction to *The Jews and Their Lies* in *LW* 47:129.

his friend Schlick, who asked him to refute it.⁵⁵ It repeated the usual Jewish charges about Mary and the Lord Jesus and clearly it incensed him. At table in summer 1542 he told his students:

> I intend to write against the Jews once again because I hear that some of our lords are befriending them. I'll advise them to chase all the Jews out of their land. What reason do they have to slander and insult the dear Virgin Mary as they do? They call her a stinkpot, a hag, a monstrosity. If I were a lord I'd take them by the throat or they'd have to show cause. They're wretched people. I know of no stronger argument against them than to ask them why they've been in exile so long.⁵⁶

ON THE JEWS AND THEIR LIES

And so we come to Luther's most infamous anti-Jewish tract, *On the Jews and their Lies*, published in 1543. Luther began preparing to write it by reading and in some cases rereading a number of significant works on Jewish arguments against Christianity and Jewish claims for their own religion. A copy of Salvagus Porchetus' classic work from around 1300, *Victory Over the Godless Jews*, survives with Luther's critical marginal notes in it.⁵⁷ However, in the midst of his preparation tragedy struck the Luther household. On September 20, 1542, Luther's beloved daughter Magdalene died in his arms. Luther was devastated. His hope in Christ remained resolute. He had inscribed on her tomb the words, "The child sleeps here in the earth as one born to die and someone lost because of sin, but thanks to Christ's blood and death she lives."⁵⁸ However, the wounds were still raw when his book on the Jews was completed near the end of December that year. The tragedy does not excuse his violent tone; yet still it is an important part of the context for this book.

On the Jews and Their Lies is the work to which all who wish to draw the link between Luther and German anti-Semitism over the centuries routinely turn. It is 155 pages long in the English translation. His proposals for what should be done about the Jews occur in 25 pages near the end of the book, addressed more generally and then repeated with special reference to

---

55. Ibid., 133.
56. M. Luther, *Table Talk* #5462 (1542), in *LW* 54:426.
57. Brecht, *Preservation*, 346.
58. Ibid., 237–8.

pastors and preachers. This small section has overshadowed the vast bulk of the book, which is concerned to refute Jewish teaching from the Scriptures.

Luther makes clear from the start that his intended audience are German Christians, not Jews. He wants to strengthen Christian faith by answering the challenges presented by Jews in the booklet he had been sent. He is intent on answering abuse of the Scriptures with faithful and forceful biblical exposition. There is no need to be unsettled by tracts such as this one. What is more, something needs to be done about the spread of lies and distortions such as these.

There are five parts to Luther's treatise. After an introduction, in which Luther gives his most pessimistic assessment of the prospects of Jewish conversions—"I do not propose to convert the Jews, for that is impossible"[59]—Luther embarks on a scriptural rebuttal of each of the so-called Jewish privileges. He deals first with the boast of Jewish lineage from the patriarch Abraham.[60] He points out that others were descended from Abraham as well: Ishmael and his descendants, the children of Keturah and all their families, and the children of Esau. He also draws attention to a most significant fact: what sets Abraham and his descendants apart is not in the final analysis a common race, but a common faith.

Luther next pays particular attention to the Jewish boast associated with circumcision.[61] He considers the reliance upon circumcision and the claim that it sets the Jews apart and puts them in a special relationship with God as "a clumsy, foolish, and stupid lie."[62] Others were circumcised besides Abraham, Isaac, Jacob and their descendants. Abraham himself circumcised Ishmael, after all (Gen 17:23). Furthermore, physical circumcision was never the most important thing, Luther argues. In his words, "Only a circumcised heart can produce a people of God, and it can do this even when physical circumcision is absent or is impossible, as it was for the children of Israel during their forty years in the wilderness."[63] When the Christian apostle Paul dismissed the necessity of circumcision, he was not doing something without precedent in the Old Testament.

---

59. M. Luther, *On the Jews*, in *LW* 47:137.
60. Ibid., 140–49.
61. Ibid., 149–64.
62. Ibid., 152.
63. Ibid., 153.

The third boast Luther deals with is the boast that the Jews possess and keep an eternal law, which God has given and calls all men to heed.[64] Here Luther repeats some of the arguments from his *Against the Sabbatarians*. The Jews do not in fact keep their law. Their own histories testify to their persistent rebellion and idolatry. What is more, what they claim as their own is at points much more universal. Luther argues that the Ten Commandments are universal. God abhors murder, adultery, theft, and covetousness wherever they may be found. Luther insists that "all Gentiles and devils are also duty-bound to keep these, or else are polluted and condemned on account of them."[65]

Luther spends the least amount of time on the fourth and final boast, the Jewish boast of having received the land of Canaan.[66] He points out that God's promise of the land was accompanied by the threat of removal from it if they turned aside from God and his word. That judgement fell briefly in the time of the Babylonians and God in his mercy restored the Jews to the land of promise. But the Roman exile continues and has continued for some 1,500 years. Still they haven't learnt the lesson and continue in this empty boast.

The second main section of this treatise is an answer to the charge that the Messiah has not yet come.[67] Luther's treatment of four key messianic texts—Genesis 49:10, 2 Samuel 23:2ff., Haggai 2:6–9, and Daniel 9:24—owes much to earlier expositions by Nicholas of Lyra and Paul of Burgos. Luther explicitly acknowledges his debt to others who have considered these things before him. Yet Luther himself is quite familiar with these texts. He had dealt with Genesis 49 and Daniel 9 at some length in 1523. He had mentioned Haggai 2 then as well. In 2 Samuel 23, the last words of David were of particular interest to him at this time. Later that year, Luther would devote a whole treatise to it. Luther's expositions, which were at the same time refutations of distortions he saw in rabbinic exegesis of these passages, point to the coming of the Messiah just prior to the fall of Jerusalem, when land, temple, and king would disappear from the pages of history. Jesus the Christ not only has come, but he came at the time appointed and declared long before.

64. Ibid., 164–72.
65. Ibid., 169.
66. Ibid., 172–6.
67. Ibid., 176–254.

The Gospel and Israel

It is in the third section of the treatise that Luther's temperature begins to rise.[68] Here he treats the lies that have been told by Jews about Christ, Mary, and consequently about Christians. Each of these pains Luther because of the preciousness of Christ and his gospel. It is blasphemy to claim that Jesus is a sorcerer and a tool of the devil. It is even worse to describe him as the son of a whore. And it does not stop there. Luther repeats the language he has heard, perhaps from the most scurrilous of sources. The defamation spreads beyond Christ and Mary of course to include those vile people who honour them. The burden that Jewish moneylenders and others lay upon Christian people is merely a sign of their contempt. They play the masters, they sit back in luxury, while ordinary Christians sweat and work because the Jews are convinced they are better and deserve better than the hated "Goyim."

And so Luther turns to what he would do about it, now that all hope of their conversion appears to be lost.[69] Perhaps there is still a sliver of hope left for some, but only with the most radical of measures. Luther begins his series of proposals this way:

> What shall we Christians do with this rejected and condemned people, the Jews? Since they live among us, we dare not tolerate their conduct, now that we are aware of their lying and reviling and blaspheming. If we do, we become sharers in their lies, cursing and blasphemy. Thus we cannot extinguish the unquenchable fire of divine wrath, of which the prophets speak, nor can we convert the Jews. With prayer and the fear of God we must practice a sharp mercy to see whether we might save at lest a few from the glowing flames.[70]

In the pages that follow Luther lists seven measures and uses language reminiscent of his harsh book against the peasants and his ferocious work against the papacy as he explains them. In brief, he calls upon those in authority to:

1. Burn all synagogues and schools—they must not be allowed to teach these things any longer.

---

68. Ibid., 254–67.
69. Ibid., 267–74.
70. Ibid., 268.

2. Raze and destroy their houses—for they teach and speak these things there as well (Luther suggests they could live in barns or under roofs like gypsies).

3. Take from them all their religious writings—the source and record of their blasphemies.

4. Forbid their rabbis to teach on pain of loss of life or limb—they are the agents of this false and blasphemous teaching.

5. Abolish safe-conduct on the highways for them—let them stay at home and not spread their lies in other places.

6. Bring an end to their money lending and usury and take their ill-gotten gains from them (interestingly at this point Luther argues that the confiscated wealth should be kept in safekeeping and used to provide for genuine converts).

7. Make them work like us, in the fields and with their hands.

If all of this failed, Luther argued, then the only remedy was to follow the example of other nations and "eject them forever from the country."[71]

The language Luther uses from this point is strong and, from our perspective as twenty-first-century readers, undoubtedly offensive (I have somewhat sanitised it in the list above). His language and the aggression he advocates towards the Jews cannot be explained away or excused, nor should it be. It bears all the marks of a man pushed too far, of disillusionment and betrayal, and even of grief. He may have explained it as "sharp mercy," but even some of his closest friends found it difficult to swallow.

In the last section of the treatise, Luther repeats his advice, this time for pastors and preachers, and this time heading the list with the instruction to "warn your parishioners concerning their eternal harm." He then closes by recapping on the nature of the Messiah and briefly mentions again the key messianic texts.

HARSH WORDS AT THE END

Luther wrote twice more about the Jews that year: in his *On the Ineffable Name and the Genealogy of Christ*[72] and his exposition of 2 Samuel 23, en-

---

71. Ibid., 272.

72. M. Luther, *Vom Schem Hamphoras und vom Geschlecht Christi* (1543), in WA 53:579–648.

titled *Treatise on the Last Words of David*.[73] In the first of these, he dealt with suggestion that Jesus performed his miracles by sorcery and magical incantations associated with the mystic name of God. He also sought to harmonise the two genealogies of Jesus in Matthew 1 and Luke 3. The same aggressive and somewhat vulgar tone in that little book horrified the reformers in Zurich.[74] The second book was an exposition of the last words of King David in which Luther emphasised the hope of the Messiah and even the divine sonship of Jesus.

But it was *On the Jews and Their Lies* that set the tone of his last years and tainted his reputation with all who live in the shadow of the Shoah. He didn't step back from it despite the reservations of some of his friends. His very last sermon included a diatribe against the Jews, notwithstanding his insistence that "still we want to practice Christian love toward them and pray that they convert."[75] His longstanding hope for Jewish converts remained, but it was overshadowed by the disappointments he had suffered, and the new threats resurgent "evangelism" on the part of the Jews themselves seemed to present to the Christian men and women. As a result, Luther's strategy for minimising the damage they could do and bringing as many of them as possible to Christ changed from "gentle dealing" to "sharp mercy."

So how do we make sense of Luther and his engagement with the Jews? As difficult as it is, we should not allow Hitler and his henchmen to determine our attitude to him, even on this issue. As everyone who has read his words immediately recognises, Luther did not recommend the extermination of the Jews. He did not recommend beating them or anything like it. He did not advocate mob violence against them. Even eviction from Germany was a last resort if the "sharp mercy" he was advocating did not stop the spread of anti-Christian teaching and result in the conversion of at least some of them. As one modern biographer puts it:

> Luther never organized any campaign against the Jews, and ... despite the ferocity of his tirades against them he never truly renounced the notion of coexistence between Jews and Christians.

---

73. M. Luther, *Treatise on the Last Words of David* (1543), in WA 54:16–100 = *LW* 15:265–352.

74. R. Marius, *Martin Luther: the Christian Between God and Death* (Cambridge, MA: Harvard University Press, 1999), 378.

75. M. Luther, "Eine vermanung wider die Juden" (February 15, 1546), in WA 51:195.39–40.

> But the fact that Luther's hostility to Jews was not the same as modern anti-Semitism does not excuse it. It was as bad as Luther could make it . . .[76]

And it was that bad because Luther saw himself in the midst of the final battle for the gospel on earth. He believed the end was near. His famous chronology of the world, published just two years before *On the Jews and their Lies*, suggested the climax of God's purposes was just around the corner.[77] Luther had long been convinced of this. The rise of the papacy as the power of antichrist confirmed it. Yet the multiple, sustained, and increasingly virulent attacks upon the gospel Luther preached was, in his eyes, the strongest proof of all. The devil will not hold back when the end is near, and Luther became convinced that it was the devil's work that meant the Jews were not only refusing to come to Christ, but were drawing Christian men and women away from him.

In the end, Luther can't be excused, nor should he be simply equated with the racial hatred that drove the Holocaust. His opposition to the Jews was never racially motivated; nor was it simply an echo of the anti-Semitism that has plagued Europe for centuries. His was a very specific concern. I'll leave the last word to Heiko Oberman:

> As Luther neared the end of his days on earth, the issue was not a Turkish crusade, or hatred of Rome or the Jews, it was upholding the Gospel against all enemies in the confusion of the Last Days [. . .] He saw in the Jews' resistance to the Reformation, to the rediscovered Gospel, an obstinately persistent estrangement from God and thus a newly formed alliance of all the forces inimical to God.[78]

---

76. Marius, *Martin Luther*, 380.
77. M. Luther, *Supputatio annorum mundi* (1541), in *WA* 53:22–182.
78. Oberman, *Luther*, 296.

5

Calvin and the Jews

—Dr. Peter Barnes

CALVIN THE JUDAIZER?

Down through the ages, Calvin has at times received brutal press, especially in the last half of the nineteenth century and the first half of the twentieth century. Adolf von Harnack is supposed to have begun his lecture on Calvin with the words, "We now come to a man who never smiled." More severely, Stefan Zweig in 1936 portrayed him as a dictator, a kind of Hitler before his time, who inspired his followers to be "hostile to beauty, happiness, life itself."[1] However, Zweig said nothing about Calvin and the Jewish question—which must be of some significance.

As the sixteenth century drew to its close, the polemical Lutheran theologian Aegidius Hunnius produced a treatise with the imposing but very comprehensible title: *Calvin the Judaizer: Judaistic Glosses and Corruptions by Which John Calvin Did Not Fear to Corrupt the Clearest Passages of Sacred Scripture and Its Witness to the Glorious Trinity, the Deity of Christ and the Holy Spirit, including the Predictions of the Prophets concerning the Coming of the Messiah, His Birth, Passion, Resurrection, Ascension to Heaven, and Session at the Right Hand of God, in a Detestable Fashion.*[2] In fact, the charge that Calvin was a Judaizer was not uncommon in the latter half

---

1. Stefan Zweig, *The Right to Heresy: Castellio Against Calvin* (New York: Viking, 1936), 224.

2. Cf. David Puckett, *John Calvin's Exegesis of the Old Testament* (Louisville: Westminster John Knox, 1995), especially 1–7.

of the sixteenth century. Another Lutheran polemicist, Georg Nigrinus, also accused Calvin, again posthumously, of siding with Jewish interpretation of the Old Testament "as if he were the intercessor of the Jews, as if he would rather align himself with Jewish rabbis than Christian teachers."[3] In his own lifetime, because of his views on the abiding significance of the law, Calvin was accused by Michael Servetus: "You place the Christians on a par with the vulgar Jews."[4]

JEWS IN SIXTEENTH-CENTURY EUROPE

From 1388 to 1520, some ninety cities took action against the Jews.[5] Jews were expelled from France in 1394 by Charles VI (who was reinstituting a previous order of 1306), with only a few remaining in Alsace and Lorraine, and in the papal possessions of Avignon and Comtat Venaissin. They were also expelled from England (1290), Spain (1492), and other parts of Europe, and were only allowed to live in sections of Italy, Germany, and Poland. Periodically there were accusations against the Jews of ritual murder (e.g., that the rabbis had killed a Christian boy in Norwich in 1144), desecration of the host (e.g., in Rottingen in 1298), and the poisoning of wells (e.g., during the Black Death of 1347–49). Jeremy Cohen points to the friars as playing a large part in spreading concern, even panic, about Jews and the Talmud.[6]

By 1514, the Parisian theological faculty was embroiled in the Reuchlin-Pfefferkorn controversy. Johannes Pfefferkorn (d. ca. 1522) was a converted Jew who adopted extreme views, arguing that the Talmud should be seized and burnt, as it had already been in a number of places in late medieval Europe. He saw the end of the world as near, and wanted to usher in the conversion of the Jews. Johannes Reuchlin was fond of a kind of Christian occultism, and answered somewhat fiercely. He inspired but did not write the *Letters of Obscure Men*, which managed to arouse Pope Leo

---

3. Cited in Achim Detmers, "Calvin, the Jews, and Judaism," *Jews, Judaism, and the Reformation in Sixteenth-Century Germany* in, eds. Dean Philip Bell and Stephen. G. Burnett (eds), (Leiden/Boston: Brill, 2006), 198.

4. Cited in Salo W. Baron, "John Calvin and the Jews," in *Essential Papers on Judaism and Christianity in Conflict from Late Antiquity to the Reformation*, ed. Jeremy Cohen (New York: New York University Press, 1991), 384.

5. Heiko Oberman, *The Impact of the Reformation* (Grand Rapids: Eerdmans, 1994), 110.

6. Cited in ibid., 133.

X's ire in 1520. In 1553, by order of the Inquisition, the Talmud was publicly burned in Rome, but in the meantime Emperor Charles V adopted a more friendly attitude to the Jews to keep them from the Protestant camp.

History merges into mythology regarding some of these issues. Erasmus, the champion of Enlightenment tolerance in Peter Gay's view, was hostile to Pfefferkorn as too much of a Jew, and was too anti-Semitic to be very staunch in his support for Reuchlin. At times Erasmus could sound a little like a Marcionite: "If only the Church would not attach so much importance to the Old Testament—it is a book of shadows, given just for a time!"[7] He actually feared a revival of Hebrew studies, yet Jerome, one of the few Hebraists in the early Church and the translator of the Vulgate, was his favourite church father!

In 1538 the Landgrave, Philip of Hesse, sought the help of Martin Bucer with regard to the organisation of the Hessian church. This included the issue of the possible toleration of the Jews. Bucer and other Hessian theologians gathered together at a synod at Cassel to discuss these issues. Catholics had accused Bucer of being the child of Jewish parents, and he denied this most vigorously, regarding it as slander.[8] The Cassel Advice was signed by Bucer, Rymeus, Melander, Lening, Winther, Pistorius, and Kauffungen. Somehow the principle of there being one true religion was to be upheld, yet the Jews had to be recognised in some way. They were to put aside Talmudic teaching, build no more synagogues, and attend to Christian preaching provided for them. Jews were to be excluded from commerce and industry, but not from subordinate and menial work.

Landgrave Philip regarded this Cassel Advice as too drastic, and pointed out that Christ was a Jew. Bucer responded that Christians should help the Jews insofar as it was possible to do so without harming others. He also claimed that the Cassel Advice would treat the Jews better than they would the Christians were they in power.[9] Bucer pointed to vicious Jewish conduct in the past, the need to curb false religion, and God's punishment of the Jews (in Deut 13, 17, 28).[10] However, Bucer did not make an issue

---

7. Oberman, *Impact*, 104. See too Charles Zika, "Reuchlin and Erasmus," *Journal of Religious History* 9 (1977) 223–246.

8. Cited in Hastings Eells, "Bucer's Plan for the Jews," *Church History* 6/2 (June 1937) 129.

9. Ibid., 134.

10. Ibid., 135

of this, and Hastings Eells writes, "It seems to have been merely a minor episode in his life."[11]

In his *Concerning the True Care of Souls*, also written in 1538, Bucer had stated:

> That is why God in his righteous judgment has arranged that, because we do not seek to win Jews, Turks and other heathen to the kingdom of Christ, but seek only to take away their temporal possessions and estates, they should rob us of our own temporal possessions and estates. Thus the Jews have sucked dry the poor Christians to a remarkable extent by means of their usury, and the Turks day by day strip us of land and people with violence, making quite alarming advances.[12]

Bucer said that such a people were to be shunned and loved; "they should be considered our enemies and our friends, to be fought against and to be cherished."[13] There is thus a two-sided aspect to the attitude of Bucer to the Jews, as there was with Calvin.

Luther in his latter years is notorious for his outbursts against the Jews, yet they were milder than those of his Catholic opponent, Johann Eck, who compiled all manner of horror stories, claiming that Jews killed Christian children. Andreas Osiander at Nuremberg—a flamboyant, somewhat egotistical, and doctrinally erratic character—was nevertheless forthright in rejecting these commonly believed accusations, and Philip Melanchthon and Justus Jonas were also embarrassed by Luther's vitriolic attacks on the Jews. In 1543, Strasbourg forbade the circulation of Luther's anti-Jewish writings, although, as we have seen, Bucer still wanted to force Jews to attend Christian sermons, to abandon the Talmud, and to be forbidden to engage in money lending.

---

11. Ibid.

12. Martin Bucer, *Concerning the True Care of Souls*, trans. Peter Beale (Edinburgh: Banner of Truth, 2009), 87.

13. R. Gerald Hobbs, "Bucer, the Jews, and Judaism," in *Jews, Judaism, and the Reformation in Sixteenth-Century Germany*, eds. Dean Philip Bell and Stephen. G. Burnett (Leiden/Boston: Brill, 2006), 161.

The Gospel and Israel

A COMPARISON WITH LUTHER

For some odd reason, Achim Detmers considers that it helps little to compare Calvin's views with the anti-Jewish outbursts of Luther.[14] Luther wrote passionately—which was both a strength and a weakness. Two of his works, separated by twenty years, might especially be compared.[15]

(a) *That Jesus Was Born a Jew* was published in 1523.[16] In it he wrote

> I hope that, if one deals in a kindly way with the Jews and instructs them carefully from Holy Scripture, many of them will become genuine Christians, and turn again to the faith of their fathers, the Prophets and Patriarchs. They will only be frightened further away from it, if their Judaism is so utterly rejected, that nothing is allowed to remain, and they are treated only with arrogance and scorn. If the apostles, who also were Jews, had dealt with us Gentiles as we Gentiles deal with the Jews, there would never have been a Christian among the Gentiles. Since they have dealt with us Gentiles in such a brotherly fashion, we in our turn ought to treat the Jews in a brotherly manner, in order that we might convert some of them.[17]

Luther added:

> So long as we treat them like dogs, how can we expect to work any good among them? Again, when we forbid them to labour and do business and have any human fellowship with us, thereby forcing them into usury, how is that supposed to do them any good? If we really want to help them, we must be guided in our dealings with them not by papal law, but by the law of Christian love. We must receive them cordially and permit them to trade and work with us, that they may have occasion and opportunity to associate with us, hear our Christian teaching, and witness our Christian life. If some of them should prove stiff-necked, what of it? After all, we ourselves are not all good Christians either.[18]

As Luther pointed out, "We are aliens and in-laws; they are the blood relatives, cousins and brothers of Our Lord." For this he was criticised as a

---

14. Detmers, "Calvin, the Jews, and Judaism," 201.

15. See Mark Thompson, "Luther and the Jews," in the present book.

16. Martin Luther, *Luther's Works*, vol. 45, ed. W. Brandt (Philadelphia: Muhlenberg, 1962).

17. Ibid., 200–201.

18. Ibid., 229.

"Half-Jew" and "Patron of the Jews." Luther was vigorous and understanding: "If I had been a Jew and had seen such dolts and blockheads govern and teach the Christian faith, I would sooner have become a hog than a Christian."[19]

By the 1530s this tone had changed, as Luther became frustrated that so few Jews converted to Christianity; those who did sometimes reverted to Judaism, and some Christians in Moravia began to observe Saturday as the Sabbath and practise circumcision. Melanchthon tells a story of how a Jew fell into a latrine on the Sabbath. His Jewish friends requested the magistrate to order some Christian officials to pull him out so that they would not have to break the Sabbath. The magistrate refused, and the poor man remained there two days.[20]

Yet even in 1537 Luther still wrote in a letter, "For my opinion was, and still is, that one should treat the Jews in a kindly manner, that God may perhaps look graciously upon them and bring them to their Messiah—but not so that through my good will and influence they might be strengthened in their error and become still more bothersome."[21] By this time, one increasingly detects in Luther what Jean-Paul Lichtenberg has most aptly called an "anti-Semitism of resentment."[22]

(b) *Concerning the Jews and Their Lies* was published in 1543.[23] Here Luther castigated the Jews as vampires, blasphemers, thieves, usurers, and devils incarnate. He recommended that the Jews be expelled—as had happened in Spain, France, and Bohemia. Luther advocated what he called "a sharp mercy to see whether we might save at least a few from the glowing flames. Avenge ourselves we dare not." He concluded with the prayer, "Christ, our loving Lord, convert them in thy Compassion!" As Roland Bainton comments, "One could wish that Luther had died before ever this tract was written."[24]

19. Ibid., 200.

20. Timothy J. Wengert, "Philip Melanchthon and the Jews: A Reappraisal," in *Jews, Judaism, and the Reformation in Sixteenth-Century Germany*, eds. Dean Philip Bell and Stephen. G. Burnett, (Leiden/Boston: Brill, 2006), 119.

21. Cited in Graham Keith, *Hated Without a Cause?: A Survey of Anti-Semitism* (Carlisle: Paternoster, 1997), 153.

22. Robert M. Healey, "The Jew in Seventeenth-Century Protestant Thought," *Church History* 46/1 (March 1977) 69.

23. Martin Luther, *Luther's Works*, vol. 47, ed. Franklin Sherman (Philadelphia: Fortress).

24. Roland Herbert Bainton, *Here I Stand: A Life of Martin Luther* (Nashville:

The Gospel and Israel

Alas, he wrote a couple of other treatises in the same vein, notably *On the Tetragrammaton* and *The Genealogy of Christ*. This latter work horrified Heinrich Bullinger, who said it reminded him of the methods of the Inquisition. A day or two before he died, Luther preached at Eisleben, and condemned the Jews for calling the Virgin Mary a whore and Christ a bastard. He claimed that they would kill all Christians if given the chance. He still called for their conversion, although the options were now two—baptism or expulsion.

Heiko Oberman saw no great change for the worse in Luther's attitude to life but this is misleading.[25] A change in tone is still a change—very much so. As Mary Sweetland Laver puts it, "Luther offered an olive branch to the Jews early in his evangelical career, only to exchange it for a whipping stick when they did not join the Reformation."[26] Oberman is, however, right to categorise Luther as anti-Jewish but not a racial anti-Semite.[27] Unfortunately, we have little to go on in gleaning Calvin's response to these works of Luther. A letter from Ambrosius Blaurer shows that Calvin was familiar with Luther's anti-Jewish writings, but not necessarily that he had read them.[28] David Puckett's summary of Calvin's view seems misleading: "While his criticisms of Jews are perhaps not as harsh as Luther's diatribes, they are still quite severe."[29] The "perhaps" is quite beguiling, and out of place.

Paul Johnson too is hardly convincing. He compares Calvin favourably to Luther in being better disposed towards the Jews, but then adds that this was "partly because he tended to agree with them on the question of lending at interest."[30] Calvin's views on usury are not easy to discern. He certainly opposed the charging of excessive interest to anybody, whether Jew, pagan, Muslim, or Christian. In 1547, the Genevan council allowed an interest rate of 5 percent, and this seems to have reflected Calvin's views on the subject. In a sermon on Deuteronomy 23:20–23 preached in 1556, Cal-

---

Abingdon, 1950), 297.

25. Oberman, *Impact*, 51, 111–12.

26. Mary Sweetland Laver, "Calvin, Jews and Intra-Christian Polemics," PhD diss. (Philadelphia: Temple University, 1987), 1.

27. Oberman, *Impact*, 76.

28. Detmers, "Calvin, the Jews, and Judaism," 209.

29. David Puckett, *John Calvin's Exegesis of the Old Testament* (Louisville: Westminster John Knox, 1995), 139.

30. Paul Johnson, *A History of the Jews* (London: George Weidenfeld and Nicolson, 1987), 242–43.

vin condemned the practice of usury. He declared, "We are all neighbours, whether we be of the same country or farther off; and of whatever condition we be, we do not cease to be of that neighbourhood which God has established between us."[31]

CALVIN'S CONTACT WITH JEWS

There were no Jews in Geneva at the time of Calvin's living there as they had been expelled in 1491, eighteen years before Calvin was born and forty-five years before he reached Geneva. In 1536, Calvin stayed briefly in Ferrara where there was a strong Italian Jewish community. In 1539, he stayed at Frankfort for six weeks, where there was a ghetto of some four hundred Jews. Especially during his time of exile from Geneva in 1538–41, Calvin stayed at Strasbourg, which was religiously tolerant, although in 1530 it forbade the Jews to engage in any financial activities.

Later, Calvin supported the converted Italian Jew Immanuel Tremellius in his failed attempt to get a position at Bern. Tremellius had been won to Catholicism by Cardinal Pole in 1540 but embraced the Reformed faith the following year. In 1558, Calvin even tried to secure him for the Genevan Academy. Tremellius sought to spread the Reformed faith amongst Jews, and so translated the Geneva catechism into Hebrew, adding a Jewish missionizing introduction. In the end, however, Calvin had rather little contact with Jews during his life.

GOD'S BLESSING TO THE JEWS

Being a faithful expositor of Scripture, Calvin saw the Jews as a privileged people whom God had chosen. On John 4:22, Calvin states that "there can be no doubt that Christ gives the preference to the Jews on this ground, that they do not worship some unknown deity, but God alone, who revealed himself to them, and by whom they were adopted as his people."[32] He connected this to Isaiah 2:2 and Micah 4:2, that the Law would go forth from Zion.

On Luke 2:32 Calvin wrote:

31. John Calvin, *Sermons on Deuteronomy* (Edinburgh: Banner of Truth, 1987), 827. NB: The wording has been modernized.
32. John Calvin, *Commentary on the Gospel according to John* (on 4:22), trans. William Pringle (Grand Rapids: Baker, 1989), 160.

The Gospel and Israel

> There is propriety in the distinction here made between the people Israel and the Gentiles: for by the right of adoption the children of Abraham "were nigh" (Eph. 2:17) to God, while the Gentiles, with whom God had made no "covenants of promise," were "strangers" to the Church (Eph. 2:12).[33]

Hence Israel is God's firstborn (Jer 31:9). Calvin, of course, saw an essential unity between the two Testaments of Scripture. Hence in *The Institutes of the Christian Religion* he wrote that "The covenant made with all the patriarchs is so much like ours in substance and reality that the two are actually one and the same."[34]

Salo Baron says, "But, as a rule, Calvin emphasised the anti-Jewish and toned down the pro-Jewish statements in the New Testament."[35] That is demonstrably inaccurate. As G. Sujin Pak has pointed out, in treating the Psalms, Calvin, unlike Augustine and Luther, did not identify the Jews as God's enemies, for example in Psalm 59.[36] Indeed, in commenting on Psalm 47:9, Calvin wrote, "When the doctrine of the Gospel was manifested and shone forth, it did not remove the Jews from the covenant which God had long before made with them. On the contrary, it has rather joined us to them."[37] Even when the Jews declared that the blood of Christ was to be upon them (Matt 27:25), Calvin resisted any temptation to launch into an attack on the "Christ-killers" who had condemned themselves. His first application was that we ought to guard against rushing headlong into rash judgments.[38]

In his commentary on Romans, Calvin wrote:

---

33. John Calvin, *Commentary on a Harmony of the Evangelists*, trans. William Pringle (Grand Rapids: Baker, 1979), 1:145.

34. John Calvin, *Institutes of the Christian Religion*, trans. Ford Lewis Battles (Philadelphia: Westminster, 1977), 2.10.2.

35. Salo W. Baron, "John Calvin and the Jews," in *Essential Papers on Judaism and Christianity in Conflict from Late Antiquity to the Reformation*, ed. Jeremy Cohen (New York: New York University Press, 1991), 387.

36. G. Sujin Pak, "A Break with Anti-Judaic Tradition?: John Calvin and the History of the Interpretation of Ps.59:11–15," unpublished typescript. See G. Sujin Pak, *The Judaizing Calvin: Sixteenth-Century Debates over the Messianic Psalms* (Oxford: Oxford University Press, 2010), 91–92.

37. John Calvin, *Commentary on the Book of Psalms* (on 47:9), trans. James Anderson (Grand Rapids: Baker, 1979), 214.

38. Calvin, *Commentary on a Harmony of the Evangelists*, 3:288.

> For the Lord had passed by all other nations, and selected them as a people peculiar to Himself, and had adopted them as His children, as He often testifies by Moses and the prophets. . . . It is the singular honour conferred on the Jewish people that they have God as their lawgiver.[39]

Indeed, the Messiah himself is a Jew, and

> It is no empty honour to be united by a natural kinship with the Redeemer of the world. If He honoured the whole human race when He connected himself with us by sharing our nature, much more did He honour the Jews, with whom He desired to have a close bond of affinity.[40]

Calvin, however, held to the biblical principle that the greater the privileges, the greater the condemnation if these privileges are abused.[41] That was not good news for the Jews. Furthermore, he noted Paul's warning in Romans 9:6 that not all Israel is Israel.

THE PRESENT STATE OF THE JEWS

E. A. Boer speaks for many when he says that "Calvin expresses himself in purely negative terms on the Jews since Christ's coming."[42] Certainly, Calvin claimed that the Jews "had treacherously set aside the covenant of eternal life which God had made with their fathers," and so "were deprived of the treasure which they had till that time enjoyed."[43] One can quite readily find comments that are critical of the Jews. Regarding the prophecy of Isaiah 60:6–7, for example, Calvin stated, "Foolishly, therefore, do the Jews, under the pretence of this prophecy, devour with their insatiable avarice all the riches of the earth." However, he was quick to move onto the Papists who "torture these words to support their luxuries, wealth, and magnificence."[44] It is probably fair to say that Calvin was more hostile to heretics than to Jews.

---

39. John Calvin, *Commentary on Romans and Thessalonians* (on Rom 9:4), trans. Ross Mackenzie (Grand Rapids: Eerdmans, 1995).

40. Calvin, *Commentary on Romans*, 9:5.

41. Ibid.

42. E. A. de Boer, *John Calvin on the Visions of Ezekiel* (Leiden: Brill, 2004), 221.

43. Calvin, *Commentary on John*, 4:22.

44. Calvin, *Commentary on Isaiah* (on 60:6), trans. William Pringle (Grand Rapids: Baker, 1979).

The Gospel and Israel

However, the Jewish religion had little to recommend it since it failed to recognise the coming of the Messiah. In Calvin's view, the Old Testament is related to the New Testament in terms of childhood to maturity (Gal 4:1–2), shadow to substance (Heb 7), letter to spirit (Jer 31:31–34; 2 Cor 3:6–11), bondage to freedom (Gal 4:22–31), and one nation to all nations (Gal 3:28; Eph 2:14).[45] Calvin did not mean that there was little genuine spirituality in the Old Testament. Quite the reverse: the Old Testament saints—most of them being Jews, of course—exhibited greater fidelity, despite being granted less light than those who live in post–New Testament times.

The Jews were criticised by Calvin for a number of reasons, occasionally with some arbitrariness. Referring to Hebrews 13:1 ("Let brotherly love continue"), Calvin speculated that "Probably he gave this command respecting brotherly love, because a secret hatred arising from the haughtiness of the Jews was threatening to rend the Churches."[46] However, it can be said that three objections stand out regarding the Jews: their reliance on their relationship with Abraham, their dependence on the works of the law, and their rejection of Jesus as the Christ.

On the first criticism, Calvin, referring to John 8:39, commented: "What they continually claim and vaunt of is, that they are Abraham's children; by which they do not simply mean that they are the lineal descendants of Abraham, but that they are a holy race, the heritage of God, and the children of God. And yet they rely on nothing but the confidence of the flesh. But carnal descent, without faith, is nothing more than a false pretence."[47]

Regarding the second criticism, Calvin noted, for example on Romans 9:31, that "Paul's use of contrasted expressions is striking, when he informs us that legal righteousness was the reason why Israel fell from the law of righteousness."[48] Finally, with regard to the third criticism, he wrote that "none of us can excuse the Jews for having crucified Christ, treated the apostles with barbarous cruelty, and for having attempted to destroy and extinguish the Gospel."[49]

---

45. See Calvin, *Institutes*, 2.7.1–12.

46. John Calvin, *Commentary on the Epistle of Paul the Apostle to the Hebrews* (on 13:1), trans. John Owen (Grand Rapids: Baker, 1979).

47. Calvin, *Commentary on John*, 8:39.

48. Calvin, *Commentary on Romans*, 10:2.

49. Ibid., 9:31.

Calvin could say harsh things about Judaism, and even of Jews themselves, but he could also write warmly about the Jews as God's ancient people: "Despite the great obstinacy with which they continue to wage war against the gospel, we must not despise them while we consider that for the sake of the promise God's blessing still rests among them."[50] Baron contrasts that with what Calvin says in his Romans commentary—somewhat unconvincingly it must be said.[51] Calvin was not always consistent—who is?—and in a sermon on Genesis 9:3–7 in 1560 he allowed himself to complain of the Jews, "Yet we know that theirs is the most pitiless, the most merciless, and the most violent and fierce nation that can possibly be found."[52]

Commenting on Romans 9:4, Calvin wrote of the Jews, "Although their ingratitude rendered them unworthy of esteem on account of these gifts of God, Paul does not cease to give them due respect." His application was: "Let us imitate Paul, who granted the Jews their privileges in such a way that afterwards he declares that without Christ nothing is of any worth."[53] Calvin tended to apply criticisms of the Jews in Scripture more to the present church rather than to Jews of biblical times, let alone Jews of his own day. Hence on Romans 9:32 he wrote, "This example of the Jews should inspire with fear all those who strive to obtain the kingdom of God by works."[54] In commenting on Paul's analysis of the Jews' zeal without knowledge, Calvin did not attack the Jews so much as urge, "let us reflect that we well deserve a thousand deaths, if having been enlightened by God, we wander knowingly and willingly from His way."[55] And "If Israel has obtained nothing by merit, what have others obtained whose case or condition was no better?"[56]

When Paul declares that his heart's desire for the Jews is their salvation, Calvin comments, "We see from this how anxiously the man of God had guarded against giving offence. To mitigate any harshness which there was in his interpretation of the rejection of the Jews, he continues as before

---

50. Calvin, *Institutes*, 4.16.14.

51. Salo W. Baron, "John Calvin and the Jews," in *Essential Papers on Judaism and Christianity in Conflict from Late Antiquity to the Reformation*, ed. Jeremy Cohen (New York: New York University Press, 1991), 387–88.

52. John Calvin, *Sermons on Genesis 1–11*, trans. Rob Roy McGregor (Edinburgh: Banner of Truth, 2009), 733.

53. Calvin, *Commentary on Romans*, 9:4.

54. Ibid., 9:32.

55. Ibid., 10:2.

56. Ibid., 11:7.

to affirm his goodwill towards them. He proves this by its effect, viz. that their salvation was a matter of concern to him before the Lord. Such affection arises only from unfeigned love."[57] Jews and Gentiles are equal in guilt, so both Jews and Gentiles can obtain salvation from no other source than the mercy of God.[58]

Commenting on Acts 13:46 and noting also Romans 1:16, Calvin stated that "under the law, before Christ was given, the Jews were not only the first, but alone." Even with the coming of Christ, "the fellowship of the Gentiles did not take from the Jews the right of the first-begotten" for "they were always the chief in the Church of God." This works both ways, for "Such greatness of grace which vouchsafed to bestow upon them, exaggerates and increases the greatness of their sin, whilst they reject that which is so mercifully offered unto them."[59] There is a double-sidedness to Calvin's outlook on the Jews, but he did see the church not so much as replacing Israel as filfiling it. With regard to Zechariah 12:8, he commented, "this blessed and happy state was promised to the Jews, because from them Christ was to arise, and also because Jerusalem was to be the mother of all Churches; for from thence the law was to go forth, and from thence God had determined to send forth the royal sceptre, that the son of David might rule over the whole world."[60]

AD QUAESTIONES ET OBIECTA IUDAEI CUIUSDAM RESPONSIO

Calvin's only specifically anti-Judaistic writing was *Ad quaestiones et obiecta Iudaei*,[61] which was unpublished in Calvin's lifetime and which Mary Sweetland Laver refers to as "an historically obscure document."[62] Detmers thinks it was probably written in the last years of his life,[63] while Baron

---

57. Ibid., 10:1.

58. Ibid., 11:32.

59. John Calvin, *Commentary on the Acts of the Apostles* (on 13:46),. trans. Henry Beveridge (Grand Rapids: Baker, 1979).

60. John Calvin, *Commentary on Zechariah* (on 12:8), trans. John Owen (Grand Rapids: Baker, 1979).

61. John Calvin, Ad quaestiones et obiecta Iudaei cuiusdam, in *Calvini opera*, 9:658–674; translated by Susan Frank in Laver, *Calvin, Jews*, 230–61.

62. Laver, *Calvin, Jews*, 220.

63. Detmers, "Calvin, the Jews, and Judaism," 216.

dates it, with considerable uncertainty, to 1539.⁶⁴ Wulfert de Greef considers that "Calvin did not provide an edition himself, probably because it was not yet ready for publication."⁶⁵

Calvin's opponent, if such existed, may have been the rabbi Josel of Rosheim, whom Heiko Oberman refers to as "the ubiquitous advocate of oppressed Jewry."⁶⁶ Unlike Baron, Detmers and de Greef see no real encounter between Calvin and Josel of Rosheim at Frankfort in 1539, or at any other time.⁶⁷ All that Josel says in his diary is that a violent, angry, and menacing Protestant in Frankfort attacked him in 1539, and Jack Hughes Robinson is content to write, "This Protestant could have been Calvin."⁶⁸ That remains guesswork, as it is not known whether Calvin knew Josel, although both men were at the Regensburg Imperial Diet in 1541.

In commenting on Daniel 2:44–45, Calvin claimed, "I have spoken with many Jews, [but] have never noticed a drop of piety, a kernel of truth, or strength of spirit—no, I have never found common sense in any Jew."⁶⁹ Calvin may have been merely alluding to medieval Jewish commentaries, but the language seems to go further than that. Having said that, the comment is passed in the context of replying to the interpretation of the celebrated Jewish rabbi Isaac Abarbanel, who died in Venice in 1508, which tried to show that Daniel's fifth kingdom could not be that of Jesus the Christ.

The treatise *Ad quaestiones et obiecta Iudaei cuiusdam responsio* is only nine pages (each page has two columns) dealing with twenty-three objections by a Jew, and it was first published in 1575, eleven years after Calvin's death. In dealing with the twenty-three queries, Calvin tended to concentrate on the Old Testament while the anonymous Jewish debater concentrated on the New Testament. For example, the Jew pointed to

---

64. Baron, "John Calvin and the Jews," 389.

65. Wulfert de Greef, *The Writings of John Calvin: An Introductory Guide*, trans. Lyle D. Bierma (Louisville: Westminster John Knox, 2008), 169.

66. Oberman, *Impact*, 111.

67. Detmers, "Calvin, the Jews, and Judaism," 201 n.19.

68. Jack Hughes Robinson, *John Calvin and the Jews* (New York: Peter Lang, 1992), 19.

69. John Calvin, *Commentary on Daniel* (on 2:44–45), trans. Thomas Myers, in *Commentaries* (Grand Rapids: Baker, 1981), 13:185 (slightly altered).

The Gospel and Israel

Matthew 5:17 and the abolition of circumcision,[70] and to Matthew 10:34 as a contradiction of Isaiah 9:6's reference to the Prince of Peace.[71]

Calvin is firm in his replies but not usually menacing. In the very first question, the Jew asked whether the crucifixion of God increased the sin of the Jews, and Calvin simply replied, "not only the Jews but also most other men turned that light into shadows by their own wickedness."[72] He is far less patient in question 14, where the Jew asks why Jesus felt hunger. Calvin fumed: "The solution is of no importance to these pigs."[73] He resorted to the same zoological term of abuse in answering question 21 on the impossibility of killing God.[74]

Calvin could be objectivity personified in dealing with Jewish claims. For example, he never pressed the point that the Hebrew word for God, *elohim*, which is plural, was a clear pointer to the doctrine of the Trinity.[75] He regarded Psalm 72 as filfiled in the coming of Christ, but also warned, "Those who would interpret it simply as a prophecy of the kingdom of Christ, seem to put a construction upon the words which does violence to them; and then we must always beware of giving the Jews occasion of making an outcry, as if it were our purpose, sophistically, to apply to Christ those things which do not directly refer to him."[76] In dealing with Psalm 35:19 he made no reference to John 15:25, and did the same in Psalm 78:24 with respect to John 6:31. Wulfert de Greef comments that "It is notable in Calvin's interpretation of the Psalms that he is not intent on relating each and every Psalm to Jesus Christ."[77]

---

70. Question 2.
71. Question 8.
72. Question 1; trans. Susan Frank, in Laver, *Calvin, Jews*, 230.
73. Question 14, in ibid., 249.
74. Question 19, in ibid., 258.
75. E.g. John Calvin, *Commentary on Genesis* (on 1:1), trans. John King (Grand Rapids: Baker, 1979).
76. Calvin, *Commentary on Psalms 72*, preface.
77. Wulfert de Greef, "Calvin as an Interpreter on the Psalms," in *Calvin and the Bible*, ed. Donald McKim (Cambridge: Cambridge University Press, 2006), 99.

A FUTURE BLESSING PROPHESIED FOR THE JEWS?

It is often contended that Calvin held no place for a future large-scale conversion of the Jews.[78] Indeed, he was rather muted and guarded on the subject. However, he warned, as did the apostle Paul, against Gentile pride, and asserted that the Gentiles in no way exceeded the Jews: "But if you forget yourself, and vaunt insolently over the Jews, the same ruin into which they fell awaits you."[79]

Calvin published his commentary on Romans in 1539—rather surprisingly it was his first! Most commentators work up to Romans; Calvin worked out from it. Calvin begins Romans 9 by pointing out that Paul has abstained from all bitterness to the Jews. Indeed, "the perdition of the Jews caused very great anguish to Paul, though he knew that it happened through the will and providence of God." Paul was no Stoic, and he believed that Christians ought to be capable of two feelings at once. Hence, "They are then much deceived, who say that godly men ought to have apathy and insensibility, lest they should resist the decree of God."[80]

Paul declared that he could wish himself anathematised if only his fellow countrymen, the Jews, could be saved. Calvin commented, "It was then a proof of the most ardent love, that Paul hesitated not to wish for himself that condemnation which he saw impending over the Jews, in order that he might deliver them."[81] Calvin disagreed with those who saw only a love of God or a love of men, for "I connect the love of men with a zeal for God's glory."[82] He considered that the fall of the Jews could be seen by some to detract from the promises of God, as found, for example, in Psalm 72:7. The Jews had disowned Paul, but Paul had not disowned the Jews.

Regarding Romans 11:11, Calvin wrote, "He [Paul] rightly denies here that the salvation of the Jews was to be despaired of, or that they were so rejected by God that there was no restoration to come, or that the covenant of grace, which God had made with them once, was completely abolished, since there always continued to remain in the nation the seed of blessing."[83] He added, "If, therefore, the design of the Lord is to provoke to envy, the

---

78. E.g., E. A. de Boer, *John Calvin on the Visions of Ezekiel* (Leiden: Brill, 2004), 221.
79. Calvin, *Commentary on Romans*, 11:22.
80. Ibid., 9:2.
81. Ibid., 9:3.
82. Ibid.
83. Ibid., 11:11.

The Gospel and Israel

Jews had not fallen in order to be cast into eternal destruction, but so that the blessing of God which they despised might reach to the Gentiles, in order that the Jews too might finally be roused to seek the Lord from whom they had fallen away."[84] He seems to treat verse 12 ("if their failure means riches for the Gentiles, how much more will their full inclusion mean") as hypothetical rather than prophetic.[85] On verse 15 he writes, "We understand resurrection here to mean the act by which we are transferred from the kingdom of death to the kingdom of life."[86]

Again, any criticism of the Jews is applied to the Gentile church, as with Paul himself in Romans 11:18–22, "We should never think of the rejection of the Jews without being struck with dread and terror."[87] Gentiles were called to "modesty and submission."[88] In all this, Calvin considered that God was not writing about individuals who were elected, but about the whole body.[89] Paul's "present purpose" is to "restrain the insolence of the Gentiles and keep them from exulting over the Jews."[90]

Calvin saw the "all Israel" who are saved in Romans 11:26 as "the entire people of God," and is usually considered not to have entertained any thoughts of a large-scale return of Jews to Yahweh through faith in the Messiah. However, Calvin wrote:

> When the Gentiles have come in, the Jews will at the same time return from their defection to the obedience of faith. The salvation of the whole Israel of God, which must be drawn from both, will thus be completed, and yet in such a way that the Jews, as the first born in the family of God, may obtain the first place.[91]

Jack Hughes Robinson has good reason to conclude that Calvin hoped for and believed in a future salvation of the Jews through their coming to faith in Jesus as the Messiah.[92] Wolfgang Capito, Theodore Beza, and Martin Bucer all saw a future salvation for the Jews, and it seems that Calvin

---

84. Ibid.
85. Ibid., 11:12.
86. Ibid., 11:15.
87. Ibid., 11:21.
88. Ibid., 11:19.
89. Ibid., 11:22.
90. Ibid., 11:25.
91. Ibid., 11:26.
92. Jack Hughes Robinson, *John Calvin and the Jews* (New York: Peter Lang, 1992), 81.

played his part in the Reformed acceptance of this interpretation of Romans 9–11.[93] Calvin's successor at Geneva, Beza, wrote, "As for myself, I gladly pray every day for the Jews."[94] Calvin never expressed himself in the same certain way, for example, that Jonathan Edwards did: "Nothing is more certainly foretold than this national conversion of the Jews in Romans 11."[95] But he believed what Edwards believed on this issue. Life is rarely tidy, and it needs to be noted that, after Calvin's death, the council of Geneva refused to allow Jewish readmission in 1582.

THE TURKS

Just as a matter of interest, Pete Wilcox maintains of Calvin, "it certainly seems never to have occurred to him to see the proximity of the Turks as an evangelistic opportunity."[96] This seems too hard on Calvin. On Deuteronomy 15:7–10 and Galatians 6:10, Calvin argued that there is a sense in which all men had now become brothers. He wrote movingly that "we are all of one flesh, and we bear a mark which ought to induce us to do all that we possibly can for one another." Albeit not in the sense suggested by liberal theologians, Calvin could speak of the brotherhood of all men, including the Moor (the Muslim) and the barbarian (the pagan).[97] He cited Isaiah 58:7 about not looking down upon our own flesh, and declared, "By that he means we cannot look upon another human being without having before us a living representation of our own selves, and if we deny him our help, it is as if we were refusing it to ourselves." He added that even the pagans have recognised "what is so difficult for us to get into our heads,"

---

93. Cf. Iain Murray, *The Puritan Hope: A Study in Revival and the Interpretation of Prophecy* (Edinburgh: Banner of Truth, 1975), for those Puritans and preachers of revival who believed in the coming salvation of Israel. See too Robert White, "An Early Reformed Document on the Mission to the Jews," *Westminster Theological Journal* 53 (1991) 93–108, which deals with a document of 1535 that may have been authored by Capito.

94. Cited in Graham Keith, *Hated Without a Cause?: A Survey of Anti-Semitism* (Carlisle: Paternoster, 1997), 181.

95. Jonathan Edwards, *A History of the Work of Redemption*, in *The Works of Jonathan Edwards* (Edinburgh: Banner of Truth, 1976), 1:607.

96. Pete Wilcox, "Evangelisation in the Thought and Practice of John Calvin," *Anvil* 12/3 (1995) 217.

97. John Calvin, *Sermons on Galatians*, trans. Kathy Childress (Edinburgh: Banner of Truth, 1997), 624–25.

The Gospel and Israel

namely that there is "a universal kinship within the human race."[98] This is a strand in Calvin's thought that is too often neglected.

CONCLUSION

It is Heiko Oberman's view that it was precisely Christianity in its most refined and revived state that has proved to be "a deadly threat to the Jews."[99] This thesis hardly fits the case of Calvin. Nor is Salo Baron's conclusion any more convincing. He compares Calvin to Balaam: "The Geneva reformer, too, set out to curse the Jews, but in the end turned out to have blessed them."[100] This was unwitting in that Baron sees Calvin as tyrannical and despotic, and the apostle Paul as antinomian. Thankfully, in Baron's view, Calvin was legalistic. Calvin encouraged the study of Hebrew, urged church-state separation, and was international in his outlook. All this, says Baron, ultimately benefited the Jews. Baron's thesis, however, is far too convoluted, harsh and negative. It is interesting that the Jews gained civil rights first in the Netherlands, then England (beginning with Cromwell), then in the New World—all places that were much influenced by Calvin.

Mary Potter Engel is content to conclude that "Calvin's relation to the Jews and Judaism is every bit as maddeningly complex as Paul's is."[101] That is surely his strength, and indicative of his commitment to the biblical revelation. As a Christian, Calvin could not be expected to sympathise with those who by definition rejected Jesus as the Messiah.[102] But we find no sustained vitriolic attacks on the Jews, nor any vehement advocacy of civil discomforts on God's ancient people. And he remained hopeful for the salvation of many of them through the one Saviour of sinners, be they Jewish or Gentile, Jesus the Messiah. Finally, noting the call of Psalm 150:6, where all that breathes is to praise the Lord, Calvin sees the consummation of God's purposes for His people, consisting of redeemed Jews and Gentiles,

---

98. John Calvin, *Sermons on the Acts of the Apostles: Chapters 1–7*, trans. Rob Roy McGregor (Edinburgh: Banner of Truth, 2008), 75

99. Oberman, *Impact*, 140.

100. Baron, "John Calvin and the Jews," 394.

101. Mary Potter Engel, "Calvin and the Jews: A Textual Puzzle," *Princeton Seminary Bulletin Supplementary* 1 (1990) 122–23.

102. For Jewish views of the Reformation, see Jerome Friedman, "The Reformation in Alien Eyes: Jewish Perceptions of Christian Troubles," *The Sixteenth Century Journal* 14/1 (1983) 23–40.

and unfallen angels: "And in this prediction we have been joined in the same symphony with the Jews, that we may worship God with constant sacrifices of praise, until being gathered into the kingdom of heaven, we sing with elect angels an eternal hallelujah."[103]

---

103. Calvin, *Commentary on Psalms*, 150:6.

6

Christian Mission to the Jews
1550–1850

—Dr. Rowland S. Ward

IN THIS LECTURE I want to address the scriptural basis of Jewish mission as it developed historically and trace, at least in outline, the way in which it led to specific Jewish mission work through organised societies. Our chief focus will be the developments from the sixteenth century onwards.

In the period we are looking at large-scale conversion of the Jews was commonly associated with end-time events, and this remains the case for many today. Differing understandings of the future prospects for the church of God affected attitudes to the Jews. Generally you were postmillennial, believing Christ would return after the millennial period, but from 1600 on there is an increased interest in Christ inaugurating a millennial reign on earth so his coming was premillennial. But whether pre- or post-, these terms did not necessarily mean what is commonly meant by them today. Given that millennial hopes of one kind or another kept Jewish mission and evangelism alive, it seems appropriate to outline the four basic views of the Book of Revelation as we begin. One should keep in mind that there may be aspects of one view that are included in forms of another, and that there are varieties within each view.

MILLENNIAL VIEWS

1. The *futurist* view places everything after chapter 4 in the future so that it describes trouble and tribulation belonging to the end times preceding a thousand-year reign of Christ on earth with his saints before the final resurrection. In Justin Martyr (103–165), about AD 150, we see belief in Christians as the true Israel, and while Jews are to be evangelised it is not evident that large-scale conversion is envisaged. Justin advocates a form of premillennial teaching in which antichrist proper was equivalent to the man of sin and was an individual—possibly a Jew—destined to overthrow the Roman Empire and establish a wicked and tyrannical rule for three and a half years based on a rebuilt Jerusalem. He would quickly be overthrown by the return of Christ, and an earthly millennial reign would follow. Justin states many held this millennial or chiliastic view, but also admits that many true Christians believed otherwise.[1] The Alexandrian school, for example, took a more allegorical approach. The literalist approach of Justin and others probably owes a great deal to pre-Christian Jewish belief in the earthly restoration of ethnic Israel modified by Justin's recognition that spiritual Israel is the true Israel of God. The eloquent Lactantius (ca. 240–320) in Asia Minor was another who taught a future literal thousand-year reign of Christ.[2]

2. The *praeterist* view sees Revelation as filfiled in the early period either in the fall of Jerusalem in AD 70 or in the collapse of the Roman Empire in the fifth century. This view had little currency beyond these events. The Jesuit scholar Luis Alcazar (1554–1613) revived it[3] and of course it was a useful counter to the general Protestant historicist interpretation which saw the papacy as the antichrist.

3. As time went on without Christ's return, the *historicist* view developed, which saw Revelation as an unfolding of history in advance so that each symbol could be identified with a specific historical event, usually taking it in chronological sequence, but sometimes recognising a structure involving recapitulation. Lactantius was neglected in the Middle Ages until his literal millennium was taken up by others influenced of Joachim of Fiore (1135–1202), such as the Franciscan Alexander Minorita, who wrote a

---

1. Justin Martyr, *Dialogue with Trypho*, 80.
2. Calvin, *Institutes*, 7.24.
3. In Luis Alcazar, *Vestigatio arcane sensus in Apocalypsi* [An Investigation into the Hidden Sense of the Apocalypse] (Antwerp, 1614).

commentary on the Apocalypse around 1240. Alexander regarded the millennium as running from 326 to 1326 or soon after.[4] Another Franciscan, Nicholas of Lyra, was influenced by Alexander, as well as by Jewish exegetes such as Rashi, and issued his lectures on Revelation in 1329. Nicholas in turn influenced Luther and Protestant approaches to interpreting Revelation in a historicist way.

4. The *idealist* view, which I regard as the substantially correct position, regards Revelation as giving the history behind history using symbolic language to describe the spiritual factors operating in every age. Augustine (354–430) at one time accepted the chiliastic futurist position. However, in his *City of God* (ca. 420) he sufficiently confuted it[5] for it to gradually die away, although, contrary to some recent claims, it was never condemned by any of the early councils of the church.[6] Tyconius, the dissident Donatist (fl. 375), and Augustine, later followed by such as the Venerable Bede (673–735), viewed the visions of the Book of Revelation as a kind of recapitulative treatment of the basic problems faced by the church in every age.[7] The millennium was generally seen as the whole period of church history until Christ returned. It was not necessarily a literal thousand years. Belief in the general conversion of the Jews near the end of history was common, based on Romans 11, but the idea that "the first resurrection" of Revelation was literal, rather than spiritual, was firmly rejected. Interestingly, it is Augustine who develops a more positive attitude to the Jews than had previously existed. He considered that they should not be persecuted for they were a witness to the truth of Scripture.[8]

---

4. Robert E. Lerner, in *The Apocalypse in the Middle Ages*, eds. R. K. Emmerson and B. McGinn (New York: Cornell University Press, 1992), 60.

5. Augustine, *City of God*, bk. 20, ch. 7.

6. Contra, e.g., Peter Toon, ed., *Puritans, The Millennium and the Future of Israel* (Cambridge: James Clarke, 2002), 14. Cf. Francis X. Gumerlock, "Millennialism and the Early Church Councils: Was Chiliasm Condemned at Constantinople?," *Fides et Historia* 36/2 (Summer/Fall 2004) 83–95.

7. Philip D. W. Krey, in *Nicholas Lyra: The Senses of Scripture*, eds. Philip D. W. Krey and Lesley Smith (Leiden: Brill, 2000), 268; Paula Fredriksen, "Tyconius and the End of the World," *Revue des études augustiniennes* 28 (1982) 59–75.

8. See this fully argued in Paula Fredriksen, *Augustine and the Jews: A Christian Defense of Jews and Judaism* (New York: Doubleday, 2008).

SIXTEENTH CENTURY

The early Protestants considered the millennium of Revelation 20 to be a period of a thousand literal years, beginning either in the first century or with Constantine in the beginning of the fourth century. The more or less universal conviction of the Protestants of the sixteenth and seventeenth centuries was that the predicted antichrist or "man of sin" was most fully and clearly expressed in the papal system as represented in the pope, and most thought this tyranny had existed since about the time of Hildebrand, who became Pope Gregory VII in 1073. They believed the Reformation to be a decisive blow against the man of sin, and in general did not think the end of the world and the return of Christ were far away. In common with much of the church of earlier ages, they thought that Romans 11 indicated a mass conversion of Jews would also occur near the end of history.

Martin Luther (1483–1645), who thought the end was near but didn't set dates, initially hoped well of the conversion of the Jews. Later his optimism changed to bitter invective due to their refusal to believe. Luther thought "all Israel" in Romans 11:26 was an ethnic description but remained puzzled over how the Jews could be saved given their stubborn rejection of Christ. He certainly did not accept that every individual Jew was included in the "all." Luther's initially dismissive view of Revelation began to change to a more positive one in 1528.

A few radicals in Luther's time thought of a future millennium, usually in the near future, and involving the earthly reign of the saints, and date setting was not infrequent among them. The first creedal condemnation of this chiliasm in its more extravagant form, as in Thomas Müntzer (1488–1525), occurs in the Lutheran *Augsburg Confession* of 1530, Article 17:

> They condemn others also, who now scatter Jewish opinions, that, before the resurrection of the dead, the godly shall occupy the kingdom of the world, the wicked being every where suppressed [the saints alone, the pious, shall have a worldly kingdom, and shall exterminate all the godless].[9]

---

9. Philip and David S. Schaff, eds., *The Creeds of Christendom: With a History and Critical Notes*, vol. 3, *The Evangelical Protestant Creeds, with Translations* (6th ed., rev., 1931; reprint, Grand Rapids: Baker, 1983), 18. The bracketed words appear in the German text.

The Gospel and Israel

Views expressed in the Peasants' Revolt of 1524/25 are in the background.

Article 41 of the *Forty Two Articles of the Church of England* (1552/53) stated similarly:

> They that go about to renew the fable of heretics called Millenarii, are repugnant to Holy Scripture, and cast themselves headlong into a Jewish dotage.

Doubtless the horror of the rebellion of radical Anabaptists, who set up the New Jerusalem at Münster in Germany in 1534–35, was also part of the background.

John Calvin (1509–64) thought of the expression "all Israel" as describing all believers in Christ, whether Jew or Gentile. Although he seems to be in the minority today, there are good reasons for this position, not least that it is difficult to see how the conversion of a particular generation of Jews can be described as "all Israel." This is especially so given Paul's stress in the preceding sections on the Gentile mission as a means to provoke some Jews to faith, his emphasis on an elect remnant, and his appropriation of the Abrahamic promises to those who are true believers (cf. Rom 9:6). Calvin does not exclude significant conversion of Jews in the course of history. He writes in 1540 in his Romans commentary:

> Many understand this of the Jewish people, as if Paul was saying that religion was to be restored to them again as before. But I extend the word Israel to include all the people of God, in this sense, "When the Gentiles have come in, the Jews will at the same time return from, their defection to the obedience of faith. The salvation of the whole Israel of God, which must be drawn from both, will thus be completed, and yet in such a way that the Jews, as the first born in the family of God, may obtain the first place."[10]

Although Calvin did not comment on the Book of Revelation as such, he viewed the millennium as referring to the trials of the church as she toiled on earth, and he dismisses futurism.[11] In other words the theology of the cross is not eclipsed in his thinking, and it looks as if he is basically Augustinian. He does recognise the papacy as the predicted antichrist. He

---

10. John Calvin, *The Epistles of Paul the Apostle to the Romans and the Thessalonians* (on 11:26), trans. Ross Mackenzie (Edinburgh: Oliver & Boyd, 1961), 255.

11. Calvin, *Institutes*, 3.25.5. This appears to be the only reference to the millennium in Calvin. For a neat summary of Calvin's eschatology see the closing sentences of *Institutes* 3.20.42 in commenting on the petition "thy kingdom come."

does not tie the millennium of Revelation 20 to a past or future age, but he does write in a very positive vein of the *present* kingly reign of Christ. Thus, in the preface to the *Institutes*, written in 1536, he states:

> We, indeed, are perfectly conscious how poor and abject we are: in the presence of God we are miserable sinners, and in the sight of men most despised... But our doctrine must stand sublime above all the glory of the world, and invincible by all its power, because it is not ours, but that of the living God and his Anointed, whom the Father has appointed King, that he may rule from sea to sea, and from the rivers even to the ends of the earth; and so rule as to smite the whole earth and its strength of iron and brass, its splendour of gold and silver, with the mere rod of his mouth, and break them in pieces like a potter's vessel; according to the magnificent predictions of the prophets respecting his kingdom (Dan. 2:34; Isaiah 11:4; Psalm 2:9).[12]

If the notion of a future millennium had some following, it was certainly not the view of the vast majority of Protestants in the sixteenth century. The Roman Church argued for a future antichrist—an individual who would harass the church for three and a half years at the close of the millennium, which spanned Christian history.[13] This approach was elaborated by two Jesuit scholars: Francisco Ribera (1537–91) and Robert Bellarmine (1542–1621). Bellarmine thought of the antichrist as a Jew who would reign in Jerusalem for three and a half years.

In summary: in the sixteenth-century Reformed community there was a historicist interpretation of Revelation with special reference to the papacy and the Turk (i.e., Islam). The millennium, in so far as it is expounded, is in the past, and the first resurrection of Revelation 20 is taken in a spiritual sense, not a literal one. There is a rather common belief in the future conversion of many Jews, usually as a prelude to further gospel blessing among Gentiles, and date setting is avoided. One can see all this in the notes to the very influential Geneva Bible (1557/1560), in Foxe's *Book of Martyrs* (1563), and in writers like Heinrich Bullinger (1557), Peter Martyr Vermigli (1558), Andrew Willet (1590) and his famous contemporary William Perkins.

---

12. Beveridge's translation. Many passages in Calvin's comments on the Prophets and the Psalms are to similar effect.

13. Note Calvin's negative comment on this view in *Commentary on 1 John*, 2:18 (1556).

The Gospel and Israel

SEVENTEENTH CENTURY

The virtually universal Protestant reading of things to come in terms of a past millennium ending around 1070 or 1300, or of a millennium equating to the whole church period to the return of Christ, broke down somewhat in the seventeenth century. The historicist view was always subject to reinterpretation, particularly when social or political upheaval and change was present.

The tumultuous times undoubtedly contributed to shifts in Protestant views about the future. The execution of Mary Queen of Scots in 1587 and the defeat of the Armada of Catholic Spain in 1588 furthered a new mood in England under Elizabeth I. Nor did the union of the crowns in 1603 dampen the interest in Britain's role in bringing about a brighter future. James VI of Scotland and I of England had written against the papal Antichrist as early as 1588, even predicting its overthrow. Perhaps the latter-day glory was at hand.

In Scotland John Napier (1550–1617), the mathematician generally regarded as the inventor of logarithms, published a commentary on Revelation in 1593. He gives detailed dates and employs the principle that a day in prophecy equates to a year. He predicted the fall of the papacy in 1639 and the return of Christ and the end of the age between 1688 and 1700. He does not appear to have a place for the future conversion of the Jews as he refers the 144,000 in Revelation 7, whom he takes to be converted Jews, to the period around AD 70. He calculates the millennium as running from 300 to 1300. His significance is that he started to predict the future with his detailed calculations.

Writing in 1602, John Welch (1570–1622) of Ayr, John Knox's son-in-law, acknowledged that Romans 11 foretold the general conversion of the Jews, and he noted that the annotations to the Roman Catholic Rheims Bible agreed. He then turned this against his opponent's view that antichrist was a Jew who would appear in the last three and a half years of history and deceive his fellow Jews for rejecting Christ. His grounds were that such was not indicated in Scripture nor was it credible given that shortly previous the Jews had been converted.[14]

In 1602 Thomas Brightman (1562–1607), a minister in Bedfordshire, wrote a very large book published posthumously in Holland (Latin 1609;

---

14. John Welch, *A Reply Against M. Gilbert Browne Priest* (Edinburgh: Robert Waldegrave, 1602), 288.

Christian Mission to the Jews

English 1611, 1615, 1616) in which he contrived to derive two millenniums from Revelation 20: (1) the period 300–1300 and, crucially, (2) a *future* period 1300–2300. About 1650 the power of Rome and the Turk would wane, the Jews would be converted, the final ruin of antichrist would occur in 1686, and triumphs of the gospel would follow until the consummation in 2300.[15] Germany was seen as like the church of Sardis; Scotland and Holland, because more thoroughly reformed, were like Philadelphia, and England like Laodicea. This was a view hardly likely to encourage the more radical Puritans to stay in England, and the exit of many to America is not unrelated. Brightman influenced Dutch thinkers as well.[16] In his *Gravissimae Quaestionis* published in 1613, Archbishop James Ussher (1581–1656) also envisaged a second millennium beginning around 1500 with the restoration of the gospel, but it appears changing political circumstances led him to refrain from publishing his detailed position on this second millennium.[17]

In 1618, the exposition by Elnathan Parr (1577–1622) of Romans 8–11 came off the press. Parr was certain of the future calling of the mass of the Jews. Commenting on 11:26 he wrote:

> ... the secret is this, that when the fullness of the Gentiles is come in there shall be a famous, notorious universal calling of the Jews .... The end of this world will not be until the Jews are called, and how long yet after that none can tell.[18]

---

15. The drift of the volume can be gathered from title of the brief epitome published in 1641: *Reverend Mr. Brightmans judgement, or prophecies what shall befall Germany, Scotland, Holland, and the churches adhering to them Likewise what shall befall England, and the hierarchy therein. Collected out of his exposition on the Revelations, printed above forty yeares since. Wonderfull to see how they are fulfilled, and in fulfilling, foreseeing and foretelling what our eyes have seen, and may see, both in the past, present and future state of our times. Declaring that the reformation began in Queene Elizabeth's dayes, is not sufficient for us under greater light. Finishing the work if we now withstand as heretofore, we are to expect, God hath a sad controversie with the land. This faithfull watchman or our English prophet (as he is cald) was persecuted and banished by the bishops, and this commentary condemned by them to the fire; which they could not effect in Queen Elizabeths raigne, till King Iames. Collected for the good of those who want time or coine, to purchase so large a volume.*

16. W. J. Van Asselt, "Structural Elements in the Eschatology of Johannes Coccceius," *Calvin Theological Journal* 35 (2000) 96.

17. Crawford Gribben, *The Puritan Millennium, Literature and Theology, 1550–1682* (Dublin: Four Courts, 2000), 88–91.

18. Elnathan Parr, *A Plaine Exposition* ... (London: George Purslowe, 1620), 406, 409.

The Gospel and Israel

He thought the conversion of the Jews will mean "life from the dead" in the sense that believers will be confirmed and also increased in number and graces.[19] He appears to represent the mainstream Puritan view in his time and his book ran to several editions. He does not connect his view with the thousand-year of Revelation 20, but interest in a future millennium was building.

In 1604, Johannes Piscator (1546–1625), the head of the important Reformed Academy of Theology at Herborn, issued his new translation of the Bible in German (the first since Luther), which had notes supporting a *future* millennium. In his Commentary on Revelation published in 1613, these views were elaborated,[20] but he was strongly criticised by David Pareus of Heidelberg.

Piscator's colleague and successor in 1625, Johann Alsted (1588–1638), was at first an adherent of the earlier position of a past millennium, but from 1622 he was moving from this, influenced by the upheavals of the Thirty Years War (1618–48), the death of Piscator, and a disastrous fire in Herborn itself. His quite brief and sober *Diatribe de mille annis apocalyptic*, published in 1627 (in English in 1643 as *The Beloved City*), advocates a full future millennium beginning about 1694, with Christ in heaven but the resurrected martyrs governing for him on earth.[21] Alsted argues for the conversion of the Jews utilising thirty-four passages mainly from the Old Testament.[22]

In 1621, William Gouge (1575–1653), Puritan minister of St. Ann Blackfriars in London, published the book by Sir Henry Finch entitled *The World's Great Restauration. Or the Calling of the Jewes and (with them) of All the Nations and Kingdoms of the Earth, to the Faith of Christ*. In the preface he states:

> Here are no Rabbinical conceits, no Jewish fables, no abrogated ceremonies, raked out of the ashes, but such a glory of the Church is here set forth as may stand with the doctrine of the Gospel, preached by the Apostles.

---

19. Ibid., 365–66.

20. Howard Hotson, *Johann Heinrich Alsted, 1588–1638: Between Renaissance, Reformation, and Universal Reform* (New York: Oxford University Press, 2000), 208.

21. Johann Alsted, *The Beloved City* (London, 1643), 13, 17.

22. Hotson, *Johann*, 198; also Howard Hotson, *Paradise Postponed: Johann Heinrich Alsted and the Birth of Calvinist Millenarianism* (Dordrecht: Kluwer, 2000), 135.

Christian Mission to the Jews

This book not only affirms the general conversion of the Jews, although not every individual, but goes further. The first conversion would occur "about the time the Turkish tyrannie shall have lasted 350 years" (i.e., 1650), and the final overthrow of the Turks would occur forty-five years later (i.e., 1695) in a battle with the Jews at Jerusalem with heavenly assistance. The twelve tribes of the Jews would flourish again in Palestine and abound in spiritual graces; all nations would be converted and honour the Jews.

King James did not like some of the content and the author and publisher were arrested and only released after apology. Gouge was to be a leading member of the Westminster Assembly in the 1640s.

Napier and Brightman were Puritans who were critical of the half-reformed Laodicean English church. On the other hand, the quiet, irenic scholar of Christ's College, Cambridge, Joseph Mede (1586–1638), was committed to the episcopal polity and worship of the Church of England under Archbishop Laud[23] but was not given preferment because he identified the papacy as antichrist: under Laud's ascendancy, 1633-40, any books making such an identification could not be published. Mede's *Clavis Apocalyptica (Key to Revelation)* was published in Latin in 1627, and in fuller form in 1632. It drew from the earlier Protestant tradition as well as from Brightman, sought to synchronise Daniel and Revelation, and advocated a future millennial rule of the saints beginning no later than 1715. His presentation was careful and measured and appealed to people from the different sections of Protestant society in England. In 1642, an English translation of Mede's *Key*, with recommendatory preface by William Twisse (1578–1646), the first chairman of the Westminster Assembly of Divines, was approved for publication by the Long Parliament. Mede's works were reprinted in the 1640s and in fuller form in 1664 and subsequently, and have impacted the more radical section of Christian thought on the last things ever since.

In the same year (1642), a fifty-nine-page booklet, *The Personall Raigne of Christ upon Earth* by John Archer appeared, advocating essentially a premillennial scheme with a literal resurrection at its beginning and a general conversion of the Jews. Archer was minister of the English Independent congregation at Arnhem, 1638-42. Despite the title, Archer

---

23. S. Hutton, "The Appropriation of Joseph Mede: Millenarianism in the 1640s," in *The Millenarian Turn: Millenarian Contexts of Science, Politics and Everyday Anglo-American Life in the Seventeenth and Eighteenth Centuries*, eds. J. E. Force and R. H. Popkin (Dordrecht: Kluwer, 2001), 3:9.

thought Christ would only appear briefly at the beginning of the millennium and then withdraw to heaven to rule this Fifth Monarchy (succeeding the Four World Empires of Daniel's visions) through believers who had died prior to the commencement of the millennium, circa 1700.

The position of Thomas Goodwin (1600–80), co-pastor with Archer, 1639–40, was the same, although who influenced whom is unclear. Goodwin's views on Revelation were derived from sermons he preached in 1639. They were posthumously published in his *Collected Works* in 1681. There is also his *Sermon on the Fifth Monarchy* published in 1654. Goodwin is generally said to be the author of the brief *A Glimpse of Zion's Glory*, published in 1642, but the content, which has Christ actually reigning on earth with his saints for a thousand years, might suggest as author another of the Independent party such as Jeremiah Burroughs.[24] Goodwin thought antichrist would be overthrown in 1666. As already noted, Alsted's work was published in English in 1643 under the title *The Beloved City: Or the Saints' Reign on Earth a Thousand Years*.

It was powerful stuff in the context of the competing parties in the English church and the outbreak of civil war in 1640. Quoting Christopher Hill, Gribben notes:

> The collapse of censorship saw a fantastic outpouring of books, pamphlets and newspapers. Before 1640, newspapers were illegal; by 1645 there were 722. Twenty-two books were published in 1640; over 2,000 in 1642.[25]

Each part tended to see the future glory in terms of the elevation of their particular view of the church. Independents and Presbyterians had been allies in 1641, but this alliance had collapsed by 1649. The Independents were not impressed with the Scots' royalist sympathies and, while there was a strong optimistic streak in Scottish thinking, it was more what we would call postmillennial than premillennial in orientation. Further, Presbyterians looked for a national church, Independents one to which only the regenerate would belong. It is no accident that premillennial and extravagant views of the future belonged mostly to Independents and Baptists, and it is no accident that the Fifth Monarchy men of the 1650s, who

---

24. Robert Baillie, *A Dissuasive from the Errours of the Time* (London: Samuel Gellibrand, 1645), 79, identifies Goodwin as the author, a conclusion that can be otherwise established; cf. A. R. Dallison, "Appendix II," in Toon, *Puritans*, 131–36.

25. Gribben, *Puritan Millennium*, 195.

talked of helping God bring in the reign of the saints by force, were drawn from their ranks.

One of the Scottish commissioners to the Westminster Assembly, Robert Baillie (1602–62), while perhaps more in the Augustinian mould as far as the millennium is concerned, was certainly not one who rejected the conversion of the Jews.[26] Referring to Romans 11:12 he wrote:

> . . . we grant willingly that the nation of the Jews shall be converted to the faith of Christ; and that the fullness of the Gentiles is to come in with them to the Christian Church; also that the quickening of that dead and rotten member, shall be a matter of exceeding joy to the whole Church. But that the converted Jews shall return to Canaan to build Jerusalem, that Christ shall come from heaven to reign among them for a thousand years, there is no such thing intimated in the Scriptures in hand.[27]

His fellow Scottish Commissioner, George Gillespie (1613–48), in a sermon before the English Parliament in 1644, suggested that 1643—the year the Assembly began—marked the beginning of the promised blessing for the church. Yet he cautions:

> That which I have said, from grounds of Scripture, concerning a more glorious, yea, more peaceable condition of the church to be yet looked for, is acknowledged by some of our sound and learned writers who have had occasion to express their judgment about it: and it hath no affinity with the opinion of an earthly or temporal kingdom of Christ, or of the Jews' building again of Jerusalem and the material temple, and their obtaining a dominion above all other nations, or the like.[28]

The influential *Commentary on Revelation* by James Durham (1622–58) appeared in 1658. Durham spoke highly of Mede,[29] but differed from him in some particulars. Durham considered that the millennium had likely begun in 1560[30]—the year of the Scottish Reformation—and that

26. Contra, in measure, A. R. Dallison "Contemporary Criticism of Millenarianism," in Toon, *Puritans*, 107.

27. Baillie, *Dissuasive*, 243.

28. George Gillespie, "A Sermon Preached before the Honourable House of Commons at Their Late Solemn Fast, Wednesday March 27, 1644," in *The Presbyterian's Armoury* (Edinburgh: Oliver and Boyd, 1844), 3:22.

29. James Durham, *A Commentarie upon the Book of the Revelation* (London, 1658), 333, 725.

30. Ibid., 727.

The Gospel and Israel

what he considered the Gentile church would come to a flourishing condition with the overthrow of the papal antichrist and the calling of the Jews following. He was cautiously of the view that the Jews would be restored to Palestine.[31]

None of these writers subscribed to a premillennial scheme and their general outlook was to be virtually universal in Scotland until the 1820s.

The Dutch Annotations of 1637 ordered by the Synod of Dort (translated into English and published 1657 at London) render Romans 11:26 (ungrammatically) as "*Then* all Israel shall be saved." As regards Revelation 20, a future millennium is rejected: the church has no promise of being free from persecution at any point before the last day, and a literal resurrection at the beginning of the millennium is repugnant to the Bible's teaching of a general resurrection at the last day. This approach is found in representative Reformed writers such as Johannes Cocceius (1603–69)[32] of Franeker and Leiden and Francis Turretin (1623–87) of Geneva,[33] although the latter is uncertain as to whether the conversion of the Jews is successive through history or simultaneous.

The English Annotations (1645), largely the work of men who were also members of the Westminster Assembly, recognise the future calling of the Jews but do not decide between the ethnic or spiritual Israel view of "all Israel" in Romans 11:26; and similarly in the 1658 edition. The millennium is thought to be a future period of a literal or non-literal one thousand years.

The documents of the Westminster Assembly are singularly careful in dealing with eschatology.[34] *The Directory for the Public Worship of God* (1644) outlines the matter of public prayer including:

> to pray for the propagation of the gospel and kingdom of Christ to all nations; for the conversion of the Jews, the fulness of the Gentiles, the fall of Antichrist, and the hastening of the second coming of our Lord; for the deliverance of the distressed churches

---

31. Ibid., 617–20.

32. W. J. Van Asselt, "Structural Elements in the Eschatology of Johannes Cocceius," *Calvin Theological Journal* 35 (2000) 95–96, 100.

33. Francis Turretin, *Institutes of Elenctic Theology* (Phillipsburg, NJ: P & R, 1997) 3:574–89.

34. Derek Thomas, "The Eschatology of the Westminster Standards," in *The Westminster Confession into the 21st Century*, ed. Ligon Duncan (Fearn: Mentor, 2009), 3:307–379, esp. 351ff.

Christian Mission to the Jews

> abroad from the tyranny of the antichristian faction, and from the cruel oppressions and blasphemies of the Turk . . .

Similarly, in Larger Catechism 191 the petition "thy kingdom come" is said to require prayer to the end that "the gospel spread throughout the whole world, the Jews called, the fullness of the Gentiles brought in . . ." but in the Confession itself (1646) there is no mention of the calling of the Jews, nor is Revelation 20 cited or referred to in any of the Assembly documents.

The *Savoy Declaration* of the English Independents (1658) does go further in its version of the Westminster Confession, stating:

> . . . so according to his promise we expect that in the latter days Antichrist being destroyed, the Jews called, and the adversaries of his dear Son broken, the churches of Christ being enlarged and edified through a plentiful communication of light and grace, shall enjoy in this world a more quiet, peaceable and glorious condition than they have enjoyed. (ch. 26.5)

In all the millennial interest in the ferment of the first half of the 17th century, it is evident that the attitude to the Jews was motivated in the last analysis by religious interest. Hence, their admission to England under the protectorate of Oliver Cromwell in 1656 was a means to bring them under the sound of the gospel that their conversion might be hastened and the reign of Christ begin.[35]

Following the restoration of the monarchy in 1660, there was a moderation of extravagant notions of things to come in England, although there remained side by side the views that Christ comes after the millennial period and that he comes before it. In 1691, the notable Richard Baxter (1615-91) published a refutation of Thomas Beverley's theories (which included the inauguration of the millennium in 1697) entitled *The Glorious Kingdom of Christ, Described and Clearly Vindicated against the Bold Asserters of a Future Calling and Reign of the Jews, and 1000 Years before the Conflagration* . . . Baxter dedicated the volume to Increase Mather (1639-1723), whose position he acknowledged was more moderate.[36] In America a generally premillennial position with emphasis on the Jews' future conversion was held by many Christian leaders, such as Mather, the first president of Harvard and the author of *The Mystery of Israel's Salvation* (1669).

---

35. Anthony Fletcher, "Oliver Cromwell and the Godly Nation," in *Oliver Cromwell and the English Revolution*, ed. John Morrill (London: Longman, 1990), 211-12.

36. J. A. De Jong, *As the Waters Cover the Sea: Millennial Expectations in the Rise of Anglo-American Missions 1640-1810* (Kampen: J. H. Kok, 1970), 89.

The Gospel and Israel

EIGHTEENTH CENTURY

Deism blighted much of the first half of the eighteenth century, although it did serve to restrain some speculations into a more rational mould, and the idea of toleration after the religious strife of the preceding century was influential. Early free thinker and human rights advocate John Toland (1670–1722) published *Reasons for Naturalizing the Jews* in 1714 drawing on the recently published, massive and pioneering *History of the Jews* by the French Huguenot Jacques Basnage (1653–1722). Unlike Basnage, Toland did not concern himself with or argue for the conversion of the Jews,[37] but believed the Jews should be able to retain the Mosaic Law minus the sacrificial system. Isaac Newton held that the Jews would be restored to Palestine and rebuild the temple some centuries hence.[38] Prominent Unitarian preacher, scientist, and philosopher Joseph Priestly (1733–1804) believed in human progress bringing about the millennium. In his *Letters to the Jews Inviting Them to an Amicable Discussion of the Evidences of Christianity* (London, 1787), he argued for his rational version of Christianity and, like Toland, believed in the perpetual obligation on the Jews to observe the Mosaic Law. He also asserted that God would restore them to Palestine when they were obedient. As late as 1819, US President John Adams expressed the wish that the Jews be again in Judea as an independent nation, but he did not operate from trinitarian Christian principles and entertained the hope that the Jews, thus restored, would become "liberal Unitarian Christians."[39]

In 1700 William à Brakel (1635–1711), the Dutch Second Reformation writer, argued at length for future conversion of the Jews and their restoration to Palestine.[40] In an appendix to his *Paraphrase and Commentary on the New Testament* (1703), English clergyman Daniel Whitby (1638–1726) agreed, but specifically linked the millennium of Revelation 20 with the future period of gospel blessedness he believed would follow on the fall of antichrist and the conversion of the Jews. He was open to the possibility of

---

37. Pierre Lurbe, "John Toland and the Naturalization of the Jews," *Eighteenth-Century Ireland / Iris an dá chultúr* 14 (1999) 37–48.

38. S. Snobelen, " 'The Mystery of This Restitution of All Things': Isaac Newton and the Return of the Jews," in *Millenarianism in early European Culture: The Millenarian Turn*, eds. J. E. Force and R. H. Popkin (Dordrecht: Kluwer, 2001), 95–118, at 110.

39. Quoted in "John Adams Embraces A Jewish Homeland," online: http://www.jewishvirtuallibrary.org/jsource/US-Israel/adams.html.

40. Wilhemus à Brakel, *The Christian's Reasonable Service* (Morgan, PA: Soli Deo Gloria, 1995), 4:510–34.

Jewish return to Jerusalem but denied that the temple would be rebuilt. He thus systematised the earlier postmillennial-type position, which had not settled on a particular position on the Revelation 20 passage. The influential Lutheran pietist and biblical scholar J. A. Bengel (1687–1752) held premillennial views. He distinguished an earthly millennium followed by a heavenly one when conditions on earth would be difficult, and calculated Christ's return to occur in 1836. John Wesley (1703–91) acknowledged his debt to Bengel, and in his early years appears to maintain a form of premillennialism, but he is not very clear or dogmatic; he certainly accepts a future calling of the Jews:

> So many prophecies refer to this grand event, that it is surprising any Christian can doubt of it. And these are greatly confirmed by the wonderful preservation of the Jews as a distinct people to this day. When it is accomplished, it will be so strong a demonstration, both of the Old and New Testament revelation, as will doubtless convince many thousand Deists, in countries nominally Christian; of whom there will, of course, be increasing multitudes among merely nominal Christians. And this will be a means of swiftly propagating the gospel among Mahometans and Pagans; who would probably have received it long ago, had they conversed only with real Christians.[41]

With a view to relieving Jews of the financial disadvantages on aliens and the prohibition of the unnaturalised owning land, the Whig English parliament passed a naturalization bill in May 1753. It was commonly called the "Jew Bill" since Jews could not comply with existing long-standing naturalisation procedures designed to exclude Roman Catholics as there was a requirement to receive communion in the Church of England. Under pressure from certain London merchants and the Tories, the act was repealed later that year. It is clear that the Whigs thought that the measure would stimulate trade but also that it was a general belief among them, but not among the Tories, that the Jews' conversion as predicted in Scripture would be furthered.

Cotton Mather (1663–1728) of New England held his father Increase's views for most of his life, and even projected the return of Christ for around 1697,[42] but in an unpublished essay some years before he died he rejects

---

41. John Wesley, *Explanatory Notes upon the New Testament* (1755; reprint, London: Charles H. Kelly, n.d.), 565, on Rom 11:12.
42. De Jong, *As the Waters*, 91.

belief in the *en masse* conversion of the Jews. He now thought the Old Testament prophecies had been filfiled in the return of the Jews from exile in Babylon in the sixth century BC and in the conversion of many Jews in the first century AD, and that now the only true Israel consists of those who worship Christ.[43]

The remarkable Jonathan Edwards (1703–58) was a prominent advocate of an optimistic postmillennial position and stated, "Nothing is more certainly foretold than this national conversion of the Jews is in the 11th chapter of Romans."[44] He was particularly influential on both sides of the Atlantic through his correspondence with John Erskine (1721–1803), a leader of the evangelicals in the Church of Scotland. Indeed, Erskine maintained a strong missionary interest and even thought that the revivals associated with George Whitefield might be a precursor of the return of Christ. Erskine also corresponded with Calvinistic evangelicals like the English Baptist John Ryland (1753–1825). Edwards himself came to think of the revivals as preparatory to the latter-day glory. The revivals certainly quickened hope for the better times many Protestants believed were predicted. Indeed, it has been suggested that the theology of Edwards and the example of David Brainerd (1718–47) were the two major forces in the missionary movement of the nineteenth century. John Ryland named his sons Jonathan Edwards Ryland and David Brainerd Ryland.[45]

With the upheavals of the American War of Independence (1776) and then the French Revolution (1789), many Protestants saw God's providence as bringing about conditions for the overthrow of the papal antichrist, the conversion of the Jews, and widespread gospel triumphs throughout the world. While there was much unfounded speculation about unfilfiled prophecy, the major leaders stressed the preaching of the gospel as the great means used by the Spirit of God to bring about these changes. Mission organisations were formed. The first was the Baptist Missionary Society by William Carey, John Ryland, and a few friends in 1792. In 1795 the interdenominational Missionary Society (later called the London Missionary Society [LMS]) followed, with the Scot Daniel Bogue (1750–1825) a driving force; but stricter Evangelical Church of England men held back until

---

43. Mel Scult, *Millennial Expectations and Jewish Liberties: A Study of the Efforts to Convert the Jews in Britain, Up to the Mid-Nineteenth Century* (Studies in Judaism in Modern Times 2; Leiden: Brill 1978), 49–50.

44. Jonathan Edwards, *A History of the Work of Redemption* (Grand Rapids: Associated Publishers & Authors, repr. n.d.), 313.

45. De Jong, *As the Waters*, 177.

1899 when they formed their own Church Missionary Society. The Religious Tract Society (1799) and the Bible Society (1804) augmented these missionary bodies.

While a common view was that the latter-day glory was about to break forth, Bogue wrote:

> But I beg you to consider that in aiming to propagate the gospel, we are to be guided by what God enjoins as a duty, not by what he delivered as a prediction.

That duty was to preach as commanded by Christ, he continued. Only through preaching would the millennium be realised, and then only in God's time.[46] There were those in the Missionary Society who thought that the conversion of some of the Jews was a necessary prelude to the widespread conversion of the heathen. In 1801, a converted German Jew, Joseph Samuel Christian Frederick Frey (1774–1850), came to London under the auspices of the Missionary Society, and continued theological studies at Daniel Bogue's Academy at Gosport. In 1805 he was set apart to preach at Aldgate (London), where a number of poor Jewish immigrants from Europe lived. The LMS encouraged this work and a collection of essays by various leaders was published by Henry Hunter in 1806 under the title *The Rise, Fall, and Future Restoration of the Jews*. It was in this same year also that Napoleon began to change the laws that restricted Jewish freedoms and rights in Europe.

Frey was not able to persuade the Society to adopt some of his schemes for providing a boarding school and employment for Jewish converts, and in 1809 he and some others formed The London Society for the Promotion of Christianity Amongst the Jews on an interdenominational basis. The interest was significant at this time, especially due to the stimulus given by Claudius Buchanan (1766–1815), an evangelical minister of the Church of England. He had investigated Jewish communities in India and fascinated many with his claims about the origin of these groups, ill-founded though those claims may have been. The highly influential Anglican leader Charles Simeon (1759–1836) was a great supporter and continued to be until his death.[47] William Wilberforce (1759–1833) was a member, as well as other

---

46. Ibid., 187

47. See Michael Eldridge, "Charles Simeon and the Jewish People: 'The Warmest Place in His Heart,'" *Olive Press Research Paper* 5 (June 2009), online: http://www.cmj.org.uk/downloads/olivepress5charlessimeon.pdf.

The Gospel and Israel

prominent people in society. The Society soon had the patronage of the Duke of Kent, Queen Victoria's father.

However, there were tensions over how to handle the ecclesiastical status of converts, given the interdenominational basis. A mutual arrangement was struck by which the non–Church of England directors withdrew and the Society became a Church of England one. Anglican supporters injected new funds to cover some £14,000 in debt incurred in erecting the Episcopal Jews' Chapel and school in Bethnal Green. Lewis Way (1772–1840), a wealthy minister of the Church of England, contributed £10,000 of this.[48]

> Following the inheritance of a large legacy from John Way (who was not related, despite bearing the same surname) Lewis Way devoted his fortune, and also his home, to religious works. . . . In 1817–18 he made a long journey through the Netherlands, Germany, Poland, and Russia, investigating Jewish communities and worship. On reaching Moscow he had four fascinating audiences with Tsar Alexander I. In 1823 Way made a further trip, to the Holy Land, where he met Lady Hester Stanhope. On his return he established the Marboeuf (English protestant) Chapel in Paris, and devoted his latter years to the idea of establishing a Hebrew college (to train missionaries to the Jews) at [his property in] Stanstead. This never came to fruition . . .[49]

It can be seen that interest in the Jews and their conversion was not the interest merely by uneducated people but attracted strong interest from all sections of society, particularly the educated.

The London Jews' Society, as it was commonly known, reported in 1861, when Anthony Ashley-Cooper (1801–85), the seventh Earl of Shaftesbury, was its president, that it maintained

---

48. For the early history see R. H. Martin, "United Conversionist Activities Among the Jews in Great Britain 1795–1815: Pan Evangelicalism and the London Society for Promoting Christianity Amongst the Jews," *Church History* 46/4 (December 1977) 437–52. For early criticism of management and activities see H. H. Norris, *The Origin, Progress and Existing Circumstances of the London Society for the Promotion of Christianity Amongst the Jews* (London: J. Mawman, 1825). Norris' assessment is very negative. He was a long-time director of the SPCK and chaplain to the Earl of Shaftesbury. The story of the London Society (now known as The Church's Ministry Among Jewish People) is told in a recent coffee-table-type book, *Restoring Israel: 200 Years of the CMJ Story*.

49. Robert Brown, "Way, Lewis (1772–1840)," *Oxford Dictionary of National Biography* online: http://www.oxforddnb.com.rp.nla.gov.au:2048/view/article/28905.

Christian Mission to the Jews

29 ordained missionaries, 26 unordained missionary agents, 61 colporteurs, scripture readers, school-masters and mistresses etc., the greater part of them Christianized Jews, distributed among 39 stations in Europe, Asia, and Africa. The work carried on at the missionary station in London indicates the course pursued by the agents generally; the Gospel is carried into the Jewish quarters, from house to house; inquirers are daily instructed; Divine service is regularly performed in the Hebrew, English, and German languages. Adjoining the chapel in Palestine Place are schools for 100 Hebrew children; 754 have been admitted. There is also a college for training Jewish missionaries. The New Testament has been translated into Hebrew, and both Old and New widely circulated among the Jews—during the last 10 years to the extent of 27,000 of the former and 15,000 of the latter. Tracts and treatises in various languages, on Jewish controversy, have been largely circulated, with which the Jews have been most favourably impressed. The society has also published the Liturgy in Hebrew. The report states, that when the society was formed, there were not 50 Christian Jews known in the United Kingdom. Now, in the Church of England and Ireland, there are nearly 70 ordained ministers of the seed of Abraham; and there are hundreds of converts. In the society's chapel in London, 881 adults and children, of the House of Israel, have been baptized. In the society's schools at home and abroad, 1,000 children are generally under regular instruction.[50]

Lewis Way's influence impacted the wealthy London banker Henry Drummond (1786–1860), who became a vice president of the London Jews' Society in 1823. It appears that Way was the first to stress that the Old Testament promises had *primary* and *literal* reference to Israel.[51] The Scottish minister and orator Edward Irving (1792–1834) had begun his meteoric ministry in Hatton Garden, London, the previous year. In 1826, Way and Irving were among the twenty or so guests at the first of a number of conferences on prophecy hosted by Drummond at his estate in Surrey. Out of these came a negative view of the future for the church. The glorious promises of the Old Testament could only be filfiled by the return of Christ and the re-establishment of Israel.

The new view did not win its way overnight. Irving and Drummond ended up in the highly liturgical Catholic Apostolic Church. But the

---

50. Sampson Low, *The Charities of London* (London: S. Low, 1861).

51. Lewis Way, *The Latter Rain* (London 1821), cited in D. W. Bebbington, *Evangelicalism in Modern Britain* (London: Unwin Hyman, 1989), 88.

The Gospel and Israel

emphasis on a premillennial advent made some headway. In particular, a strongly futurist and dispensational form advanced among some of the followers of John N. Darby (1801–82), who propounded also the idea that before what he regarded as a coming seven-year tribulation believers would be raptured away from the earth. As evangelicalism suffered eclipse in the second half of the nineteenth century and lost itself in a mere social gospel, the allegedly literal interpretative method and premillennial dispensational approach became a very strong reaction among American evangelicals, it and remains so. But among others, including Bishop J. C. Ryle (1816–1900) and C. H. Spurgeon (1834–92), a moderate premillennial view was found very commonly.

Of course this historicist approach with a literalistic method also resulted in the specific predictions of Christ's return as by William Miller (1782–1849), an American Baptist preacher who considered 1843 or 1844 was the date of the Second Advent. The failure of the date led to some of his followers (but not Miller himself) forming groups with other peculiarities. The most significant and successful was the Seventh-day Adventist Church, dating from 1844 but organised under that name in 1860. It continues a futurist and historicist interpretation of prophecy but regards the formation of the state of Israel as a political rather than a prophesied event. The Millerite excitement tended to polarise opinion and discredit futurism and historicism among the mainstream, leaving its advocacy to the fringe.

In Scotland there had never been great interest in a premillennial approach, and the fact of Irving's excesses only ensured that remained the case except for a few, such as the saintly brothers Horatius Bonar (1808–89) and Andrew Bonar (1810–92). Their friend Robert Murray McCheyne (1813–43) certainly believed that the restoration of the Jews to their own land and their conversion would occur soon,[52] but it is difficult to find specific premillennial teaching in his writings.

We have seen that the London Jews' Society was operated from 1809. It had many auxiliaries in other parts of the United Kingdom. From its beginning in 1810, the *Edinburgh Christian Instructor*, edited by Rev. Dr Andrew Thomson (1778–1831), regularly included articles and reports related to Jewish missionary endeavour, but it was not until 1837 that the

---

52. For example, note the sermon on Hosea 2:14, preached in December 1839, applied to Israel's return in R. M. McCheyne, *The Passionate Preacher* (Fearn: Christian Focus, 1999), 73–78. N. R. Needham, in *Dictionary of Scottish Church History and Theology*, ed. N. M. de S. Cameron (Edinburgh: T. & T. Clark, 1993), 563, classifies McCheyne as postmillennial.

Christian Mission to the Jews

General Assembly of the Church of Scotland, now with an evangelical majority, appointed a Committee on the Conversion of the Jews to the Faith of Christ. In 1838, it was decided to send a commission of enquiry to Palestine and Eastern and Central Europe. Those sent were Rev. Dr Alexander Keith, who had written much on prophetic subjects, Rev. Professor Alexander Black of Aberdeen, a brilliant linguist, and Rev. Robert Murray McCheyne of St. Peter's Dundee, then convalescing in Edinburgh, and his friend Rev. Andrew Bonar. McCheyne and Bonar were the only two to complete the entire missionary journey, and their very large book-length report was duly published in 1842.[53]

But already the Church of England had resolved on mission work to the Jews. In 1841, Rev. Daniel Edward (d. 1896) was sent to work in Iaşi, now within the borders of Romania, while a few months later Rev. Dr. John "Rabbi' Duncan (1796–1870) and two assistants went to Budapest, where the first Jewish mission centre was established. There were many encouragements. Two notable converts were Alfred Edersheim (1823/4–1889) and Adolf Saphir (1831–91), the latter more in the theological line of the Brethren although serving as a Presbyterian minister.

A meeting was held in the National Scotch Church, Regent Square, London—the church built for Edward Irving—on November 7, 1842 to form the British Society for the Propagation of the Gospel among the Jews. Those present included Robert Murray McCheyne. It was agreed to co-operate with the Church of Scotland's mission to the Jews. The society later became known as the International Society for the Evangelisation of the Jews, and ultimately merged with the Barbican Mission to the Jews (founded 1879) to form Christian Witness to Israel.

CONCLUDING REMARKS

It will be seen from this review that there was significant impetus to Jewish evangelism from understandings of Scripture that are defective. However, the point to remember is that Jewish evangelism is an obligation however one reads Romans 9–11 or Revelation 20. Commitment to Jewish evangelism does not require one to believe: (a) that there is a future millennial

---

53. Reprinted in slightly abbreviated form (446 pages) in Andrew Bonar and R. M. McCheyne, ed. Allan M. Harman, *Mission of Discovery: The Beginnings of Modern Jewish Evangelism: The Journal of Bonar and McCheyne's Mission of Inquiry* (Fearn: Christian Focus, 1996).

period of great peace and prosperity for the church on earth before or after Christ's return climaxed by the last judgment. After all, the millennium of Revelation 20 looks to be much more a recapitulation of the inter-advent period showing the blessedness of the departed saints reigning with Christ in heaven as conflict continues on earth.[54]

Nor is one required to believe: (b) that only some future period before Christ's return is one of great tribulation for the church rather than the whole period of the church's time on earth; or (c) that one is to understand the Old Testament promises in a basically literalistic way so that rather than being filfiled in and through the church as the Israel of God composed of believing Jews and Gentiles, they are to be filfiled in some future earthly restoration of ethnic Israel; or (d) that one should be agnostic or pessimistic about future prospects for the gospel this side of Christ's return, rather than optimistic based on the lordship of Jesus and the promise of a rich harvest, despite losses, from the sowing of the seed of the word of God.

In the period reviewed, the foundation of various still-current positions can be found. Calvin appears to have regarded the gathering of Jews and Gentiles by gospel preaching as occurring throughout the ages according to God's gracious election resulting in the final total Israel of God. N. T. Wright provides a recent robust argument for this position.[55] Others, particularly in the Scottish and earlier Puritan tradition, are positive for a future widespread calling of the Jews and consequent further blessing of the Gentiles without tying this to a particular view of Revelation 20. This is the kind of position argued for in Iain Murray's popular book *The Puritan Hope*, published in 1971,[56] although I suspect a lot of sympathisers with this approach would class themselves today as optimistic amillennialists rather than as postmillennialists. Some think the return of many Jews to Palestine was the specific fulfilment of biblical prophecy, while others see it merely as occurring in God's providence without claiming that it has an unequivocal biblical warrant. There are those who are futurist in some measure, while others, such as the present writer, see the classic signs operating throughout Christian history, so that for them there are no clear chronological indicators still to occur to signal the return of Christ.

54. Note the classic treatment in B. B. Warfield, "The Millennium of the Apocalypse," in *The Works of Benjamin B. Warfield* (Grand Rapids: Baker, repr. 2003), 2:643–64.

55. N. T. Wright, *The Climax of the Covenant* (Edinburgh: T. & T. Clark, 1991), 231–57.

56. Iain H. Murray, *The Puritan Hope: Revival and the Interpretation of Prophecy* (Edinburgh: Banner of Truth, 1971).

Many earnest Christians in the forefront of Jewish evangelism advocate some form of premillennialism. I think there are substantial objections to that approach, particularly when the basic unity of the people of God as a people saved by grace in both Old Covenant and New Covenant times, emphasised so well by the olive tree illustration in Romans 11, is denied. I recognise that by no means do all premillenialists do so. Nevertheless, there are points for all Christians to keep in mind: the organisation of Jewish believers into distinct churches can only at best be a temporary expedient; the spotlight in Jewish evangelism must not be on prophecy and Middle East politics but on Jesus Christ; we can never claim God's special approval of Israel while she persists in unbelief, nor suppose she is beyond criticism; we must not only speak, but practice, the truth in love; and we need an even hand for Jew and Gentile, for Israeli and Palestinian. United in this way as the church of Jesus, and confident in the lordship of Christ, the authority of his Word and the power of the Spirit, let us be up and doing!

7

The Israel/ Palestine Conflict

—Martin Pakula

INTRODUCTION: A CONTROVERSIAL TOPIC

The topic of the modern state of Israel and the "Palestinian question" is one that is often in the news. Often as Christians we don't know what to make of all this and there are a wide variety of views even among evangelicals. The topic can be quite controversial and involve various views about the end times. However as evangelicals we should not shy away from a topic just because it is controversial. We should be seekers after the truth and in that respect we should ask what the Bible says about this topic.

This topic is of course political. The Israel-Palestine conflict is also part of a wider Middle East instability and it will be necessary to review some political history in order to understand the conflict. We will need to know some of the historical facts before reviewing what the Bible has to say on this topic.

This topic is also theological. Those who are pro-Israel accuse the other side of spiritualising the Bible and not taking it literally. But those who are pro-Palestinian see the other side as refusing to read the Old Testament through its New Testament fulfilment in Jesus. At the heart of this topic for us as Christians is a battle over the Bible and how we should interpret it, particularly the Old Testament (OT).

Many Christians today, especially in the United States, are very pro-Israel. Their reading of the Bible leads them to view the ancient promised land as belonging uniquely to the Jewish people. Sometimes, when one reads pro-Israel material, it seems that Israel as a country can do no wrong and that all Palestinians are terrorists. That was the sort of view that I heard when I grew up in a Zionist Jewish youth group. It saddens me to see so many Christians with this view, especially amongst my fellow Jewish Christians. I can understand what must be an immense frustration on the part of Palestinian Christians when they see their brothers and sisters in Christ effectively disown them in favour of unbelieving Jewish people.

On the other hand there is a recent wave of propaganda in the media and in books that is pro-Palestinian, anti-Israel, and either borders on anti-Semitism or *is* simply anti-Semitism disguised as anti-Zionism. I do love Israel myself (mainly because there are many of my fellow Jews there), and when I hear Israel being compared to the Nazis I find that deeply offensive.

So it can seem like there are two extremes on this topic: a pro-Palestinian stance, which might mean that you have replacement theology[1] and even that you are anti-Semitic; or a pro-Israel stance, which might mean that you are a premillennial dispensationalist with all sorts of strange views about the end times. I hope to put forward a balanced view somewhere in between these extremes.

This article will aim to cover an enormous topic quite briefly. But for those who do not know all the ins and outs of the topic I will need *first* to go through the background history of the Israel-Palestine conflict. After that, *secondly*, I will discuss what the Bible says on this topic, albeit briefly. *Thirdly*, I will address some of the key issues involved in the conflict today and possible solutions. Let's start then with an overview of the background history.

1. HISTORICAL BACKGROUND

Pre-Mandate years

Before modern times Jewish people had lived in the promised land since the conquest under Joshua. They lost control of the land in the Roman-Jewish War when the temple was destroyed in AD 70. Different powers have ruled the land since then. After the Romans, the Muslims ruled the land most of the time from the seventh century onwards. The Ottomans ruled it from the sixteenth century until WWI.

---

1. The view that the church has replaced Israel and that the Jewish people no longer have a part in God's plans (cf. Rom 11).

The Gospel and Israel

During that time, in the nineteenth century the land was often owned by absentee landlords. Waves of Jewish migrants came to the promised land after 1880, buying the land from these absentee landlords. Before this time the Jewish population in the land was quite small, although there had been a continual Jewish people there. But by 1947 Jews comprised 31 percent of the population. From WWI until 1947 the Jewish population increased almost tenfold: from 57,000 to 555,000.[2]

Many Jewish people have longed to return to their promised land since the second century AD. However this was not meant to happen, according to traditional Jewish belief, until the Messiah returned. Thus before the nineteenth century there was no major drive for the Jewish people to return to the land. Modern nineteenth- and twentieth-century Zionism therefore is a repudiation of this traditional Jewish doctrine. Hence Jewish Zionism has a predominantly secular basis: it arose in the nineteenth century as a solution to the problem of anti-Semitism and persecution. Many Jewish people felt that having their own homeland would provide a safe haven from persecution.

Michael Rydelnik, in his book *Understanding the Arab-Israeli conflict*, defines Zionism as "the right of Jewish people to their ancient homeland."[3] Zionism was made famous by Theodore Herzl, a Hungarian journalist working in Austria. There were Jewish people before him who advocated a Jewish return to the promised land. But Herzl wrote independently of them, being unaware of their writings. Herzl wrote *Der Judenstaat* (*The Jewish State*) in 1896 and formed the World Zionist Organization, which held its first conference in 1897. Their aim was to strive to establish a home in Palestine for the Jewish people.

The Balfour Declaration

During WWI, the British proposed to the Arabs in the Middle East that after they defeated the Turks (the Ottoman Empire) they would recognise and uphold the independence of the Arab countries and their inhabitants. This agreement was encapsulated in what is called the McMahon-Hussein Correspondence (1915). There is debate about whether Palestine was

---

2. The Palestinian population doubled in that period, from 660,000 to 1.2 million.

3. M. Rydelnik, *Understanding the Arab-Israeli Conflict* (Chicago: Moody, 2004), 62.

The Israel/Palestine Conflict

included in this agreement. The British later argued that Palestine was not included.

In November 1917 the British put forward the famous Balfour Declaration, which stated:

> His Majesty's Government views with favour the establishment in Palestine of a national home for the Jewish people, and will use their best endeavours to facilitate the achievement of this object, it being clearly understood that nothing shall be done which may prejudice the civil and religious rights of existing non-Jewish communities in Palestine.

The Palestinians view the Balfour Declaration as a repudiation of the earlier McMahon-Hussein agreement. But the Balfour Declaration was accepted by the League of Nations in 1922. The League then set up the British Mandate in 1923: the temporary rule of the land by the British until the people in that land could rule themselves. However various white papers were issued by the British government during the Mandate years that softened or even repudiated the Balfour Declaration of 1917. This means that both sides can claim a right to the land on a historical and political basis.

The Mandate Years

During the Mandate years (1923–47) there were at times Arab riots or strikes in response to Jewish migration. There was a large revolt during 1936–39 and hundreds were killed on all sides in 1938. During this time Jewish terrorist and counter-terrorist groups were formed. The Haganah was a counter-terrorist group formed to combat violence from the Arabs. Formed in 1920, it became active after the Arab riots of 1929. This was the birth of what is called "militant Zionism." The Irgun was a smaller group that attacked both Arabs and the British using terror tactics. The Stern gang (or Lehi) broke off from the Irgun and were even more extreme.

The attacks of such groups on the British, and the continued violence and unrest, caused the British to withdraw after WWII. They handed over their Mandate to the UN. Thus in 1947 the UN proposed ending the Mandate and partitioning the land between the Jews and the Palestinians, with Jerusalem as an international city under UN control. The Jews accepted this proposal, but the Palestinians rejected it, because they felt that they had not been consulted and that it was unfair.

The Gospel and Israel

From the end of 1947 to May 1948 there was continued violence. Atrocities were committed on both sides. The Irgun and Stern gang perpetrated a massacre of Palestinians at Deir Yassin. More than a hundred Palestinians were killed. Jewish organisations condemned the massacre. The Palestinians in retaliation attacked a medical convoy, killing many Jewish doctors, nurses, and university lecturers.

During this time and after independence there is some evidence that the Israelis deliberately drove out many Palestinians from their homes and land.[4]

1948: Independence and War

The Mandate ended May 14, 1948. Israel immediately declared independence. Several Arab armies and nations (Lebanon, Syria, Iraq, Egypt) attacked Israel forthwith, managing to secure the old city of Jerusalem and the West Bank. But by January 1949 Israel was victorious and the fledgling state of Israel had survived. Their new borders comprised about 78 percent of the land. The Arab nations refused to recognise the new state of Israel.

1956: The Suez War

During 1956 Egypt blocked the Straits of Tiran, which was a major trade route for Israel, and nationalised the Suez Canal. Britain and France wanted control of the Suez as a conduit for oil. Britain and France, together with Israel, plotted to attack the Sinai and the Suez Canal because of the perceived threat to their interests. The attack was successful. The US demanded that Israel withdraw, which they eventually did, having been given the assurance that the Straits of Tiran would be kept open after that.[5]

1967: The Six-Day War

The next event was a very major one: the 1967 Six-Day War. In the lead up to the war the Syrians were lobbing bombs into Israel from the Golan

---

4. See C. G. Chapman, *Whose Promised Land?* (rev. ed.; Oxford: Lion, 2002), 81–84.

5. The US was worried it would lead to a wider war with the USSR, which at that time backed Egypt.

Heights, and there were skirmishes between Syria and Israel in April of that year. In May the USSR warned Syria that Israel was building up its forces on their border (which was not true). Syria then formed an alliance with Egypt and prepared to attack Israel, both speaking at the time of "wiping out" Israel. Jordan joined this coalition a short while later (on May 30).

Israel was worried that it would not survive such an attack and launched a pre-emptive strike on June 5. They destroyed the air forces of Egypt and Jordan and more than half of Syria's, which ensured air superiority. They captured Sinai in four days, defeating what was at the time the largest and most heavily equipped Arab army (the Egyptian army). Israel captured the West Bank and Jerusalem. Though it cost them many casualties, they fought and took the Golan Heights.

These spectacular defeats were a humiliation for the Arab world. But Israel offered back the lands for peace. However, at an Arab summit in August of that year the Arabs refused to recognise Israel and refused peace. After the war, UN Resolution 242 called for Israel to withdraw from the occupied territories and for the Arab nations to recognise Israel and cease from war.

1973: The Yom Kippur War

In 1973 Egypt and Syria launched a surprise attack on Yom Kippur—the most holy day in the Jewish calendar, when the country comes to a virtual standstill. At first the war went badly for Israel. However in time Israel prevailed and won. After this, in 1978, Egypt met with Israel for peace talks and signed a peace treaty in 1979. Israel returned the Sinai to them in exchange for this peace. The Arab League was outraged at Egypt and expelled them. Anwar Sadat, the president of Egypt, was then assassinated two years later (1981).

1982: The Lebanon War

During the 1970s the Palestine Liberation Organisation (PLO) had been shelling Israel from southern Lebanon. On several occasions they crossed the border and made attacks, killing children. Israel invaded Lebanon in 1978 to stop these attacks. Their intention was to push the PLO back from the southern border of Lebanon. However in response to the UN they withdrew later that year. Then in June 1982, to put an end to the shelling from

The Gospel and Israel

the PLO on northern Israeli towns, Israel invaded Lebanon again. The aim as before was to push back the PLO from the border.

In September, Lebanese Christian militia, who were allied with Israel, killed hundreds of Palestinians in a revenge attack in the refugee camps of Sabra and Shatila. The Israeli Defence Force (IDF) under Ariel Sharon stood by, allowing the massacre to take place. An Israeli investigation found that Sharon was therefore indirectly responsible and he resigned from his position as defence minister.

Hezbollah is a militant Islamist group in Lebanon that arose in 1983 in opposition to Israel's invasion. When Israel finally withdrew from Lebanon in 2000, Hezbollah claimed this as their victory.

1987: Intifada I

"Intifada" is Arabic for "uprising." The first Intifada began in December 1987. It was characterised by rock-throwing youths, but also civil disobedience, boycotts, demonstrations, and strikes. Israeli soldiers often used force against these youths, but later gained better control with anti-riot techniques that saw fewer casualties. But the harsh Israeli response against rock throwing youths resulted in media favour towards the Palestinians.[6]

The first Intifada fizzled out by 1991. This occurred during the First Gulf War in Iraq. When Iraq sent Scud missiles into Israel, many Palestinians were seen cheering for Saddam Hussein and Iraq. Yasser Arafat, the leader of the PLO, lost a great deal of credibility as a result. One result of the first Intifada was the formation of Hamas in 1987.

1993: The Oslo Peace Accords

The 1993 Oslo Accords were preceded in 1991 by the peace talks in Madrid. There were no breakthroughs at this time, but afterwards there were secret negotiations between senior PLO officials and Israeli academics. In 1993 Israel recognised the PLO, and the PLO recognised Israel.[7] The Oslo Accords were signed on September 13. According to this agreement, gradual withdrawal by the Israelis was to result in self-rule by the Palestinian Authority (PA) in the West Bank and Gaza, and the PA in turn agreed to com-

---

6. 159 children below the age of 16 were killed, many being shot by soldiers.
7. The PLO had in fact already recognised Israel in 1988.

bat terrorism. Contentious issues were temporarily put to one side. These included the status of Jerusalem, the Israeli settlements, and the Palestinian refugees.

However after Oslo the Palestinians violated the accords by increasing their acts of terrorism. And the Israelis violated the accords by increasing their settlements in the West Bank and East Jerusalem. Writers like Mark LeVine and Gabriel Tabarani believe that the Oslo process was doomed from the start. LeVine says that neither side trusted the other.[8] A minority on either side genuinely wanted peace, but, as Tabarani says, "The rest of the people, including the leadership, saw the agreements either as betrayal of the cause, or as a means to wage war by other (diplomatic) means."[9] Some believe that the PA never wanted peace and used the peace process as a stepping stone towards defeating Israel. Tabarani writes, "the avowed goal of many was, it seems, to obtain an agreement that would be a springboard for the destruction of Israel."[10] Arafat and the PLO committed themselves to non-violence at Oslo, but the organization they led was committed to violence and to an end of Israel. But the Israelis were also to blame. They sought to maximise their settlements and so maximise the area they would retain and the security that would result. Not surprisingly the Oslo peace process is now dead.

2000: Camp David and Intifada II

In July 2000, however, both sides met at Camp David. The contentious issues that had been put off were addressed. Israeli Prime Minister Ehud Barak offered 95 percent of the West Bank and all of Gaza, and compensation for the 5 percent of the West Bank that would be kept (for security reasons). He offered to remove some settlements and to allow 100,000 refugees to return. He offered shared sovereignty over Jerusalem. Arafat demanded the return of all refugees and that East Jerusalem be ruled by the Palestinians (with Israeli authority over Jewish religious sites). In short, Arafat rejected Barak's offer. The right of return of refugees was a key sticking point. In the

---

8. M. LeVine, *Impossible Peace: Israel/Palestine since 1989* (Halifax, Winnipeg: Fernwood, 2009), 46.

9. G. G. Tabarani, *Israeli-Palestinian Conflict: From Balfour Promise to Bush Declaration* (Bloomington, IN: AuthorHouse, 2008), 199.

10. Tabarani, *Israeli-Palestinian Conflict*, 203.

end, for the PA Israel didn't offer enough, and for Israel they could not offer more.

In September 2000, after the failed Camp David talks, Ariel Sharon visited the Temple Mount. Sharon's visit seemed to many ill advised or even provocative. Nevertheless his visit was approved by PA officials beforehand. Furthermore Sharon did not do anything to offend Muslim sensibilities. However demonstrations and riots broke out in response. And so the second Intifada began. Intifada II was much more severe than Intifada I. It was characterised more by terrorism and suicide bombings than by rock-throwing youths. Hundreds were killed on both sides.

2003: The "Road Map"

In 2002 US President Bush called for a Palestinian state. He also called for an end to the use of terrorism by the Palestinian side. These points constitute the "Road Map" that was agreed to by both sides in 2003. The Road Map was overseen by the quartet of the UN, US, EU, and Russia. However the PA has been unable to stop the terrorism on their side; their leaders believe that an attempt to do so would lead to civil war. Thus the Road Map also lies in ruins.

Since 2003 . . .

Israel, having given up on the peace process, decided on unilateral action that would separate the Palestinian and Israeli communities. One such action was the building of the Israeli West Bank security barrier. The barrier wall follows the boundaries between Israel and the West Bank in many places, but elsewhere it encroaches into Palestinian territory to surround Israeli settlements in the West Bank. This barrier is very controversial. Israel erected it for security reasons, but the Palestinians say that it is an illegal land grab. For example, the UN Office for the Coordination of Humanitarian Affairs estimates that 10 percent of the West Bank will fall on the Israeli side of the barrier. The International Court of Justice declared in 2004 that the wall violated international law. As of mid-2010, 61 percent of the wall had been built.

The construction of roads between settlements in the West Bank has also resulted in the loss of land to the Palestinians. There are many check points set up along these roads. This results in Palestinian territory being broken up into what LeVine calls "cantons" that are separated from one another. Thus a unified Palestinian territory is impossible and their economy is undermined by the restrictions that impede the flow of commerce from area to area.[11] The wall therefore separates not only Israelis from Palestinians, but also Palestinians from Palestinians. The result of this, according to Israeli human rights organization B'Tselem, was that Israel had prevented "any real possibility for the establishment of an independent, viable Palestinian state."[12]

In 2005 Israel pulled out from Gaza unilaterally. In January 2006 elections were held for the Palestinian Legislative Council and Hamas won a majority of seats. Hamas was formed in 1987 from the Palestinian Muslim Brotherhood. Hamas is viewed by many nations (including Australia) as a terrorist organisation. By 2007 Hamas took full control of Gaza. They and the PA have been at odds with one another. So there have been effectively three states, not just two: Israel, the PA in the West Bank, and Hamas in Gaza.

Peace remains elusive. Is that a massive understatement? That then is a summary of the background history. I will now examine all too briefly what the Bible says about the issue of the land today.

2. THE BIBLE AND THE LAND

Christian Zionists believe that the modern state of Israel is a fulfilment of Old Testament prophecy. Such prophecies are typically read as future predictions that are filfiled in our time. And this perceived fulfilment of Old Testament prophecies is seen as a precursor to the return of Jesus. As Paul Wilkinson says:

> . . . the key motivating factor" behind Christian Zionism is "belief in the *imminent* return of the Lord Jesus.[13]

Calvin Smith, a moderate Christian Zionist, injects a note of caution. He says:

---

11. LeVine, *Impossible Peace*, 93–94.
12. Quoted in LeVine, *Impossible Peace*, 91.
13. C. L. Smith, ed., *The Jews, Modern Israel and the New Supercessionism* (Lampeter, UK: King's Divinity, 2009), 99.

> ... unless one maintains categorically that we are indeed in the last days, biblically-speaking one cannot declare with certainty that modern Israel represents fulfilled prophecy.[14]

Christian Zionists point out that in the OT the land is given *eternally* to Abraham's descendants (Gen 17:8), therefore the land must still belong to the Jewish people today. But this ignores what the New Testament says about the land. We need to consider how the NT deals with such OT as a whole. For instance, the law is also eternal; however in Christ the law is filfiled in such a way that it has been *transformed*—and that transformation is the key point: we are no longer under the eternal law of God. For example we do not take sacrifices to a temple in Jerusalem because Jesus' sacrifice has atoned for sins once and for all. There is no need for any more sacrifices. Jesus' sacrifice has transformed what we do with OT sacrifices.

The NT likewise sees the coming of Jesus as transforming how we view the promised land. We cannot just quote OT verses out of context of the whole Bible, which comprises both Old and New Testaments, and insist that we are reading it literally. The theme of land has been transformed in the NT, and reading the OT literally means reading it in the context of the NT. What is missing in other words is good biblical theology. The writings of Graeme Goldsworthy on biblical theology are very important in this respect.[15] The biblical theology approach does not "spiritualise" the OT since we are dealing here with typology, not allegory. Allegory sees truths in the words of Scripture without reference to its context and original historical setting; that is, it *spiritualises* the text of the Bible. A typological approach, however, reads a passage literally in its original context and then moves forward from there to its fulfilment in the NT; that is, the original passage is read in light of the context of the *whole Bible*—that is, *literally*. Biblical theology gives us a reading of the OT that is Christian: that understands the OT in light of its fulfilment in Jesus. It is crucial that we read the OT in light of its fulfilment in the NT.

I was frustrated in reading both sides of this debate that neither side seemed to have very good biblical theology. The Christian Zionist side seemed to ignore the NT fulfilment of the OT and so have no biblical theology at all. But the other side seemed to have poor biblical theology as

---

14. Ibid., 40.

15. G. Goldsworthy, *Gospel and Kingdom* (Exeter: Paternoster, 1981), and G. Goldsworthy, *According to Plan: The Unfolding Revelation of God in the Bible* (Leicester: InterVarsity, 1991).

well. I did not particularly like the way Colin Chapman or Stephen Sizer handled the biblical passages. Stephen Sizer in particular frustrated me.[16] He seemed to polarise two groups only. Either you had full-blown replacement theology like him or you were a Christian Zionist. Because I continue to see a place for Jewish people in God's plans, he would call me a Christian Zionist! I find this lack of nuance frustrating.

Although I believe, from Romans 9–11, that the Jewish people are still important in God's plans today, I do not believe the same when it comes to the promised land. Now someone might ask: can we not have good biblical theology but still have a place for the land in God's purposes today? Logically this could be argued. Consider the following. In the NT the theme of God's people broadens out to all people, not just Israel. That is, the Gentiles are included in the kingdom of God. But the church does not *replace* Israel: Israel continues and the church is made up of the usual remnant of Israel along with a remnant of the nations (Romans 11). Likewise in the NT the theme of God's place broadens out to the whole earth, not just the promised land. However if there is still a special chosen people, the Jews (and I am convinced by Romans 11 that this is indeed the case), then why not still have a special chosen land for them as well? If the universalisation of God's people does not exclude the specificity of God's people the Jews, why should the universalisation of God's land exclude the specificity of the promised land? Indeed some would argue that we cannot separate God's people from their land. So even though Romans 11 does not mention the land, it surely assumes it, or so some would argue. Theoretically this could indeed be the case. Biblical theology does not demand per se an end to the promised land.

Donald Robinson, who introduced biblical theology to Australia, has written about the importance of the Jewish people in God's plan of salvation (Romans 11).[17] Like me, he also repudiates replacement theology. However he believes that the NT does *not* continue to give importance to the physical land in God's purposes today.[18] I am convinced he is right. I will briefly explain why I believe this to be the case.

---

16. S. Sizer, *Christian Zionism: Road-map to Armageddon?* (Leicester: InterVarsity, 2004).

17. See chapters 1–11 in *Donald Robinson: Selected Works*, eds. P. G. Bolt and M. D. Thompson, vol. 1, *Assembling God's People* (Sydney: Australian Church Record/Moore College, 2008).

18. Ibid., 179–90.

The Gospel and Israel

There is a trajectory from the OT to the NT regarding the theme of land. The theme of land narrows in the OT from all the earth (Genesis 1) to the promised land, to Jerusalem, to the temple. The temple is ultimately the place where God dwells. But in John 1 we find that Jesus is God in the flesh who tabernacled among us (John 1:1, 14). Jesus is the place where God dwells. The temple was a visual symbol of this reality. So, Jesus equates himself with the temple:

> Jesus answered them, "Destroy this temple, and in three days I will raise it up." The Jews then said, "It has taken forty-six years to build this temple, and will you raise it up in three days?" But he was speaking about the temple of his body.[19] (John 2:19–22)

The sacrifice that atones for our sin and the place where God dwells is Jesus himself. So once Jesus comes there is no more holy place—neither Jerusalem nor Mt Gerizim:

> "Our fathers worshiped on this mountain, but you say that in Jerusalem is the place where people ought to worship." Jesus said to her, "Woman, believe me, the hour is coming when neither on this mountain nor in Jerusalem will you worship the Father. You worship what you do not know; we worship what we know, for salvation is from the Jews. But the hour is coming, and is now here, when the true worshipers will worship the Father in spirit and truth, for the Father is seeking such people to worship him. (John 4:20–23)

The theme of land follows a trajectory from OT to NT, finishing in the person of Jesus himself. Once he has come he filfils the theme of land in such a way that there is no more holy land. Romans 4:13 makes it clear that Abraham was to inherit the whole earth, not just the promised land. As Jesus' followers, Jew and Gentile, we have God's Spirit dwelling in us. Paul says:

> Do you not know that you are God's temple and that God's Spirit dwells in you? If anyone destroys God's temple, God will destroy him. For God's temple is holy, and you are that temple. (1 Cor 3:16–17)

So we are now the temple in Christ and we inherit the whole earth (1 Cor 3:16–17, 6:19; Eph 2:19–22).

---

19. Unless otherwise indicated, Bible quotations in this essay are taken from the ESV.

The Israel/Palestine Conflict

Even in the OT itself, the land and Jerusalem and the temple start to merge (Ezek 40–48). The new covenant will bring a new heaven and a new earth (Isa 65:17–25). There will be a new Jerusalem. But the new temple and the new Jerusalem are almost synonymous with the new promised land. In the NT these images are fused together. The new Jerusalem in Revelation has no temple and is synonymous with the new heaven and earth (Rev 21–22). This is why there is no expectation in the NT of another temple or another Jerusalem.

On the other hand, the earthly Jerusalem, Jerusalem below, is in slavery (Gal 4:25). Stephen Sizer quotes J. C. De Young:

> "Gal. 4:21ff represents, perhaps, the sharpest polemic against Jerusalem in the NT . . . Far from being pre-occupied with hopes for a glorification of the earthly Jerusalem, Paul's thought represents a most emphatic repudiation of any eschatological hopes concerning the earthly city."[20]

Christians are not to look to an earthly Jerusalem; instead Christians belong to the Jerusalem above (Gal4:26).[21] The earthly Jerusalem is referred to figuratively as Sodom (Rev 11:8). Ray Pritz says of this verse, "'the joy of the whole earth' is now consigned to the category of those places where wickedness reigned and from which God's people had to escape."[22]

Christian Zionists accuse biblical theology of spiritualising the OT. But are they not unwittingly accusing the NT of spiritualising the OT? Biblical theology is seeking to interpret the OT the way the NT does. This is a true *literal* hermeneutic. The Christian Zionist hermeneutic is a literalising hermeneutic that does not interpret Scripture by Scripture. For Sizer,

> the question is not whether the promises of the covenant are to be understood literally or spiritually, it is instead a question of whether they should be understood in terms of old covenant shadow or new covenant reality. The failure to recognize this principle is the basic hermeneutical error which Christian Zionists make.[23]

---

20. J. C. De Young, *Jerusalem in the New Testament*, quoted in Sizer, *Christian Zionism*, 170.

21. Note that these verses in Galatians are not against Jerusalem per se. Paul is against the Jerusalem that stands opposed to Jesus. However, much of modern-day Jerusalem would fall into the latter category.

22. Ray Pritz, "Jerusalem, the Holy City?," *Mishkan* 26 (1997) 41.

23. Sizer, *Christian Zionism*, 135.

The Gospel and Israel

The error of some Christian Zionists is to view the modern state of Israel, to quote Sizer, as "the consummation of God's purposes on earth rather than the atoning work of Christ."[24] I have had Christian Zionists say to me that if the modern state of Israel ceased to be, they could no longer believe the Bible and be a Christian. Instead of putting their hopes in Jesus as the fulfilment of the OT, they have put their hopes in the modern state of Israel as the fulfilment of the OT. But the hopes of the OT prophets are filfiled in Jesus. Looking forward to the fulfilment of prophecy in a return to the land after the time of Jesus is missing a profound truth that the NT is making. Christian Zionists often claim, like unbelieving Jews, that the OT prophecies have not found their fulfilment yet in Jesus, and that therefore we should look to a future fulfilment, such as they claim has happened in 1948 and 1967. That unbelieving Jews would use the OT only to come up with Zionism makes sense. That Christians would do the same is bewildering in light of what the NT says.

Given the historical background to this conflict, and if, as I believe, Christian Zionism is mistaken, how should we approach the current issues involved in the Israel-Palestine conflict? Our approach will be biblical, in that it will seek to uphold justice for both sides. But our approach will also be political, as it would be with any other international conflict. A Christian Zionist view will affect how one deals with these issues so that justice is not upheld, and this is due to a misunderstanding of how the promises of the OT are filfiled today. An appeal to the fulfilment of the promises of the Bible should result in the proclamation of the gospel to both sides. But regarding the political conflict the promises of the OT will not be pertinent, except in their teaching about such things as fairness, generosity, forgiveness, and peace.

3. KEY ISSUES IN THE CONFLICT

The Settlements

The building of settlements in the West Bank began after the 1967 war. Many Jews in Israel are secular and moderate, but others are religious. The latter mostly believe that the whole land belongs to them and not to the Palestinians. They have used the opportunity of Israel ruling over the West Bank to build settlements in it to claim back what they see as their own

---

24. Ibid., 204.

land. After 1977, when Likud came to power (the first right-wing government in Israel), there was a great increase in the number of settlements built in occupied land.[25]

According to LeVine, during the Oslo years (1993–2000) Israel "massively expanded the settlements and their population."[26] He also cites a 2006 study that says that "40 percent of settlement land is composed of privately owned Palestinian land that has . . . been 'illegally confiscated' from the owners."[27] The settlements are considered to be illegal by the International Court of Justice (2004), the EU, and the General Assembly of the UN. They are said to violate the fourth article of the Geneva Convention,[28] which concerns occupying powers transferring its civilians into occupied territory.

Why is Israel doing this? At its narrowest point Israel is only nine miles (14.5 km) across without the West Bank, and is vulnerable to an invading force. For strategic reasons Israel has planted settlements and roads to ensure its future security. Settlements remain a key issue in this conflict.

Refugees

The second issue is that of Palestinian refugees. In 1948 during the war of independence (and again in 1967) many Palestinians fled from their homes and became refugees. Palestinians claim that one million were driven out in 1948.[29] Some refugees were forcibly removed. For example, 60,000 were forcibly evacuated from Lydda and Ramla.[30] This was done for security reasons. Pro-Israel sources blame Arab propaganda, which caused a panic that resulted in most of these refugees fleeing. An example of the latter is the flight from Haifa: the Arab Higher Committee ordered some 15,000–25,000 Palestinians to leave, but the Jewish leaders urged them to stay.

25. In 1977 when the first right wing government gained power in Israel, there were 4,400 settlers living in 31 settlements. In 2001 there were 198,000 settlers in 123 settlements.

26. LeVine, *Impossible Peace*, 9.

27. Ibid., 76.

28. Tabarani, *Israeli-Palestinian Conflict*, 312.

29. Rydelnik claims there were not one million refugees, but a maximum of 650,000 or even only 450,000 (Rydelnik, *Understanding the Arab-Israeli Conflict*, 169). Tabarani claims 750,000, and 400 villages depopulated (Tabarani, *Israeli-Palestinian Conflict*, 62–63). The numbers are still colossal either way.

30. Tabarani, *Israeli-Palestinian Conflict*, 68.

Whether the refugees fled because of propaganda from their own side or were forcibly removed is a moot point in the end. Such refugees have the right to return to their homes or to be compensated for their loss. UN Resolution 194 states that "refugees wishing to return to their homes and live at peace with their neighbours should be permitted to do so at the earliest practicable date." It also states that "compensation should be paid for the property of those choosing not to return." I assume Israel refuses to allow refugees to return due to continued acts of terrorism, which they interpret as the Palestinians refusing to "live at peace" with them.

The problem for Israel is that if they allow the return of all the Palestinian refugees (four to five million), Israel by population would cease to be a Jewish state since Jewish inhabitants would be in the minority. Tabarani notes that the right to self-determination is guaranteed in international law and should override other considerations: return of refugees "would negate the Jewish right to self-determination."[31]

Rydelnik and Tabarani view the peace process as a means for the PA to bring an end to the state of Israel through insisting on the right of return of refugees. To quote Tabarani again, "Not only Fatah but also Arab leaders and media have unabashedly admitted that the refugee issue and right of return are being used as a means to destroy Israel."[32]

There is also the problem of Jewish refugees. After 1948 many Arab countries became hostile to their Jewish citizens. In total 400,000 came to Israel from Arabic countries in the first decade of Israel's existence, and a further 200,000 came in the decade after that. Many were forced to leave. If compensation is given to Palestinians, the same must be given to these displaced Jewish people. Many who left, whether willingly or not, left behind property that was appropriated by the government.

Refugees, both Palestinian and Israeli, are a key issue in the conflict.

Justice

Thirdly, arising from the issues of settlements and refugees is the issue of justice. Edward Said states, "I see no way of evading the fact that in 1948 one people displaced another, thereby committing a grave injustice."[33] Some would argue that if Israel is going to claim that the OT gives it the

31. Ibid., 80.
32. Ibid., 82.
33. Quoted in C. Chapman, *Whose Promised Land?*, 11.

The Israel/Palestine Conflict

right to the land, then we must also apply to Israel the standards of morality and justice that are found in the OT; and on these Israel falls far short. Stealing land from the Palestinians is wrong according to the OT. Justice is important in the OT prophets. Christian Zionists highlight what they see as the predictions of prophecy but largely ignore what those same prophets say about justice.

David Torrance, who is pro-Israel, writes, "Israel needs continually to be reminded, in a spirit of love and humility, of the teaching of their own Scriptures about God's command to live righteously, justly, and to welcome the stranger in their midst."[34] In other words, Christian Zionists need to become far more balanced in their approach. Mitch Glaser, in a pro-Israel book, says that "some evangelical Christians have been pro-Israel to the point of losing objectivity—and this certainly needs to be rebalanced."[35] Calvin Smith says, in the same book, "Neither can we justify an 'Israel right or wrong' mentality, as some Christians seek to do. Israel sinned even in biblical times, so to ignore her present injustices and sinful behaviour is wrong."[36]

The Holocaust is often highlighted by pro-Israel writers. The Holocaust was horrific and totally wrong, but that does not justify Jewish people doing the wrong thing now—in fact the very opposite is true. The terrible suffering of Jewish people in the Holocaust should make them very reluctant to cause suffering to others.

On the other side, Palestinian terrorism is completely unacceptable. Terrorists seek to kill or injure as many civilians as possible. Israel, I believe, seeks to minimise civilian casualties. The media is completely out of line whenever it suggests that Israel's actions are terrorist-like or Nazi-like. Israel may be flawed, but it is a democracy. Terrorism on the part of the Palestinians is completely unjust. Those who have done wrong on both sides will face God's judgment for their misdeeds.

Elias Chacour is a Palestinian Christian who has written very movingly about his life as a Palestinian living in Israel in his book *Blood Brothers*.[37] He and his family were driven out of their village of Biram in 1947 by Israeli soldiers, who later blew up his village. Chacour was angry about

---

34. D. W. Torrance and G. Taylor, *Israel, God's Servant: God's Key to the Redemption of the World* (London: Paternoster, 2007), 37.
35. C. L. Smith, ed., *The Jews, Modern Israel*, xi.
36. Ibid., 43.
37. E. Chacour, and D. Hazard, *Blood Brothers* (Grand Rapids: Chosen Books, 1984).

The Gospel and Israel

what happened, but trusts in God for justice. He blesses; he does not curse. He views violent retaliation as totally wrong. He works for peace and is prepared to suffer injustice, as his own Lord did.[38] He believes that Israel will never achieve peace as long as it uses violence.

Both sides need to recognise the suffering of the other side and not claim suffering only for themselves, thinking that their suffering justifies wrong actions against the other. In fact Colin Chapman calls on both sides to *accept* suffering as the way to overcome evil.[39] There is no solution for peace that will not involve some injustice and compromise to both sides. Peace therefore cannot be achieved without an acceptance of suffering and loss.

This third issue of justice, on both sides, is also a key issue.

Islam and Anti-Semitism

I need to raise as a fourth and more minor issue: Islam and anti-Semitism. Israel is viewed by Islam as holding a Muslim land, which can never be lost and therefore must be won back. Once a land is under Muslim control it can never be allowed to pass under non-Muslim authority. Hamas therefore will never agree to a peace process or to compromise because they are under the Quran as their authority. This is not the case with the PLO. During the Oslo years the differing views of Hamas and the PLO divided the Palestinians. Hamas is popular with the Palestinians because of their charitable and social work. Their popularity resulted in their election victory in 2006 and mid-2008. They have used their budget to improve social services. There is far less corruption among them than in the PA. They believe though in violent resistance to Israel and view terrorism as legitimate. Hamas and other terrorist groups have used suicide bombings that target civilians. They have used children as young as fourteen as suicide bombers and have used ambulances to hide explosives.

Hamas are also anti-Zionist and anti-Semitic. Islamic anti-Semitism has taken the forms of Holocaust denial and anti-Semitic polemics. The latter includes use of the known forgery of the Protocols of the Elders of Zion and blood libels. Anti-Zionism is sometimes used as a mask for anti-Semitism, but not always; so the two should not always be equated.

---

38. He has twice been nominated for the Nobel Peace Prize.
39. Chapman, *Whose Promised Land?*, 221–26.

The Israel/Palestine Conflict

Conclusion: Can There Be Peace?

Stephen Sizer says that for many Christian Zionists "efforts to achieve a lasting peace in the Middle East are spurned as counterfeit and a Satanic ploy to beguile Israel."[40] Thus it is not only Muslim fundamentalists who are against peace, but sometimes Jewish and Christian fundamentalists too. However Calvin Smith, a moderate Christian Zionist states, "just as biblical Israel existed in Babylonian exile, or Persian, Greek, and Roman occupation, so today giving up some land for peace does not dilute Israel's nationhood."[41]

After the failure of the Road Map some private peace proposals have been put forward. The impasse however continues. Most would agree that both sides need to look forward and not backward; there can be endless recriminations on both sides when looking to the past. Most also agree that Israel and the Palestinians cannot solve their problems themselves. Outside help is needed, particularly from the US, which needs to be more sympathetic to the Palestinians and less one-sided in its support of Israel. The US needs to become a fair mediator between both sides and use its influence to bring about a real solution. Very hard compromises will be needed on both sides.

Tabarani so rightly says that "the substantial majority of Israelis and Palestinians recognize that their future is intertwined with the other. Most deeply desire a better future for their children and grandchildren and are willing to make substantial concessions if peace and security can be achieved."[42] But there are no easy solutions and it will take decades, at best, to establish peace.

The most popular solution seems to be the two-state solution. I particularly like Tabarani's specific suggestions for what will need to happen for peace to be achieved. He suggests the following.[43]

First, *the refugee issue*. Compensation must be given and accepted by the Palestinians as an alternative to repatriation. Compensation will be huge: in the order of many billions of dollars. The US and the international community will have to help here. Other countries must be willing to take

---

40. Sizer, *Christian Zionism*, 202.
41. C. L. Smith, ed., *The Jews, Modern Israel*, 43.
42. Tabarani, *Israeli-Palestinian Conflict*, xiii.
43. Ibid., 392f.

in refugees, including Australia. Compensation must also be paid by Arab countries to Jewish people who were forced to leave and lost property.

Second, *the settlements issue*. Some settlements will need to be dismantled. Land exchange can be given for other settlements that do not affect Palestinian life and sovereignty. The barrier must also come down.

Third, *the issue of Jerusalem*. Tabarani suggests West Jerusalem as the Jewish capital and East Jerusalem as the Palestinian capital.

The main enemy to peace, according to Colin Chapman, is fundamentalism, and I think he is right. The problem with fundamentalism is that such people are so ideologically driven that they cannot hear what the other side is saying and are completely and implacably one-sided. This means that a real conversation or negotiation cannot take place.[44]

So, can peace be achieved politically this side of heaven? I think so: there are examples throughout history. And so we need to pray for peace. We need to pray for Christians who are Palestinian and for Christians who are Israelis. We ourselves also need a right understanding of the Bible. A wrong understanding of OT prophecy in the last century has driven US policy and has not helped the situation in the Middle East.

Most of all we need to focus in this area, as in all others, on Jesus and his death on the cross: that is the answer. The cross alone is what can bring real peace—peace with God and peace with one another. There are great examples of brothers and sisters in Christ from both sides who are reconciled in Christ. Jews and Arabs will achieve this peace when they hear the gospel and accept Jesus as their Lord and Saviour, becoming one new man in Christ, reconciled to God and to one another.

I have supported Christian Witness to Israel for many years because it is a Reformed Evangelical organisation that seeks to take the gospel to the Jewish people. Real peace in the end is only achieved by Jesus' death on the cross. If we want Jewish people to have peace we need to tell them the good news of their own Messiah Jesus, who has died on the cross to pay for their sins and bring them peace with God. If we want Palestinians to have peace we need to tell them the good news of Jesus, who died on the cross to pay for their sins and bring them peace with God. That is a peace that cannot be broken, and I have experienced it myself with my brothers and sisters who are Jewish and with those who are Arab and Palestinian. And so my prayer is that God would bring peace and reconciliation to both Jew and Arab in the promised land today.

44. Chapman, *Whose Promised Land?*, 304.

8

The Yes to All God's Promises
Jesus, Israel and the Promises of God in Paul's Letters

—Dr. David Starling

CHRISTIAN WITNESS TO ISRAEL?

A GROUP THAT EXISTS for the sake of "Christian Witness to Israel" faces questions and criticisms directed to it on two fronts, each of which represents a significant challenge to the validity and importance of its reason for existing.

On the one hand, there is the position taken by those who deny the continuing theological significance of the category "Israel" this side of Christ, except for its use with reference to the church as the new Israel. Those who view the issue from this vantage point are generally open, at least in theory, to the idea that there ought to be a continuing Christian effort to evangelise individual Jewish people, and may be prepared to concede the continuing legitimacy of some of their brothers and sisters becoming "as a Jew . . . to the Jews . . . in order to win Jews" (1 Cor 9:20),[1] as a matter of evangelistic strategy. But the boldest hopes supported by such a perspective rarely stretch beyond the possibility of the occasional Jewish convert to Christianity, assimilated into the life of a Gentile congregation or perched on its periphery as an exotic anomaly. Nor does this perspective

---

1. Unless otherwise indicated, all Scripture quotations in this essay are taken from the NRSV.

provide much of a basis for placing a high priority on any responsibility that contemporary Christians might have for participating in or supporting Jewish evangelism; after all, the number of Jewish people in the world today is a drop in the bucket compared to the countless millions of Gentiles.

On the other hand, there are the arguments of those who happily grant the continuing theological significance of Israel as the elect people of God, but deny the validity or necessity of any "Christian witness" to them. Many, of course, of those who take this viewpoint do not believe in Jesus as Messiah at all. But alongside them, sharing this opinion, there are also those who grant the legitimacy of Christian faith for Gentiles but insist on a *Sonderweg*—a separate path, under a different covenant—for Jews, and those who enthusiastically embrace the idea of Messianic Judaism but insist that its stance toward the wider community of Israel should be a "post-missionary" one.

My aim in this lecture is to lay some of the groundwork for the beginnings of a response to the criticisms that might be directed against the idea of a Christian witness to Israel arising from each of these directions. The scope of the lecture will be quite narrow: I will be focusing exclusively on Paul's letters, and on one recurring theme within those letters: the relationship between Jesus, Israel, and the promises of God.

A comprehensive New Testament rationale for Christian witness to Israel would of course require much more than that. Within the corpus of Paul's letters a string of other issues could be investigated, such as his views on election, final judgement, circumcision, "Israel" language, messiahship, covenant, land, and the law. Beyond Paul's letters, in the rest of the New Testament, there are big and important discussions to be entered into about topics including the portrayal of the Jewish nation and its leaders in John's Gospel, the missions of Jesus and his disciples in the Gospel of Matthew, the theology of temple and land in Luke/Acts, the identity of the recipients of 1 Peter and the 144,000 in Revelation, and the relationship between old and new covenants in the Letter to the Hebrews. And lurking behind and beneath all these questions of New Testament interpretation are the hermeneutical and biblical-theological questions about how the Old Testament should be interpreted—whether, for example, it ought to be read by Christians (exclusively) through a New Testament lens or (also) interpreted independently of and prior to the New Testament.

But for the purposes of this lecture all of those wider questions will be left for another day and my focus will be narrowly concentrated on one question: how does Paul encourage his readers to understand the implications of the coming of Jesus for the inheritance and fulfilment of the promises of God? My plan will be to deal one by one with the four main letters in which Paul makes use of the language of "promise,"[2] asking in each case what Paul wants his readers to understand about the relationship between Jesus, Israel, and the promises of God given in the Old Testament, and the effect that Paul intends this understanding to have in the lives of his readers.

GALATIANS 3: PROMISE, OFFSPRING, AND INHERITANCE

Within the collection of Paul's letters, the earliest extended discussion of the promises of God and the people who inherit them is to be found in Galatians 3–4. It comes within the context of an urgent warning to the Gentile churches of Galatia against the teachings of a group of rival teachers who have come among them, urging them to submit to circumcision (6:12) and preaching a message that, in Paul's eyes, amounts to "a different gospel" from the one the Galatians originally received (1:6).

We do not have any direct access to the arguments of the rival teachers that had "confus[ed]" and "unsettle[d]" the Galatians (5:10, 12), but it is possible to piece together a tentative account of what it might have been, based on how Paul responds to it. Whilst the amount of energy that Paul expends in chapters 1–2 on defending his character and apostleship would suggest that these were at least called into question by his rivals, they do not appear to have presented themselves as calling for the Galatians to reject everything they had heard from Paul: their appeal seems to have been framed as an encouragement to complete or perfect through circumcision and works of Torah what they had 'started' through Paul's gospel (3:2). Their motivation, according to Paul, included a desire to "make a good showing in the flesh" and avoid persecution for the sake of the cross of Christ (6:12)—presumably by maintaining the sort of connection with the local synagogue that would have shielded Jewish Christians from synagogue discipline and given communities of believers in Jesus a measure of protection under Roman law. But their message (as it was heard and understood by the Galatians) was not just presented as an argument from prudence and pragmatism, or an encouragement toward ethical progress

---

2. For reasons of space I will be leaving out the brief reference in Titus 1:2 to "the hope of eternal life that God . . . promised before the ages began."

or a deeper experience of the Spirit: some at least among the Galatians had concluded that circumcision and subjection to the law would be necessary for them to obtain and secure a verdict of divine justification (2:21; 4:21; 5:4; cf. Acts 15:1).

Somewhere in the discussion—whether as part of the message of the rival teachers or as part of Paul's response—the question of how and by whom God's promised blessings come to be inherited emerged as a key issue of debate. It is likely, though not certain, that the rival teachers' argument included an appeal to the story of Abraham and the function that circumcision played as a sign of the "everlasting covenant" that God made with him and his offspring (Gen 17:9-14). If the Galatians are to become proper descendants of Abraham and full inheritors of the promises that God made to him and to his offspring, then—the argument would have been—they need to submit to the sign that was described by God to Abraham as "my covenant . . . in your flesh" (Gen 17:13).[3]

Whatever place arguments from the scriptural story of Abraham occupied within the message of the teachers in Galatia, they were certainly prominent in Paul's response. The bulk of Paul's argument about promise and inheritance is contained within 3:6-29.[4] Within this section of the letter, Paul offers an account of the overarching narrative of Scripture to serve as an interpretation and confirmation of the argument that he makes in 3:1-5 from the Galatians' experience of receiving the Spirit.

Paul's language within these paragraphs oscillates freely between the singular "promise" (vv. 14, 17, 18, 19, 22, 29) and the plural "promises" (vv. 16, 21). Whilst the primary promise in view is the promise of Genesis 12:3 that "all the Gentiles shall be blessed in you" (cf. Gal 3:8), the plural "promises" in verse 16 suggests that it is not that verse alone which Paul has in mind; this impression is immediately confirmed when Paul goes on to say that the promises were made to Abraham "and to his offspring," quoting this time not from the promise of blessing to the Gentile nations in Genesis 12:3 but from the promise of land in Genesis 13:15 and 17:8. To further complicate the picture, Paul's argument in 3:6-14 is constructed in

---

3. Cf. the reconstruction of their message proposed in Richard N. Longenecker, *Galatians* (WBC; Dallas: Word, 1990), cxvii.

4. Also relevant is the extended metaphor of slavery, minority, and sonship in 4:1-7, which recapitulates the main point of the scriptural arguments in 3:6-29, and the allegory of Hagar and Sarah in 4:21-31, in which the Galatian believers are described as being, like Isaac, "children of the promise" (4:23, 28) and reminded that "the child of the slave will not share the inheritance with the child of the free woman" (4:30).

a way that draws a close correlation between the restoration promises of the prophets and the original divine promises to Abraham: the outpouring of the Spirit promised by the prophets is understood by Paul to be equivalent to, or at least included within, "the blessing of Abraham" (v. 14), and Habakkuk's promise that "the one who is righteous will live by faith" is placed in parallel with the reckoning of righteousness to believing Abraham (vv. 6, 11).

The promises in view within these paragraphs, then, include not only the promise of blessing to the Gentiles but also the promise of the land and the prophetic promises of restoration and the outpouring of the Spirit. All of these promises, it seems, are understood by Paul as constituting a single inheritance promised by God "to Abraham and his offspring . . . that is, to one person, Christ."[5] Furthermore, because the inheritance of the promises belongs to "one person . . . Christ" (v. 16), it is those "in Christ Jesus" who receive the blessing of Abraham (v. 14)—in Christ "there is no longer Jew or Greek" (v. 28).

The basic point, therefore, that Paul's argument in Galatians about promise and inheritance is intended to support is an emphatic assertion of the full inclusion of Gentile believers—apart from the law and irrespective of their uncircumcision—among the justified people of God and the heirs of his promises. All that was promised—blessing, land, life, righteousness, the Spirit—is inherited "through faith in Christ Jesus" and given "to those who believe" (3:22). Stated positively, it is a claim about the justification of uncircumcised, believing Gentiles and their inclusion among the people of God. Stated negatively, it is a strong rejection of any idea that Torah observance or Abrahamic ancestry is a sufficient basis for inheritance of the promises.

2 CORINTHIANS 1:19-20: THE YES TO ALL GOD'S PROMISES

If we read Paul's letters in chronological sequence, the next place within the collection in which we meet the language of "promise" is in 2 Corinthians.

---

5. Paul's claim in 3:16 about the singular seed is not a hermeneutical rabbit pulled out of the hat, but an expression of a traditional Jewish understanding that the messiah fulfils the Abrahamic promise. Cf. 2 Sam 7, Ps 72, and the discussion in James M. Scott, *Adoption as Sons of God: An Exegetical Investigation into the Background of ΥΙΟΘΕΣΙΑ in the Pauline Corpus* (WUNT 2/48; Tübingen: Mohr Siebeck, 1992), 180-82.

The Gospel and Israel

The language of "promises" occurs at two places within the letter and plays a vital part in Paul's rhetoric on each occasion.

The first occurrence is in 1:19–20, where Paul (in the context of a defence of his own integrity) reminds the Corinthians that in Jesus Christ every one of God's promises is a "yes." In doing so, Paul not only points to Jesus Christ as the one in whom all the promises of God (presumably including, among others, the Abrahamic promises, the promises to David and his descendants, and the restoration promises given to exilic and post-exilic Israel) find their divine confirmation; he also offers a hint (confirmed in the immediately following verses) that it is those "in Christ" (whether Jew or Gentile, circumcised or uncircumcised) who inherit the promises, so that they become the "amen" to his "yes." That this is the case is evidenced, according to Paul, by the "seal" and "guarantee" of the Spirit (v. 20). Thus, as Paul goes on to say later in the letter (in an obvious allusion to the restoration promises of Isaiah), "So if anyone is in Christ, there is a new creation" (5:17).

Paul's assertion in 1:20 is not necessarily intended as a claim that the Christ event, in and of itself, is the total fulfilment of all of the Old Testament promises of God. The "yes" to a promise is not so much its fulfilment as its confirmation—in this case, the answer to an implied question about the willingness or ability of God to bring it to fulfiment.[6] Paul's intention is to draw an analogy between God's commitment to his promises and his own: "Was I vacillating when I wanted to do this? Do I make my plans according toordinary human standards, ready to say 'Yes, yes' and 'No, no' at the same time? As surely as God is faithful, our word to you has not been 'Yes and No'" (1:17–18)

The "yes" that is spoken by God, then, is not the fulfilment of all the promises within the Christ event itself, as if the content of the promises were no longer live and pending; it is the partial fulfilment in Christ and in the pouring out of his Spirit on his people, as a "first instalment" and a guarantee of the remainder. Paul is confident that God has "established" the Corinthian believers with him in Christ, and has anointed and sealed them, along with him, with the Spirit. The implication is that the promises of God to Israel are inherited by those who are "in Christ"—a line of reasoning analogous to the argument that Paul makes in Galatians 3 about the singular seed, the experience of the Spirit, and inclusion in Christ Jesus. But for the Corinthians, as for the Galatians (cf. Gal 5:5), there is still something

---

6. Cf. J. Duncan M. Derrett, "Nai (2 Cor 1:19–20)," *FN* 4 (1991) 206.

more to wait for, a future fulfilment that will deliver on the promise that was reconfirmed in the first instalment.

2 CORINTHIANS 7:1: SINCE WE HAVE THESE PROMISES

The second reference to the promises of God in 2 Corinthians comes at the conclusion of an exhortation in 6:14—7:1, warning the readers urgently against the danger of being "mismatched with unbelievers" (6:14). Within the space of the five tightly-structured, rhetorically forceful verses that follow the warning, Paul confronts his readers with a string of rhetorical questions about the impossibility of fellowship between "righteousness and lawlessness ... light and darkness ... Christ [and] Beliar ... a believer [and] an unbeliever ... the temple of God [and] idols" (6:14b–16a) and reminds them of a catena of Scripture citations that speak of their identity as the temple of God and the call to separate from uncleanness (6:16b–18). The paragraph concludes in 7:1: "Since we have these promises, beloved, let us cleanse ourselves from every defilement of body and of spirit, making holiness perfect in the fear of God."

Whatever conclusion we draw about the identity of the "unbelievers" referred to in verse 14 and the intended function of the paragraph within the broader argument of the letter,[7] the most significant feature of the paragraph for our purposes in this lecture is the ease with which the promises gathered together among the verses of the Scripture catena in 6:16–18 are applied by Paul to the (mainly) Gentile readers of his letter.

The texts in the catena come from a variety of different sources within the Old Testament. Four of them (the citations or citation fragments from Ezek 37:27; Isa 52:11; Ezek 20:34; and Isa 43:6) are promises or commands addressed in their original context to the exiles of Judah, and speak about

---

7. Amongst those who argue for the Pauline authorship of the paragraph and its integrity within the letter, something of an impasse exists between those who read "unbelievers" in 6:14 as a reference to the Gentile pagans of the city (and interpret the call to separation as a reprise of the instructions concerning cultic and sexual purity that feature prominently in 1 Corinthians) and those who read it as a reference to the false apostles spoken of elsewhere in the letter (and interpret the call to separation as a plea for the Corinthians to break their allegiance with the false apostles in order to be reconciled to Paul). Whilst the former view makes best sense of the language of the paragraph, the latter view offers a far more convincing account of how it relates to its context in the letter. For one possible resolution of that scholarly impasse, see David I. Starling, *Not My People: Gentiles as Exiles in Pauline Hermeneutics* (BZNW; Berlin: De Gruyter, 2011), 71–75.

The Gospel and Israel

return to the land and restoration as God's covenant people. The other two promises (Lev 26:11–12 and 2 Sam 7:14) are addressed, respectively, to the nation of Israel at the foot of Mount Sinai and to David, concerning the son who will come after him.

The form and structure of the catena suggests, however, that these various scriptural promises, originally given at different points in Israel's history, are closely interconnected in Paul's understanding. In a manner reminiscent of a number of other Second Temple readers of these and other texts,[8] Paul indicates by the way in which he merges the citations together that the Sinaitic and Davidic covenant formulas are applied to his readers not directly but second-hand, refracted through the lens of the end-of-exile prophecies of Ezekiel and Isaiah. The promise of Leviticus 26:11–12 ("I will place my dwelling in your midst, and I shall not abhor you. And I will walk among you, and will be your God, and you shall be my people") is reworded and merged with the repromulgated promise given to the exiles in Ezekiel 37:27 ("My dwelling place shall be with them; and I will be their God, and they shall be my people"). Similarly, the promise of 2 Samuel 7:14 ("I will be a father to him, and he shall be a son to me") is merged with the language of Isaiah 43:6 ("Bring my sons from far away and my daughters from the end of the earth").

For Paul's Gentile readers in Corinth, the summons of Isaiah 52:11 and the associated promises are intended to function as an urgent divine address to the readers. The effect is to situate the readers, typologically, in Babylon on the last day of exile, summoned homeward by divine promises (7:1). The promises are invoked by Paul in order to reinforce his call to the Corinthians to separate from the unequal yoke still binding them to the mind and mores of their Gentile neighbours and keeping them from wholeheartedly embracing his gospel of the grace of God in the weakness of the cross.

ROMANS 4: THE HEIRS OF THE PROMISE

Paul's Letter to the Romans opens with a claim that the gospel of God for which Paul was set apart was "promised beforehand" by God "through his prophets in the holy scriptures" (1:2; cf. 3:21), but it is not until chapter 4 that the language of "'promise" comes to the fore in his argument, as he

---

8. E.g. the combined citation of Lev 26:11–12 and Zech 8:8 in *Jub.* 1:17 and the combined citation of 2 Sam 7:14 and Hos 2:1 in *Jub.* 1:24.

turns to an extended discussion of the promise of God and the identity of its heirs.

The references within the chapter to the scriptural stories of David and Abraham work at two levels. At one level (particularly in vv. 1–8) David and Abraham function as parallel exempla of righteousness "credited" not to the one who works but to the one who believes. At another level, Abraham functions not simply as the exemplary believer but as the father of all believers—at stake in Romans 4 is both "how Abraham got himself justified" and "whose father he is and in what way his children are related to him."[9]

At this second level, a story of Israel is implied within chapter 4, in which the engine that drives the story forward is "the promise to Abraham and his offspring that he would be heir of the world" (v. 3). Paul's point is not only that righteousness was credited to Abraham before he was circumcised (vv. 9–12) but also that Abraham was appointed the father not just of Israel but of "many nations" (v. 17) and that the promise given to Abraham was given to be inherited not through the law but through "the righteousness of faith" (vv. 13–16).

The reason for this assertion, according to verses 14–15, is bound up in the fact that "the law brings wrath." This assertion is probably not (at least in its primary sense, in this context of argument from salvation history) a generalising, universal statement about the function of "law" but a reflection on the shape of Israel's history under the law of Moses as a history in which the nation and the individuals within it inherited not the blessings offered by the law but the wrath of which it warned.

It is this reflection on the plight of Israel under the curses of the law that leads into Paul's explanation in verse 16 that the promise depends on faith "in order that the promise may rest on grace and be guaranteed to all his descendants, not only to the adherents of the law but also to those who share the faith of Abraham (for he is the father of all of us . . ." The "grace" in the first half of the verse is thus explicitly connected not only with the plight of the otherwise-excluded Gentiles but also with that of the otherwise-condemned Israel. "If it is the adherents of the law who are to be the heirs," Paul argued in verse 14, "faith is null and the promise is void."

---

9. Richard B. Hays, *The Conversion of the Imagination: Paul as Interpreter of Israel's Scripture* (Grand Rapids: Eerdmans, 2005), 83. Hays' argument is that the critical issue in Rom 4 is the second of these and *not* the first, but the structure of Paul's argument gives serious weight to both.

The Gospel and Israel

Throughout these verses, Paul's language consistently refers to "the promise" in the singular, but (as is the case in Gal 3) the content of what the word refers to seems to embrace a number of different promises given to Abraham within the Genesis narrative, swept up together into a single inheritance. In verses 17–21 the promises in view are the promise implied by his renaming as "the father of many nations" and the promise of offspring as numerous as the stars (cf. Gen 17:5; 15:5). In verse 13, however, Paul strikingly describes the promise given to Abraham and his offspring as "the promise that he would inherit the world." The vast, expansive scope of Paul's language goes beyond any single promise that can be found within the text of Genesis, and seems to pull together the promise of the land (cf. Gen 12:7; 13:15; 15:18; 17:8; 24:7; 26:3), the promise that Abraham would be "the father of many nations" (cf. Gen 17:5) and the promise that Abraham's offspring would "possess the gate of their enemies" (Gen 22:17).

This idea that the inheritance of Abraham's offspring was not just the land of Canaan but "the world" was not a new thought; within the writings of Second Temple Judaism analogies can be found in Sirach, *Jubilees*, *First Enoch*, and the writings of Philo.[10] Paul's understanding shows both similarities and differences when compared with the understanding implied in these earlier interpretations; he not only expands the scope of the promise of land from Canaan to the world, but also speaks of its inheritors as "all [Abraham's] descendants—not only ... the adherents of the law but also ... those who share the faith of Abraham" (Rom 4:16; cf. vv. 11–12). In doing so he is not replacing a material promise of land with a "spiritual" or "a-territorial" fulfilment,[11] but he is certainly rejecting a narrowly nationalistic view of worldwide Jewish imperial domination, and probably also rejecting a *bounded* territorial fulfilment, in which the promise is inherited by an Israel regathered around a restored Jerusalem temple and separated from the nations by territorial borders and laws of symbolic purity.[12]

---

10. Cf. Sir 44:21, *Jub* 17:3; 22:14; 32:19; *1 En.* 5:7; Philo, *On Dreams* 1.175 and Philo, *On the Life of Moses* 1.155. See also *4 Ezra* 6:59; *Ap. Const.* 8.12.23, *2 Apoc. Bar.* 14:13; 51:3 and the rabbinic references in Strack-Billerbeck 3.209, cited in James D. G. Dunn, *Romans* (Dallas: Word, 1988), 1:213.

11. For the language of "a-territorial" fulfilment, see W. D. Davies, *The Gospel and the Land: Early Christianity and Jewish Territorial Doctrine* (Berkeley: University of California Press, 1974), 179.

12. A similar point could be made from the way in which Paul applies the promises of temple and restoration to the land in 2 Cor 6:14—7:1.

The Yes to All God's Promises

Positively, the vision that he paints in Romans 4 is one in which the promises of God originally given to Abraham (land, covenant relationship, blessing) are gathered up together into a single, enormous inheritance—"the world" (v. 13)—which is received not "through the law" but "through the righteousness of faith," and belongs to "[all] those who share the faith of Abraham" (vv. 13, 16).

The discussion of the promises of God in Romans 4 is not the last time that the topic surfaces within the letter. We will return to Romans shortly, to examine the return of "promise" language in Romans 9 and 15. But before we do so, in order to complete the sequence of texts about Gentile inclusion and inheritance, it will be necessary to jump ahead to the last of our four letters, Ephesians.

EPHESIANS 1–3: SHARERS IN THE PROMISE

In Paul's letter to the Ephesians, he is once again addressing a Gentile readership, and a crucial concern of the letter is to help the readers understand how they relate to the promises of God originally given to the nation of Israel.

According the prayer in 1:16b–19, Paul is eager for his Gentile readers to be given "the Spirit of wisdom and revelation" so that the eyes of their heart might be enlightened to know "the hope to which he has called you . . . the riches of his glorious inheritance among the saints, and . . . the immeasurable greatness of his power for us who believe."

The close connections between the language of "wisdom and revelation" in v. 17 and the vocabulary that Paul employs in 1:9–10 and 3:3–10 suggest that a crucial dimension of the wisdom and revelation that he prays for his readers to be granted is an understanding of the "mystery" that is at the heart of the message Paul has been given to proclaim (3:9).[13] The content of the mystery, according to 3:6, is the story of how the Gentiles have become heirs in Christ of a promise that was originally tied to covenants to which they were strangers. At the climax of that story, in the centre of the narrative in 2:11–22, "a reading of which will enable you to perceive

13. This impression is reinforced by Paul's description of what he desires the readers to understand; the reference to "hope" recalls the account in 1:11–14 of how "we who were the first to hope in Christ" were joined by "you [Gentiles] also" and "the riches of his glorious inheritance among the saints" recalls both the Jewish "inheritance" into which the letter's Gentile readers have entered (1:11–14) and the scriptural language in which the people of Israel are described as the "inheritance" of God.

157

my understanding of the mystery of Christ" (3:4), is Paul's account of how the estrangement of the Gentiles was overcome. According to these verses, the abolition of the "dividing wall of hostility" between Jew and Gentile (including the abolition of the Gentiles' estrangement from the covenants of promise) has taken place in the death of Jesus, which has "abolished the law of commandments in ordinances" (2:15). For Paul, the death of Christ is thus not only a soteriological event (reconciling Jew and Gentile to God) and an ecclesiological event (reconciling Jew and Gentile to one another within the "new humanity" of the church) but also a hermeneutical event, transforming the relationship of his readers to the scriptural promise, law, and covenants.[14]

Although Paul does not tell us precisely how it is that the death of Christ had this effect, we are told that it involved reconciling Israel to God (2:16) as well as the Gentiles to God and to Israel. This picture in 2:16 of the reconciliation of Israel to God through the cross presupposes the narration in 2:3–10 of how an Israel made up of people who were "by nature children of wrath," living among the Gentiles in a typological or spiritual exile, were raised with Christ from a predicament of "death" that was the common plight of Jew and Gentile outside of Christ. The abolition of the law as a commanding authority over the people of God and as a dividing wall between Jew and Gentile went hand in hand with the overcoming of the "death" and "wrath" that had come upon Israel through the law's curses.

The appropriation of the promises originally given by God to Israel and their application to the Gentiles are therefore best understood in the light of Paul's reminder in 2:1–3 of the solidarity of Jew and Gentile in the spiritual death that was the continuation or the antitype of Israel's exile. Gentiles can find themselves addressed in promises of restoration originally given to exiled Israelites—and older covenant promises repromulgated to the exiles—because the predicament of exile that the promises addressed corresponded so precisely with their own predicament as Gentiles, spiritually dead and far off from God.

The "mystery" of the inclusion of the Gentiles (which "in former generations . . . was not made known") is thus—paradoxically!—made known to the readers through a retelling of the ancient scriptural story of Israel's exile and promised restoration, and both are located within a larger story

---

14. For a brief discussion of the implications of that understanding for the hermeneutical questions that arise in Eph 6:2–3, see Starling, *Not My People*, 185–86.

of universal human sin and a salvation that is "by grace . . . not your own doing . . . the gift of God . . . not the result of works" (2:8–9).

THE STORY SO FAR

The passages that we have examined so far—in Galatians 3, 2 Corinthians 1, 7, Romans 4 and Ephesians 1–3—all contain a number of similarities and point in a common direction. The status and identity of Gentile believers in Christ as inheritors of the scriptural promises originally given by God to Abraham and his descendants is emphatically defended by Paul in Galatians and Romans, and is presupposed and applied in 2 Corinthians and Ephesians.

But the reading of Scripture that underlies Paul's assertions about Gentile inheritance has implications for Israel as well as for the Gentiles. The basis on which Paul defends Gentile inheritance of the promises is not simply an expansion of the circle of covenant privileges, as if Gentiles were incorporated into the Israel of the old covenant through circumcision and law adherence. The shape taken by the saving kindness of God to the Gentiles, even in their uncircumcision, is a forcible reminder of truths that were already written into the history of Israel under the law: that "a person is not a Jew who is one outwardly, nor is true circumcision something external and physical" (Rom 2:28) and that "'no human being will be justified in his sight' by deeds prescribed by the law" (Rom 3:20).

These truths raise obvious questions for the continuing identity and final destiny of national Israel. If the promises of God are inherited by a people defined not by Torah adherence or physical Abrahamic descent, then is the category "Israel" abolished forever, apart from its application to those who belong to the "new Israel" of the church? Does Gentile inheritance imply Jewish disinheritance, and is that disinheritance to be viewed as irreversible?

ROMANS 9–11: TO THEM BELONG THE PROMISES

It is to questions of this sort that Paul turns in Romans 9–11, commencing with a heart-wrenching expression of his own anguish over the issue. But Paul's anguish over the situation of Israel is not only an expression of the fact that they are his "kindred" (9:3), or of his empathetic identification with their plight. It is exacerbated by their identity as the covenant people

The Gospel and Israel

of God: "They are Israelites, and to them belong the adoption, the glory, the covenants, the giving of the law, the worship, and the promises" (9:4). The nation of Israel, according to Paul, is the people to whom the promises of God belong. This remains true even in Paul's own time, after the coming of Christ. If they are cut off, then questions arise about the trustworthiness of God himself.

For much of chapters 9–11, as Paul addresses these questions, the answer that he gives seems to hold out little hope for national Israel. Paul's assertion in verse 9:6 that "it is not as though the word of God had failed" is supported in the immediately following verses by a reminder that "not all Israelites truly belong to Israel," and "it is not the children of the flesh who are the children of God but the children of the promise" (9:6, 8). A series of biblical examples follows, illustrating this principle and affirming the freedom of God to "[have] mercy on whomever he chooses, and ... [harden] the heart of whomever he chooses" (9:18).

In 9:22–24 Paul poses a shocking rhetorical question:

> What if God, desiring to show his wrath and to make known his power, has endured with much patience the objects of wrath that are made for destruction; and what if he has done so in order to make known the riches of his glory for the objects of mercy, which he has prepared beforehand for glory—including us whom he has called, not from the Jews only but also from the Gentiles?

The implication of the question is hard to miss: if it turns out to be the case that national Israel was nothing more than an "[object] of wrath ... made for destruction," in order to serve as part of a divine plan directed toward the salvation of others, then even that would be within the rights of God the creator. After all, as Paul has just asserted, the potter has the right to make whatever he wishes out of the clay (9:21).

The immediate impression conveyed by the verses that follow, at first reading, is that this is indeed what God has done. Gentiles, who once were "not my people," have been called "my people" (9:25–26) and Israel—in a manner analogous to the judgement prophesied in Isaiah 10:22—has been reduced to a tattered remnant (9:27–29). In the paragraphs that follow (9:30—10:21) Paul mulls over the reasons why Israel "stumbled over the stumbling stone" (9:32), concluding with a gloomy image, drawn from Isaiah, of the nation of Israel as "a disobedient and contrary people" (10:21).

In the opening verses of chapter 11 the image of "stumbling" resurfaces and Paul turns to the question of whether Israel's rejection is final and

The Yes to All God's Promises

irreversible. He puts the question twice, with deliberate repetition: "I ask, then, has God rejected his people?" (v. 1). "So I ask, have they stumbled so as to fall?" (v. 11). Both times, the immediate answer he gives is the same: "By no means!" (vv. 1, 11). But the arguments with which he supports these two emphatic denials differ.

In the first instance, within verses 1–10, his answer is a reiteration of the earlier arguments about the remnant of Paul's own day: "Israel failed to obtain what it was seeking. The elect obtained it, but the rest were hardened" (v. 7). But the second answer, in verse 11–32, is more ambitious, pushing beyond the preservation of a remnant in the present to a larger, more audacious hope.

The depiction of "jealous" Israel in verses 11–15 draws on an image already evoked in 10:2, 19 as part of an argument for Israel's culpability. Now, however, that same jealousy is portrayed as a force through which Paul hopes that salvation will come to "some" within Israel (v. 14)—a hope flanked by even more optimistic references to the "fulness" of Israel (v. 12)[15] and an "acceptance" that will amount to "life from the dead" (v. 15). In support of this hope, the twin analogies of the first fruits and the batch of dough and the root and the branches in v. 16 echo the arguments from Scripture about the remnant of Israel in the preceding chapters, and now uncover their latent implications for the rest of the nation. "If the part of the dough offered as first fruits is holy, then the whole batch is holy; and if the root is holy, then the branches also are holy" (v. 16).

Likewise, the olive tree metaphor of 11:17–24 begins by recalling the various citations from Scripture in 9:6—11:10 concerning the judgements of God on hardened Israel and the inclusion of Gentile believers in the place they once occupied: "Branches were broken off, and you, a wild olive shoot, were grafted in their place" (11:17), Now, however, having spoken in chapters 9–10 about the way in which Gentiles were grafted by grace into the fulfilment of promises not originally given to them, Paul makes explicit the question of whether, by the same grace, the "natural branches" pruned because of unbelief could be grafted back into the fulfilment of the same promises (11:23–24).

In the verses that follow, the original reference of the language of the restoration-of-Israel promises (in this case, Isa 59:20; 27:9) reasserts itself emphatically. It would be over-reading "all Israel" in 11:26 to see in it an expectation of each and every Israelite embracing salvation in (or apart from)

---

15. NRSV: "full inclusion."

Christ[16]; if that were the case, why the anguish and lament of the preceding chapters? Nor, on the other hand, is it convincing to read the "Israel" of verse 26a as referring to the mixed Jewish-Gentile church as the "new Israel,"[17] against the drift of Paul's argument in the preceding paragraphs. The most plausible reading of the verse is to take Paul's *houtō*[<macron>]*s* in its commonest sense as "thus," and read the verse as describing an extension and fulfilment of the hope that Paul has expressed in verses 13–14—that *in this manner* (by the paradoxical means of the Gentile mission and the incitement of Israel to jealousy) God will extend salvation beyond the tiny remnant to the hardened majority of the nation. What Paul has in mind here may not embrace the salvation of each and every Israelite, but it does seem to require a sufficient proportion of those who are currently "hardened" and outside the believing remnant to constitute a "fulness" of Israel (v. 12) comparable with the "fulness" of the Gentiles (v. 25).[18]

ROMANS 15: A SERVANT OF THE CIRCUMCISED

The final reference in Romans to the promises of God comes in 15:8, in the context of a one-verse summation of the shape of salvation history offered by Paul in support of his urgings to the believers in Rome to "welcome one another ... just as Christ has welcomed you, for the glory of God" (15:7). "For I tell you," Paul reminds his readers, "that Christ has become a servant of the circumcised on behalf of the truth of God in order that he might confirm the promises given to the patriarchs, and in order that the Gentiles might glorify God for his mercy" (15:8–9).

Two things about Paul's summation stand out. The first is the way in which Paul retains the indispensable place of Israel within the story of salvation: "Christ has become a servant of the circumcised ... in order that the Gentiles might glorify God for his mercy." The second is the way in which Christ's servant work for Israel is directed not only toward the saving of the nations but also, and primarily, toward the vindication of God's truth: "Christ has become a servant of the circumcised on behalf of the truth of

---

16. As is argued, for example, in Robert Jewett, *Romans* (Hermeneia; Minneapolis: Fortress, 2007), 701–2.

17. As is argued, for example, in N. T. Wright, *The Climax of the Covenant: Christ and the Law in Pauline Theology* (Edinburgh: T. & T. Clark, 1991), 249–50.

18. Cf. Dunn, *Romans*, 681, Douglas J. Moo, *The Epistle to the Romans* (NICNT; Grand Rapids: Eerdmans, 1996), 723.

God in order that he might confirm the promises given to the patriarchs." For Paul, both dimensions matter and both belong together. It is through the same work of Christ the servant that God fulfils both his saving purposes through Israel for the nations and his saving purposes for Israel herself.

CHRISTIAN WITNESS TO ISRAEL

What conclusions can we draw?

In the first place, Paul's argument in Romans 9–11 is a forceful reminder of the continuing significance of hardened, unbelieving Israel within the saving purposes of God. Paul's answer to the question "Has God rejected his people? . . . Have they stumbled so as to fall?" is an emphatic, twice-repeated "By no means!" "Israel," for Paul, is not a superseded category, or one that has been swallowed up without remainder by the church.

But hope for Israel is not to be found in the law of Moses, or in Abrahamic descent alone—this much is made equally clear by Paul's arguments in Romans 4 and Galatians 3–4. If the "unbelief" for which branches were cut off was unbelief in Christ (cf. 9:33; 11:20), then the faith and repentance that will be an essential part of the story of Israel's final salvation (cf. 11:23, 26–27) will take the form of trusting in and turning to Christ. Whilst the narrative sequence of 11:25–26 seems to imply a climactic turning of Israel to Christ at the end of the age, in close connection with the time of his return, the "so" of verse 26 suggests that this miraculous turning should not be viewed as something disconnected from the long history of gospel proclamation, Gentile conversion, and Israelite jealousy that precedes it.

It is important to read the references to "jealousy" in Romans 10–11 against the background of how the language of "jealousy" and "zeal" function elsewhere in Paul's letters and in the literature of Second Temple Judaism.[19] The form that Paul's own "jealousy" took within his journey toward salvation (cf. Gal 1:13–14; Phil 3:6) is a forceful reminder that the kind of Christian mission Paul has in mind is not the coercive proselytising of an arrogant Christendom but the kind of courageous, suffering, vulnerable testimony exemplified within the Book of Acts by the story of Stephen and by the apostolic labours and sufferings of Paul himself.

Paul's argument in Romans 9–11 is not itself a direct argument for Christian evangelistic witness to Israel. The principal implication Paul wants his Gentile readers to draw from his argument in that chapter is not a

19. Cf. Jewett, *Romans*, 674–75.

call to evangelise their Jewish neighbours but a warning against presumptuousness and boasting (11:17–25). The only evangelism that is immediately in view within the climactic paragraphs of the argument is the evangelism of Gentiles, through which Paul (as apostle to the Gentiles) hopes to incite the jealousy of Israel, with saving consequences (11:13–14).

But Paul's mission to the uncircumcised (according to Gal 2:1–10) was conducted in conscious partnership with the parallel mission of Peter, James, and John to the circumcised, and even Paul, the apostle to the Gentiles, seems also to have maintained a vigorous commitment to the evangelism of the diaspora synagogue communities.[20] This continuing personal commitment of Paul to the evangelism of his fellow Jews is not something that he wishes his readers to view as a solo pursuit; it needs to be placed alongside the way in which he describes his (mainly Gentile) converts as "partners" with him in the cause of the gospel (e.g., Phil 1:5), urging them to emulate his concern for the salvation of others (e.g., 1 Cor 10:31—11:1), even to the extent of persuading Timothy to undergo circumcision "because of the Jews" (Acts 16:3).

When these considerations are taken together, a strong case can be made for the importance of a humble, persevering, gracious partnership of Jewish and Gentile believers in Christ in making known the gospel of Jesus the Messiah to the people of Israel—in other words, for Christian witness to Israel. For Paul, the Israel of our own time remains the people to whom the promises of God were first given and therefore (along with us) the people to whom the promises of God belong. For them to enter into the inheritance of those promises will require a repentant faith in Jesus as Messiah, which will, in turn, require the testimony of the gospel.

For those of us who are believers in Jesus, Paul's argument in Romans 9–11 is aimed at inducting us into both his anguish and his hope—the shared hope and the shared anguish of those who have tasted the mercy of God, who are zealous for his truth to be vindicated, and who long for his promises to be fulfiled among the people to whom they were originally given. Christian witness to Israel is driven by those twin passions—by the confluence of that anguish and that hope—and is directed toward the day

---

20. On this point, the evidence of Paul's own writings (e.g., 1 Cor 9:19–23) is strongly supported by the account of Paul's commissioning and activity in the Book of Acts. Cf. the discussion in I. Howard Marshall, "Luke's Portrait of the Pauline Mission," in *The Gospel to the Nations: Perspectives on Paul's Mission*, eds. Peter Bolt and Mark Thompson (Leicester: InterVarsity, 2000), 107–9.

when (to paraphrase Paul's words in Rom 15:10) the Gentiles will rejoice with God's people Israel, and God's people Israel with the Gentiles.[21]

---

21. This chapter originated as the 2012 Edersheim Lecture, and was subsequently published as an article in *Reformed Theological Review* 71 (2012) 185–204. It is republished here with the kind permission of the original publishers.

9

Pentecost and the Plan of God

—Mike Moore

Shavuot, or Pentecost, according to the Bible falls exactly fifty days after the Sabbath following Passover, so it is the only festival of the Lord to which no date is assigned. Israel was to count fifty days from Passover, so that in celebrating Pentecost they would never forget the festival of their redemption.

According to Jewish reckoning, Pentecost this year [2013] falls on Wednesday, May 15, so the Christian tradition of always celebrating Pentecost on a Sunday is more in line with the biblical injunction to celebrate the festival on the day after the seventh Sabbath after Passover.

The purpose of this lecture is to explore the relevance of the festival of Shavuot today in order to relate the events that took place on the Day of Pentecost in AD 33 to the plan and purpose of God for the world he created. You don't have to be Pentecostal or Charismatic to recognise that the Day of Pentecost in AD 33 was one of the most momentous events in the history of redemption. However, to many Christians, the coming of the Spirit as recorded in the second chapter of Acts was nothing more than "the birthday of the church" and few would read more into the text of Acts 2 than that.

According to Jewish tradition Pentecost, or Shavuot, the Feast of Weeks, is *Zeman Matan Torateinu*: the "season of the giving of our Torah." In Acts 2, Luke appears to depict the events of the Day of Pentecost as a second "Mount Sinai experience" for Israel. For example, both the Torah

Pentecost and the Plan of God

and the Spirit were given on mountains: the Law at Sinai and the Spirit on the Temple Mount in Jerusalem.

In the account of the giving of the Torah in Exodus 19:18–20, fire and the sound of a trumpet accompanied the descent of God on Mount Sinai. In Acts 2:2–3, the descent of the Spirit was accompanied by fire and a sound; a sound "like a rushing, mighty wind." It is significant that Luke does not say there *was* a "rushing, mighty wind" but a *sound* "like a rushing, mighty wind."

According to the rabbis, the world was divided into seventy nations and in tractate *Shabbat* 88b the Talmud states, "Every single word that went forth from the Omnipotent was split up into seventy languages for the nations of the world." In Acts 2:4–5, the disciples of Jesus spoke words in the languages of "devout men *from every nation under heaven*."

There was, however, a significant contrast between the giving of the Torah and the giving of the Spirit. In Exodus 32, after Moses came down from Mount Sinai with the Ten Commandments, three thousand men of Israel died because of the sin of the golden calf. By contrast, in Acts 2:41, when the Holy Spirit was given, three thousand "received the word" and were baptised; in other words, three thousand people became spiritually alive in Messiah. This contrast is developed by Paul in 2 Corinthians 3, where he contrasts the old covenant and the new covenant, the law and the gospel, "the letter" and "the Spirit." The old covenant, says Paul, ministered death whereas the new covenant ministers life. The outpouring of the Spirit of God on that momentous day generated a movement that was to spread through the world, toppling an empire and ministering life to countless millions until ultimately the whole earth will be "filled with the knowledge of the glory of the LORD as the waters cover the sea" (Hab 2:14).[1]

What I propose to do in this lecture is to demonstrate that the events recorded in the second chapter of Acts reveal that Pentecost was the fulfilment of five distinct Old Testament elements: a Promise, a Psalm, a Pattern, a Plan and, finally, Pentecost itself.

PENTECOST WAS THE FULFILMENT OF A PROMISE

From the very first page of the Bible God's *Ruach*—his "Spirit" or "Breath" or "Wind"—is at work at pivotal points such as creation, when the *Ruach*

---

1. Unless otherwise noted, Scripture quotations in this essay are taken from the ESV.

hovered over the unformed and unfilled earth. At the exodus, the Spirit of God empowered Bezaleel and his helpers to construct the tabernacle and the things pertaining to the worship of God; in Numbers 11, the Spirit empowered the seventy elders of Israel, and Eldad and Medad, to prophesy—an event that made Moses wish all God's people were prophets, a wish that came true at Pentecost. The *Ruach* was also at work at the establishment of the Hebrew monarchy when he came upon David in power and enabled him to conquer the Philistine giant Goliath. The work of God is never accomplished by human might or power but always by the *Ruach* of God.

In the New Testament, the Spirit was central in the ministry of Messiah and his apostles. In Luke 1:35 the Spirit overshadowed Mary causing her to conceive Messiah; in Matthew 3:16 the Spirit anointed Jesus at the Jordan River, setting him apart as Messiah; in Matthew 12:28, Luke 11:20, and Acts 10:38 the Spirit empowered Jesus for his messianic ministry; in Hebrews 9:14 the Spirit sustained Jesus for his atoning death, and Romans 8:11 states that the Spirit raised Jesus from the dead. It is hardly surprising, therefore, that the Spirit of God was present at the beginning of the God's mission to the nations. The pouring out of the Spirit on the Day of Pentecost was the fulfilment of at least two biblical promises made to Israel, the first being the promise of Joel 2:28–32:

> And it shall come to pass afterward, that I will pour out my Spirit on all flesh; your sons and your daughters shall prophesy, your old men shall dream dreams, and your young men shall see visions. Even on the male and female servants in those days I will pour out my Spirit. (2:28–29)

However, Joel 2 was not the only prophetic scripture fulfiled at Pentecost. The proclamation of the word of the Lord to the house of Israel and the *Ruach* breathing life into three thousand souls was surely a fulfilment of Ezekiel 37:1–14, where Israel is pictured as a heap of dry bones. In the vision, God promises to recall his people from exile, following which he will breathe life into them and cause them to become a great army. According to Ezekiel 37:27–28, God's dwelling place will be among resurrected Israel; he will be their God, they will be his people, and, when his sanctuary is in their midst forever, the nations will know that he is "the LORD who sanctifies Israel." Israel's promised resurrection was to have an effect on the nations.

Pentecost and the Plan of God

PENTECOST WAS THE FULFILMENT OF A PSALM

Commentators on the Book of Acts recognise a symbolic significance in the sound like a wind and the tongues of fire, and various interpretations of the symbols have been suggested but few interpreters, if any, link the phenomena to Psalm 104:4, which states that God "makes his messengers winds, his ministers a flaming fire."

In the readings for Pentecost, the Church of England's *Book of Common Prayer* includes verses 25–37 of Psalm 104 but, interestingly, not verse 4! But how fitting that with the coming of the Spirit, God's messengers and servants should be initiated into their roles by the very elements God uses as his messengers and servants. God had spoken to Elijah eight hundred years before the events of Acts 2 through a "still, small voice" rather than through fire and a howling wind, but at Pentecost he spoke with the unrestrained might and power of a spiritual tornado that uprooted three thousand observant Jews and Gentile proselytes from the kingdom of darkness and transferred them into the kingdom of God's Son.

PENTECOST WAS THE FULFILMENT OF A PATTERN

One of the most divisive issues within evangelicalism today is supersessionism, or as it is more commonly known, "replacement theology." Put simply, replacement theology is the idea that the church has replaced Israel in the plans and purposes of God and that all the promises and privileges that belonged to the Jewish people prior to the coming of Messiah have been spiritualised and transferred to a new "spiritual Israel." Some years ago, on Whit Sunday, the churches in a small town on the south coast of England organised a street party, complete with party games and jelly and ice cream, to celebrate "the birthday of the church." The idea was to attract locals in the hope (I presume) that they, like the crowd that gathered at Pentecost in Jerusalem two thousand years ago, would want to know how to be saved. Apart from the fact that the Holy Spirit is a hard act to follow, was the church really born on the Day of Pentecost in AD 33?

Look up the word "church" in any English dictionary and you will probably read that the word is based on a medieval Greek term *kuriakon doma*, meaning the "Lord's house." Ask a Christian what "church" is and the response will more than likely be that "church is people, not a building." Ask a non-Christian what "church" is and the answer will probably be that

The Gospel and Israel

it is a building. Theologically, the Christian is correct, but from the point of view of linguistics, the non-Christian is right.

How would the disciples of Jesus have understood his declaration in Matthew 16:18, "I will build my *church*"? Although Matthew 16:18 is the first occurrence of the word "church" in English translations of the Bible, none of the apostles asked the Lord what a "church" was. The Greek word *ekklesia*, translated "church" in Matthew 16, means an "assembly" or "congregation." But Jesus, of course, would have been speaking in Hebrew or Aramaic, not in Greek, and the term he would have used was one with which his Jewish disciples would have been very familiar—*qahal*.

In the Old Testament, Israel was God's *qahal*, his "assembly." When the Hebrew Scriptures were translated into Greek in the third century BC, the translators of the Septuagint, as the Greek version was known, used *ekklesia* to translate *qahal*. "Church," in that sense, therefore, was a concept with which the disciples of Jesus were very familiar and, according to Stephen in Acts 7:38, God had an *ekklesia*, a "church" or "assembly," in the wilderness; that assembly being Israel. We must not think, therefore, that the church was born on the Day of Pentecost in AD 33 or that the church has replaced Israel as the people of God. From the time of the exodus, Israel was God's "church," or assembly, and continues to be so.

If that sounds confusing, it might be helpful for us to look at the subject from another perspective.

Jeremiah 11:16 depicts Israel as "a green olive tree, beautiful with good fruit," and in Romans 11:16–22 Paul draws on Jeremiah's imagery to speak of Israel as an "olive tree" of which Jewish individuals are the branches. Those Jews, or "natural branches," who refused to embrace their Messiah were broken off, but believing Gentiles, like branches from an uncultivated olive tree, were grafted onto the cultivated olive tree of Israel. Whether cultivated or uncultivated, both varieties of branch are joined to the same tree—Israel—and are nourished by the same sap that comes from the roots of the tree, namely the patriarchs. At Pentecost, God did not cut down one olive tree and plant a new one called "the church"; instead, he began to call people from all nations, not just from Israel, to be part of his beautiful green olive tree in order they might produce good fruit.

Something new did come into existence at Pentecost, however: a spiritual temple. In the Old Testament, a developing pattern may be discerned in the way God meets with his people. Before the fall, God met and communed with Adam and Eve in the Garden of Eden. After the expulsion from Eden, Cain and Abel approached God as individuals, each at their own altar. After the call of Abraham, worship began to take place at a family altar and the mark of the faith of the patriarchs, as we observe in Genesis 12:8; 13:12; 26:17, 25; 33:18–20, was that they each pitched their tent, built their altar, and called on the name of the Lord

At the exodus, the family altar was replaced by a national shrine. The people lived in tents and, under the direction of the Lord, a tabernacle was constructed where his people might meet with their God and he might meet with them. When the people settled in the land and began to live in permanent dwellings, Solomon erected a temple of stone to serve as the house of God.

Following the destruction of the temple in 586 BC, God foretold in Ezekiel 40–48 that a better, bigger, and perfect temple would be constructed, out of which would flow a river of healing water (47:1–12). There are biblical interpreters who insist Ezekiel's vision must be interpreted in a strictly literalistic manner but such an approach raises a number of serious difficulties. According to Ezekiel's measurements, the temple will be so large that both the Temple Mount and the Mount of Olives will have to be enlarged and expanded in order to accommodate it. A clue to understanding the true nature of Ezekiel's vision can be found in John 2:19, where Jesus speaks of his body as the temple. And in John 7:38, on the final day of the Feast of Tabernacles, Jesus declares, "Whoever believes in me, as the Scripture has said, 'Out of his heart will flow rivers of living water.'"

"This," says John, Jesus "said about the Spirit, whom those who believed in him were to receive, for as yet the Spirit had not been given, because Jesus was not yet glorified." The Spirit was "given," of course, at Pentecost but which "Scripture" foretold the Spirit flowing like a river of living water out of the hearts of those that believe in Messiah? The only Old Testament passage that speaks of "living water" flowing out of anything is Ezekiel 47:1–12, in which a river of water flows from the temple of God bringing life to wherever it flows.

A series of New Testament texts—including Matthew 24:1–2; 26:61; Acts 6:14; Ephesians 2:19–22; 1 Peter 2:4–8; Revelation 22:1–5—lead us to conclude that the Body of Messiah, comprised of living stones, is the new temple, a "habitation of God in the Spirit," out of which flows living water for the healing of the nations. At Pentecost, the Spirit began to flow from the followers of Jesus in the temple, where multitudes were observing

The Gospel and Israel

Shavuot, to Jerusalem, Judea, Samaria, and, ultimately, to the uttermost parts of the earth.

In Exodus 40, when the tabernacle was erected, a cloud of glory authenticated it as the dwelling place of God. When Solomon dedicated the temple in 2 Chronicles 7, fire fell from heaven and the glory of God filled the place. In Acts 2, God authenticated his new, living temple with a glory even greater than that of the previous temples. At Pentecost, God dedicated and authenticated his living temple that was destined to fill the entire world, not simply the Temple Mount and the Mount of Olives. And whereas in times gone by God was encountered in particular locations such as Eden, the altar, the tabernacle, and the temple, since Pentecost Jews and Gentiles may meet with him not so much in a universal temple but as living stones in that temple.

The temple reminded people of Eden. It was built on a mountain from which flowed the Kidron stream, and its architecture included cherubim, palm trees, gourds, and other plants and flowers. It was a representation of the Garden of Eden from which had flowed four rivers. The single river that flowed from Ezekiel's temple caused trees to grow in the wilderness, the leaves of which brought healing. In John's parallel vision in the final chapter of the Bible, the river flows from a temple city, the New Jerusalem, and on either side of the river grows the tree of life with twelve kinds of fruit, yielding fruit every month. Even the leaves of the tree bring healing to the nations. Little wonder, then, that the hymn writer Isaac Watts wrote that in Jesus "the tribes of Adam boast more blessings than their father lost"!

PENTECOST WAS THE FULFILMENT OF A PLAN

Immediately after the fall of humankind, in Genesis 3:15, God announced his plan to redeem his fallen creation. The call of Abraham was part of the divine redemptive plan, the end of which was that all the families of the earth would be blessed (Gen 12:3). Israel's calling was a missionary calling and the nation is described in Jeremiah 2:3 as "the firstfruits of [the Lord's] increase," that is, the firstfruits of God's harvest from among all nations.

In Jeremiah 4:1–4, the Lord declared that Israel's relationship to him would have a beneficial effect on the Gentiles:

> "If you will return, O Israel," says the LORD, "Return to Me; and if you will put away your abominations out of My sight, then you shall not be moved. And you shall swear, 'The LORD lives,'" in

Pentecost and the Plan of God

truth, in judgment, and in righteousness; the nations shall bless themselves in Him, and in Him they shall glory." (NKJV)

God's plan of redemption is fundamental to understanding Psalm 67:

God be merciful to us and bless us, and cause His face to shine upon us, that Your way may be known on earth, Your salvation among all nations. Let the peoples praise You, O God; let all the peoples praise you. Oh, let the nations be glad and sing for joy! For you shall judge the people righteously, and govern the nations on earth. . . . Then the earth shall yield her increase; God, our own God, shall bless us . . . and all the ends of the earth shall fear Him. (NKJV)

The first two verses of Psalm 67 remind us of the High Priestly benediction of Numbers 6:24–26:

The LORD bless you and keep you; The LORD make His face shine upon you, and be gracious to you; The LORD lift up His countenance upon you, and give you peace. (NKJV)

They also bring to mind Genesis 12:1–3:

Now the LORD had said to Abram: "Get out of your country, from your family and from your father's house, to a land that I will show you. I will make you a great nation; *I will bless you* and make your name great; *and you shall be a blessing.* I will bless those who bless you, and I will curse him who curses you; and in you all the families of the earth shall be blessed." (NKJV)

God repeated the promise to Isaac in Genesis 26:4: ". . . in your seed all nations of the earth shall be blessed." He made the same promise to Jacob in Genesis 28:14: ". . . in you and in your seed all families of earth shall be blessed" (NKJV).

According to Genesis, before the nations could be blessed, Abraham, Isaac, and Jacob had to be blessed. At every festival the high priest blessed the people and in Psalm 67 the promise of the blessing of the nations is clarified. The blessing God has in mind for the nations is nothing less than their salvation. Could God have had anything less in mind when he promised to bless Abraham, Isaac, and Jacob and their descendants? Could he have anything less in mind when he blessed the people through their high priest?

The Gospel and Israel

The psalmist recognised that although God had blessed Israel in many ways, the nation did not possess the blessings invoked by the high priest in their fulness. Moreover, the nations were not saved.

Israel could not enjoy the blessings of Numbers 6:24-26 in their fulness, nor could the nations be saved until Messiah, the seed of Abraham, came. And Psalm 67 is a prayer that Israel will be blessed fully and that the nations will know God's salvation, his Yeshua! In the songs recorded in the first two chapters of Luke's Gospel, it becomes evident that with the birth of Yeshua the invocations of the Aaronic benediction and the pleas of Psalm 67:1-2 were being answered.

In Psalm 67:1, the Hebrew poet appeals to God to show *chanan*—grace or mercy—to Israel. In the Magnificat of Luke 1:46-55, remembering that Mary spoke Hebrew, she sings:

> My soul magnifies the Lord, and my spirit rejoices in God my Saviour. . . . his *mercy* [which in Hebrew would have been *chanan*] is for those who fear him from generation to generation. . . . He has helped his servant Israel, in remembrance of his mercy [*chanan*], as he spoke to our fathers, to Abraham and to his offspring forever. (NKJV)

In Luke 1:67-79, the blessings of Psalm 67, the high-priestly blessing, and the promise to Abraham all come together in the Song of Zechariah:

> "Blessed be the Lord God of Israel, for he has visited and redeemed his people and has raised up a horn of *salvation* for us in the house of his servant David, as he spoke by the mouth of his holy prophets from of old, that we should be *saved* from our enemies and from the hand of all who hate us; to show *the mercy promised to our fathers* and to remember his holy covenant, the oath that he swore to our father Abraham, to grant us that we, being delivered from the hand of our enemies, might serve him without fear, in holiness and righteousness before him all our days. And you, child, will be called the prophet of the Most High; for you will go before the Lord to prepare his ways, to give *knowledge of salvation* to his people in the forgiveness of their sins, because of the tender *mercy* of our God, whereby the sunrise shall visit us from on high *to give light* to those who sit in darkness and in the shadow of death, to guide our feet into *the way of peace*. (NKJV)

According to Psalm 67, as it goes with Israel so it goes with the nations, and the psalmist appeals to God to bless Israel in order that the nations might be saved. Before the nations can be blessed through the knowledge

Pentecost and the Plan of God

of Yeshua, Israel must be blessed, and the New Testament constantly emphasises the principle "to the Jew first," as Peter declares in Acts 3:24–26:

> And all the prophets . . . proclaimed these days. You are the sons of the prophets and of the covenant that God made with your fathers, saying to Abraham, "And in your offspring shall all the families of the earth be blessed." *God, having raised up his servant, sent him to you first, to bless you* by turning every one of you from your wickedness.

There is a pattern in Psalm 67: Israel is blessed; then the nations are saved; then Israel's God blesses Israel. Paul reveals a similar framework of thought in Romans 11: Israel has been blessed but has rejected the blessing; the nations are being saved and are rejoicing in God's salvation, and this will "provoke Israel to jealousy." At the moment, says Paul, only a remnant of Israel believes the gospel, but that will not always be the case. There will be a fulness. "All Israel will be saved."

God has called Gentiles to provoke Israel to jealousy. That is our duty.

Although tongues might at first reading appear to be the predominant phenomenon on the Day of Pentecost, tongues were not most important feature; the preaching of the gospel was the crucial factor on that day. The gospel was preached to the Jews first but by the time the Book of Acts closes the nations are blessing themselves in the Lord and glorying in him. Pentecost was the launch pad for the final stage of God's plan for world redemption—a plan that has nothing less as its goal than the salvation of the nations and the liberation of the cosmos from the effects of the fall of Adam.

PENTECOST WAS THE FULFILMENT OF PENTECOST

Shavuot/Pentecost, like the other festivals of the Lord, was a highly symbolic festival. It was the second of the annual pilgrim festivals at which every male Israelite was to appear before the face of God at the house of God in Jerusalem. The "place" in which the 120 believers were when the Spirit fell on the Day of Pentecost in Acts 2 was the temple. The temple was the only place in which observant Jews would have been on the morning the *Ruach* of God came upon the disciples of Jesus. Had the 120 been in an upper room in another part of Jerusalem, those in the temple would have been unaware of the sound of the wind and the tongues of fire, and Peter certainly would not have been able to address thousands of his fellow Jews in the confines of Jerusalem's narrow streets.

Shavuot was originally a harvest festival but by the first century of our era, as the Jewish people had become scattered among the nations, the festival had lost its primary harvest significance and become "the season of the giving of the law" at Sinai. It is surely significant, then, that at the time when the Torah passage for Shavuot was being read in the temple the Spirit came down on Mount Zion. The Torah reading would have included Exodus 19:18–20a:

> Now *Mount Sinai was wrapped in smoke because the LORD had descended on it in fire.* The smoke of it went up like the smoke of a kiln, and the whole mountain trembled greatly. And as *the sound* of the trumpet grew louder and louder, Moses spoke, and God answered him in thunder. The LORD came down on Mount Sinai, to the top of the mountain.

Nevertheless, the harvest significance had not disappeared and two wheat loaves made from the firstfruits of the wheat harvest were waved before God in the temple.

At both Passover and Pentecost, firstfruits were presented to God as wave offerings in the temple. The offering presented the day after the Sabbath of Passover week, as specified in Leviticus 23:10–14, was the firstfruits of the barley harvest, and barley was considered the poor man's food. The firstfruits offering at Shavuot was from the wheat harvest, and in Psalm 81:16 wheat is the rich man's food. In 1 Corinthians 15:21–23, when Paul describes Messiah as the "firstfruits from the dead" he is likening Messiah's resurrection to the Passover firstfruits offering, which was presented to God on the very day Jesus rose from the dead.

The Shavuot firstfruits offering was a different picture. The firstfruits of the wheat harvest were offered in the form of two loaves baked with leaven. It would seem that this offering is a picture of the believers—Jews and Gentiles—being incorporated into the Body of Messiah at Shavuot. And as the poor man's food signified Messiah and the rich man's food represented believers in Messiah, we are reminded that, as Paul says in 2 Corinthians 8:9, Messiah became poor for our sakes that we might become rich in him.

There is a further significance to the fact that two loaves were offered. The number two is strongly associated in the Bible with witness. In Deuteronomy 19:15, at least two witnesses were required for an acceptable testimony in a court of Israelite law. and the principle finds a variety of

Pentecost and the Plan of God

applications within the new covenant as, for example, in Mark 6:7 when Messiah sent out his disciples by twos in order to preach the good news. According to 1 Timothy 5:19, congregations are not to receive an accusation against an elder without at least two witnesses, and, says Peter in 1 Peter 3:7, in the marriage partnership there has to be agreement between both spouses for prayer to be accepted by God. Without two witnesses there is only opinion and, following Pentecost, God had both Jews and Gentiles as his witnesses to the world.

Moreover, the offering of the loaves was accompanied by a number of sacrifices, including, as we read in Leviticus 23:19, a peace offering, in Hebrew a *shalom*. When the Apostle Paul speaks to Gentile believers at Ephesus, he says in 2:14–16:

> For [Messiah] himself is our peace [offering], who has made us both [Jews and Gentiles] one and has broken down in his flesh the dividing wall of hostility by abolishing the law of commandments expressed in ordinances, that he might create in himself one new man in place of the two, so making peace, and might reconcile us both to God in one body through the cross, thereby killing the hostility.

The sages of Israel recognised that the nation's destiny was to bless the world, and regarded the coming of Ruth the Moabitess into Israel as a foreshadowing of the coming of the Gentiles into the blessings of Israel. That is why the Book of Ruth, which celebrates the coming of a Gentile into the commonwealth of Israel at harvest time, is read in synagogues at Shavuot. Ruth was blessed by becoming a member of Israel, and Israel in turn was blessed by her becoming the ancestor of King David and Messiah. At Pentecost in AD 33, Gentile proselytes as well as natural Jews were incorporated into the commonwealth of Israel. According to Romans 11:11–15, 25–26, Gentiles have been blessed by Israel and are, in turn, called to be a blessing to the Jews, not least by provoking them to jealousy.

The three thousand Jews and proselytes who believed Peter's preaching on the Day of Pentecost were the firstfruits of a harvest that would culminate in a worldwide ingathering from all lands. Revelation 7:9 refers to the Gentile converts as a "great multitude which no man could number, of all nations, tribes, peoples and tongues" (NKJV; note the many "tongues" of Acts 2). In Revelation 14:4 the 144,000 are identified as "firstfruits to God and to the Lamb" (NKJV) and it is to them, the first generation of Jewish believers, that James addresses his epistle. According to James 1:1,

The Gospel and Israel

his readers were from "the twelve tribes which are scattered abroad" and "a kind of firstfruits of His creatures" (1:18; NKJV). While Peter, James, John, and the other apostles continued to reap the firstfruits of God's harvest within the house of Israel, Paul says in Galatians 2:9 that he and his companions were reaping a harvest from among the nations.

***

What, then, do the events of the Day of Pentecost as recorded in Acts say to us? The events of that day bring together a number of threads from the Old Testament scriptures that hint (some more strongly than others) at God's plan and purpose for his creation. The teaching of Pentecost encourages us to trust that God's purposes for creation will continue to unfold until at last all Israel is saved, the people of God from all nations are gathered into the kingdom, and "the earth shall be full of the knowledge of the LORD as the waters cover the sea."

However difficult the task, however dark the days, the harvest nature of Pentecost encourages us to pursue mission in the knowledge that the firstfruits of God's harvest, which was presented to him on Mount Zion two thousand years ago, guarantees a full harvest from all nations that no person can number. Therefore, we cannot afford the luxury of pessimism. In all our service, we can "be steadfast, immovable, always abounding in the work of the Lord, knowing that in the Lord your labour is not in vain" (1 Cor 15:58). The kingdoms of this world have become the kingdom of our God and his Messiah!

www.ingramcontent.com/pod-product-compliance
Lightning Source LLC
Chambersburg PA
CBHW071448150426
43191CB00008B/1278